EXPLAINING CRIMINAL CAREERS

CLARENDON STUDIES IN CRIMINOLOGY

Published under the auspices of the Institute of Criminology, University of Cambridge; the Mannheim Centre, London School of Economics; and the Centre for Criminological Research, University of Oxford.

RECENT TITLES IN THIS SERIES:

Tough Choices: Risk, Security, and the Criminalization of Drug Policy
Seddon, Williams, and Ralphs

Breaking Rules: The Social and Situational Dynamics of Young People's Urban Crime
Wikström, Oberwittler, Treiber, and Hardie

Discovery of Hidden Crime: Self-Report Delinquency Surveys in Criminal Policy Context
Kivivuori

Serious Offenders: A Historical Study of Habitual Criminals
Godfrey, Cox, and Farrall

Penal Abolitionism
Ruggiero

Explaining Criminal Careers

Implications for Justice Policy

JOHN F. MACLEOD
PETER G. GROVE
DAVID P. FARRINGTON

OXFORD
UNIVERSITY PRESS

OXFORD
UNIVERSITY PRESS

Great Clarendon Street, Oxford, OX2 6DP,
United Kingdom

Oxford University Press is a department of the University of Oxford. It furthers the University's objective of excellence in research, scholarship, and education by publishing worldwide. Oxford is a registered trade mark of Oxford University Press in the UK and in certain other countries

First Edition published in 2012

Impression: 1

British Library Cataloguing in Publication Data
Data available

Library of Congress Cataloging in Publication Data
Library of Congress Control Number: 2012940891

ISBN 978–0–19–969724–3

Printed in Great Britain by
CPI Group (UK) Ltd, Croydon, CR0 4YY

General Editor's Introduction

Clarendon Studies in Criminology aims to provide a forum for outstanding empirical and theoretical work in all aspects of criminology and criminal justice, broadly understood. The Editors welcome submissions from established scholars, as well as excellent PhD work. The Series was inaugurated in 1994, with Roger Hood as its first General Editor, following discussions between Oxford University Press and three criminology centres. It is edited under the auspices of these three centres: the Cambridge Institute of Criminology, the Mannheim Centre for Criminology at the London School of Economics, and the Centre for Criminology at the University of Oxford. Each supplies members of the Editorial Board and, in turn, the Series Editor.

This book addresses an important, central area of criminological enquiry—namely, the theory of criminal careers. Two of the authors—John F. MacLeod and Peter G. Grove—are former scientific researchers who undertook important criminal career research at the Home Office in the first years of this century and the third—David P. Farrington—has a very long and distinguished history of path-breaking and sophisticated research in the field. Drawing upon their combined expertise, which includes psychology, statistics, and mathematical modelling, the present volume examines the validity of existing criminal career theories and proposes a theory and consequent mathematical models to explain offending, conviction, and reconviction.

Their research analyses the criminal careers of about 100,000 serious offenders drawn from official databases and the datasets of existing longitudinal studies to test propositions about the nature of criminal careers. Central issues addressed by the authors include: the number of offenders in the population; the number of crimes each commits, on average, each year; the length of their criminal careers; the numbers of persistent offenders; and the proportion of crimes that they commit. Their research tackles difficult questions about the onset, persistence, decline, and ending of criminal careers; the factors that explain criminal career duration; the effects of conviction and punishment (particularly imprisonment); and the effects of aging upon desistance. Central too are questions about what can safely be predicted about future crime rates, numbers of offenders, and prison populations. The common contention that offenders simply 'grow out' of crime is challenged by their findings, which instead suggest that the most important factor in desistance is neither aging nor sentence type but conviction.

On the basis of their analysis, the authors develop a clear picture of different categories of offender with different reconviction rates. Subsequent chapters in the book set about explaining these differences. The resulting model is shown to provide a reliable basis for making forecasts about the number of offenders and size of the prison population. The importance of such models to penal policy planning should not be underestimated, not least because they furnish a mechanism for sound predictions and provide the theoretical basis for the evaluating policy initiatives. Given the importance of these findings and their significant implications for policy development, it is especially welcome that the technicalities of their research and analysis are presented in an accessible way. The authors always keep their wider audience both within the academy and in public life in mind by using non-technical language wherever possible; by formulating their ideas in a conceptually clear and highly logical way; and by presenting much of their data in graphical form. They prudently place further details of the mathematical and statistical analysis upon which their findings rely in an appendix of 'mathematical notes' aimed at the technically competent, interested reader.

This important addition to the Clarendon Studies in Criminology Series makes a very significant contribution to criminological knowledge. It will be of interest not only to advanced students and scholars of criminology and other social scientists, but also to those working in criminal justice agencies as policymakers, analysts, researchers, and statisticians.

For all these reasons, the Editors welcome this new addition to the Series.

Lucia Zedner
University of Oxford
May 2012

Foreword

The construct of a 'criminal career' is a powerful approach for accumulating rich knowledge about offenders and using that knowledge for developing rational policies for dealing with crime. This book makes a major advance in pulling together that knowledge and pointing to directions for improved use and for expanding that knowledge. The basic thrust of criminal career research is to look at the characteristics of individual offenders and to use that information for dealing with a particular individual, but also to look at aggregates of offenders and their collective characteristics for guidance on how criminal justice policies can best respond to their offending patterns.

The predominant structure of an individual criminal career looks first at the envelope of the offending pattern, the initiation and termination of the career, and then at the pattern of offences within that envelope. The characteristics of those offences would be the mix of crime types, their frequency, and the way that mix varies over the course of the career.

There are some clear relationships between these characteristics and policy choices by the criminal justice system. The interval between initiation and expected termination, or the duration of the career, should have an important influence on sentencing policy. In particular, it would make little sense for sentences to be longer than the residual duration, or the time from any point of intervention to expected termination. As one examines different offenders in terms of their threat to public safety, those with a highest offending frequency, especially of the most serious crime types, represent prime candidates for incarceration in order to achieve the largest crime-reduction effect through incapacitation.

The authors of this volume have done an impressive job of analysing a large body of longitudinal UK data on individual criminal careers, have accumulated a prodigious amount of analytic insight into a wide variety of aggregate criminal career characteristics, and have gone well beyond criminal careers in the issues on which they have generated important understanding. Their volume is replete with a rich array of models on many aspects of individual criminal careers and aggregate implications of those careers. The results are strengthened by examining the careers in multiple cohorts drawn at different times, with a striking consistency of the results across the cohorts.

The authors have also done an impressive job of capturing many important facets of individual criminal careers. They find it sufficient to characterize the population of offenders into three categories. There is one low-risk category with a low-offending frequency (frequency is often denoted by the Greek letter lambda, λ). There is a high-risk category with considerable heterogeneity in its offending frequency, and that heterogeneity is captured sufficiently by partitioning them into two subcategories: a high-λ subcategory and a low-λ subcategory.

Where others have tended to describe the envelope of the career in terms of its duration, the authors find that unsatisfactory and instead characterize the termination process by a desistance probability or its complement, a reconviction probability. This approach captures the aggregate decline in criminal participation without requiring any change in the individual offending frequency, which some criminologists have assumed must occur because of the well-established aggregate decline in the age–crime curve (a measure of the rate of arrest or conviction as a function of age, which rises rapidly to a peak in the late teen years and then declines more slowly than the teenage rise). Importantly, the authors attribute the aggregate decrease in crime to the declining participation in offending rather than to a slowing down by a roughly constant population of offenders.

With this basic structure, they are able to capture many aspects of careers such as survival distributions (the fraction of an offending cohort still active at any time after initiation), disentangling the contributions of prevalence and λ to the widely known age–crime curve. They also examine the degree of specialization or generality in a career based on the mix of crime types included (emerging with the intriguing finding that the number of different crime types in a career involving K offences is given by the logarithm of K). Then they go further to develop estimates of the mix of anticipated types of crimes included in a career based on information on types they already know to be included. They also derive estimates of the fraction of the population in each offender category who ever get convicted, a fraction that they find impressively constant across birth cohorts. In their models, since participation is reduced after each conviction, that highlights the importance of conviction as a means of crime control and downplays any significant effect of incapacitation.

The impressive richness of their analysis of the many facets of criminal careers is exceeded by the extent to which they are able to link information on the criminal career structure to a wide variety of other features about offenders and aspects of criminal justice policy. They obtained psychological information on offenders and find a variety of intriguing associations between those psychological characteristics and the offending category. They also emerge with an intriguing array of policy insights and approaches for the criminal justice system. Then, by identifying a variety of policy approaches they can estimate trends in prison population and emerge with an intriguing variety of recommendations about how to reduce crime and make the criminal justice system more efficient and effective.

This volume is a powerful example of the richness of the variety of models that could be developed by people with strong mathematical skills, multiple sources of large samples of relevant data on individual criminal careers, and strong insights into the dynamics of crime and the criminal justice system. Of course, any such modelling inevitably involves a wide variety of assumptions. Most of the authors' assumptions seem quite reasonable, but some may have an unanticipated strong influence on their conclusions. For those who would like to challenge their conclusions, the modelling analysis provides the opportunity. Those who would like to draw other conclusions have the challenging task of identifying which assumptions were most influential in generating the conclusion they didn't like. They could then suggest other assumptions and their implications. Then, others could choose the most reasonable assumptions, preferably by data analysis or experiment. The volume provides rich opportunities for such debates and comparative tests.

While this volume should stimulate criminal career research in all countries, I would find it particularly fascinating to apply some of the modelling perspectives generated in this volume to the wide variety of individual criminal career data available in the US. All the states maintain repositories of individual arrest histories and one could readily generate cohorts of first-time arrestees in different time periods and in different states and pursue very similar analyses, perhaps substituting arrest events, which are well recorded in the US, for the conviction events that are much better recorded in the UK (and which are not as well recorded in the US). It would be particularly interesting to contrast criminal career patterns and their implications in three or four different large states characterized by different aggregate levels of criminal activity. For example, California, New York, Illinois, Pennsylvania, and Texas all have excellent criminal record information, and are different in many aspects of their policies and demography. A replication of at least some of the approaches presented by this volume would be intriguing in the results obtained in each state, in contrasting results in different states, and in contrasting results with the UK.

It would be particularly appropriate and desirable for the National Institute of Justice, the research arm of the US Department of Justice, to pursue some of this criminal career research. There was considerable effort along those lines in the 1970s and 1980s, and those early efforts provided some of the initial starting points for the much fuller developments in this volume. Nevertheless, very little of that research has been supported more recently. It is entirely possible that criminal career patterns could well have changed in the US since those earlier results. Has the proportion of serious offenders in the population changed to any significant degree, and are offending frequencies or career durations or other aspects of criminal careers significantly different from 30 or 40 years ago? And how do they compare to those characteristics in the UK developed in this volume?

A particularly challenging finding in this volume is the observation that incapacitation effects are negligibly small, largely because time spent in prison serves merely to lengthen the criminal career by that amount of time. That observation could well be a consequence of the assumption that there is a fixed recidivism (or, non-recidivism) probability following each conviction (or arrest in the US case), and the absence of arrests in prison could be what keeps the career going after release. Or it could be a consequence of the criminogenic effects of incarceration resulting from interaction with criminal peers or the difficulty of gaining successful employment after release, all of which might even contribute to lengthening the career or leading to more serious crimes after release.

These are the kinds of issues that could well be taken up by researchers skilled in the kinds of modelling that is so admirably displayed in this volume. Even more interesting would be the degree to which the volume will serve to recruit skilled modellers who are currently much more immersed in finance and business matters.

They will find the models developed here challenging their skills and thereby serve to enrich the population of criminologists in all countries with the analytic skills demonstrated by MacLeod, Grove, and Farrington. That would be a most useful and desirable outcome of this demonstration of analytic prowess and creativity.

Professor Alfred Blumstein,
H. John Heinz III College Carnegie-Mellon University,
Pittsburgh, PA

Acknowledgements

First and foremost our thanks must go to the Home Office statisticians who, in the early 1960s, conceived and set up the Offenders Index and to the generations of their successors who have painstakingly updated and maintained the database over a period of nearly 50 years. In particular we would like to thank Chris Kershaw and Julian Prime for their help and assistance in providing us with the data required for the analysis and research reported on in this volume. We would also like to thank David Godfrey, Christine Harper, Gerard Sheldon, and Kathryn Glaser for their contributions to the prison projection modelling project. There are also many former colleagues in the Home Office and the wider research community including Chris Lewis, Pat Dowdswell, Richard Price, Paul Wiles, and Robin Marris who are all due our thanks for their encouragement in this endeavour. We particularly wish to acknowledge the inspiring work of Professor Alfred Blumstein, who developed criminal career research in the 1970s and 1980s. We are also very pleased that he agreed to write a foreword to our volume. David Farrington particularly wishes to thank Alfred and Delores Blumstein for their warm hospitality in accommodating him on his many visits to Pittsburgh. We also thank Alex Piquero and Alan Lindfield for their constructive comments on early drafts of the manuscript, and an anonymous reviewer for his/her helpful suggestions and in particular for pointing out that what seems obvious to us is not necessarily clear to others.

Much of the work reported in this volume was undertaken while two of us, Grove and MacLeod, were employed by the Research, Development and Statistics Directorate of the Home Office. But, while our results may have been influential in several areas of policy and management, the views expressed herein are those of the authors and not necessarily those of the Home Office or Ministry of Justice (nor do they reflect UK Government policy, either now or in the past).

Contents

1

Criminal Career Research, Mathematical Models, and Testing Quantitative Predictions from Theories

Background

Unlike theories in the physical sciences, theories in criminology, as in the other behavioural and social sciences, rarely make exact quantitative predictions that can be tested empirically. For example, Moffitt's (1993) theory specifies that there are two types of offenders: life-course-persistent, who have an early onset and a long criminal career, and adolescence-limited, who have a later onset and a short criminal career. However, this theory does not predict such quantities as the exact fraction of any birth cohort who will become life-course-persistents compared with adolescence-limiteds; the frequency of offending of each category of offenders at each age; or the distribution of ages of onset and criminal career durations of each category. In a true science, exact quantitative predictions should be made by theories and tested empirically. In this book, we propose and test simple theories that make exact quantitative predictions about key features of criminal careers.

A number of theories and mathematical models have been proposed in psychology (see eg Atkinson, Bower, and Crothers 1965; Laming 1973) and criminology (see eg Greenberg 1979; Piquero and Weisburd 2010) that make exact quantitative predictions. The most important of these theories of criminal careers have been inspired by the work of Alfred Blumstein. Blumstein, who was originally trained as an engineer and operations researcher, came to criminology more than 40 years ago when he was recruited to Washington to lead a task force on science and technology for the

US President's Commission on Law Enforcement and Administration of Justice. In the early days of computers in the 1960s, he developed the first major model of the criminal justice system (the JUSSIM model) which was a flow diagram that predicted, for example, the effects of changes in the numbers of offenders or changes in sentencing policies on the prison population (see Belkin, Blumstein, and Glass 1971; Blumstein and Larson 1969). This was subsequently used in other countries, for example as the CANJUS model in Canada (see Cassidy, 1985).

Before describing Alfred Blumstein's work on criminal careers, we should point out that, following Blumstein et al (1986), we define a criminal career as a longitudinal sequence of offences committed by an individual offender. Therefore, the study of criminal careers requires longitudinal data on offending, whether obtained from official records or from longitudinal surveys such as the Cambridge Study in Delinquent Development, in which over 400 London boys have been followed up in interviews and records from age 8 to age 48–50 (Farrington, 2003; Farrington et al 2006, 2009). Dictionary definitions of the term 'career' specify two different concepts: a course or progress through life (our use of the term) or a way of making a living. We make no necessary suggestion that offenders use their criminal activity as an important means of earning a living.

We define 'crimes' as the most common types of crimes that predominate in the official criminal statistics of Western industrialized democracies, principally theft, burglary, robbery, violence, vandalism, minor fraud, and drug use. We do not focus on 'white-collar crimes', although these have been studied within the criminal career perspective (see eg Piquero and Benson 2004; Weisburd and Waring 2001). Much criminal career research that we will review is based on official records of offending, because these contain exact information about the timing of offences, but criminal career research can and should also be based on self-reports of offending (see eg Greenwood and Abrahamse 1982). We now consider Alfred Blumstein's contributions in more detail.

Blumstein and Cohen (1979)

In the 1970s, Alfred Blumstein became very interested in estimating the incapacitative effects of imprisonment, following the work of Shinnar and Shinnar (1975), and he chaired the US National

Academy of Sciences Panel on Deterrence and Incapacitation (Blumstein et al 1978). He became convinced that, in order to address key policy issues such as incapacitation, it was crucial to advance knowledge about key features of criminal careers. Blumstein and Cohen (1979) published a landmark paper on 'Estimation of Individual Crime Rates from Arrest Records' that addressed many of the most crucial issues in criminal career research. Blumstein and Cohen (1979, p 561) began:

> Despite an enormous volume of research into the causes and prevention of crime, very little is known about the progress of the individual criminal career. In particular, neither the number of crimes an individual commits each year, the individual crime rate, nor the changes in that rate as a person ages and/or accumulates a criminal record is known. Such knowledge about individual criminal careers is basic to our understanding of individual criminality, and in particular, to our understanding of how various social factors operate on the individual either to encourage or to inhibit criminal activity.

Basic knowledge about individual criminality also has immediate practical import for developing effective crime control policies. For example, incapacitation—or physically preventing the crimes of an offender (eg through incarceration)—has emerged as a popular crime control strategy. But the benefits derived from incapacitation in terms of the number of crimes prevented will vary greatly, depending on the magnitude of the individual's crime rate; the higher an individual's crime rate, the more crimes that can be averted through his/her incapacitation.

One incapacitative strategy calls for more certain and longer imprisonment for offenders with prior criminal records. But if individual crime rates decrease as a criminal career progresses, there would be fewer crime-reduction benefits gained from incapacitating criminals already well into their criminal careers than from incapacitating those with no prior criminal record. Clearly then, evaluating the crime control effectiveness of various incapacitation strategies requires information about the patterns of individual offending during criminal careers.

Blumstein and Cohen (1979) used λ to indicate the individual offending frequency (the average number of crimes committed per year by active offenders) and μ to measure the individual arrest frequency (the average number of arrests per year of active offenders). λ is the true (underlying) frequency of offending, while μ is the measured frequency of offending. λ and μ were linked by q, which was the probability of arrest following a crime:

$$\mu = \lambda * q \qquad (1.1)$$

(where * indicates multiplication)

After comparing the number of arrests with the number of crimes recorded by the police and the probability of reporting a crime to the police according to an early victim survey, they estimated that q varied from 0.025 for larceny to 0.111 for aggravated assault, while λ averaged 10 index crimes and 24 crimes of all kinds per year per active offender.

Blumstein and Cohen's (1979) analyses were very sophisticated. Most importantly, they took account of co-offending in linking up crimes and offenders to make their estimates (see Tonry and Farrington 2005). They also took account of time not at risk of offending because of incarceration. They pointed out that λ and μ were stochastic variables that varied randomly about a mean value, so that an active offender (a person in a criminal career, between onset and termination, with a non-zero λ or rate of offending) nevertheless had a certain probability of committing no crimes in a particular year. They concluded that there was little evidence of specialization in types of crimes, and that λ and μ stayed tolerably constant at different ages.

The National Academy Panel

Alfred Blumstein chaired the path-breaking US National Academy of Sciences Panel on Criminal Career Research, which documented the new criminal career paradigm in great detail (Blumstein et al 1986). This defined a criminal career as a longitudinal sequence of crimes committed by an individual offender, and distinguished it from a 'career criminal'. The Panel was funded by the US National Institute of Justice (NIJ) probably because of NIJ's interest in career criminals and selective incapacitation (see later), but Alfred Blumstein's main interest was in advancing fundamental knowledge about the new criminal career paradigm. The Panel defined many criminal career features: not only λ, μ, and q, but also T (criminal career duration), a_0 (age at onset), a_T (age at the termination of a career), d (participation rate or prevalence of offending per year), C (the aggregate crime rate per year), and δ (the fraction of active offenders who terminate at each age).

The Panel emphasized the need to divide aggregate crime rates into prevalence and frequency, bearing in mind the following equation:

$$C = \lambda * d \tag{1.2}$$

For example, an increase in the overall crime rate may be caused by an increase in the prevalence of offenders (d) or by an increase in the frequency of offending by active offenders (λ) or by both. In implementing criminal policies, it is important to know what is happening, because an increase in the prevalence of offenders would call for primary prevention targeted at the whole community or secondary prevention targeted at high-risk persons, whereas an increase in the frequency of offending would call for tertiary prevention targeted at the most active offenders.

The Panel pointed out that the peak in the aggregate rate of offending in the teenage years was largely driven by a peak in prevalence, since the individual offending frequency did not vary much with age. The aggregate rate of offending decreased in the 20s and beyond because offenders desisted and dropped out, not because the average frequency of offending, by active offenders, decreased with age. It is always important to investigate whether aggregate changes with age reflect changes within individuals or offenders dropping out. For example, the aggregate rate of co-offending (the average number of offenders committing each crime) decreases steadily with age. Is this because the people who have co-offenders in their teenage years change to become lone offenders in their 20s, or is it because one population of co-offenders desists and a different population of lone offenders appears in the 20s? The empirical evidence suggests that people change, not that changes in the aggregate co-offending rate are caused by dropping out processes and changes in the composition of offenders (see Reiss and Farrington 1991).

The Panel emphasized the importance of estimating the residual criminal career duration (TR) of offenders at each age and after each serial number of offence. In general, the average duration of criminal careers was of the order of 5–15 years, depending on how this was measured (eg the definition of a crime). The Panel presented the first estimate of residual career duration and showed that it increased from about 5 years for 18-year-old offenders to 10 years for 28-year-old offenders, remaining at this level (10 years) until age 40, and then decreasing again to 5 years for 55-year-old offenders (see Blumstein et al 1986, p 93). Thus, the age versus residual career duration curve was quite different from the age–crime curve, possibly because less committed offenders were desisting and dropping out between ages 18 and 28. Information about residual career duration is crucial for criminal justice policy, especially for sentencing and parole decisions. For example, it would be a waste of scarce prison resources to lock up someone for eight years if they would desist naturally after four years. Despite the importance of residual career duration, it has rarely been estimated (but see Kazemian and Farrington 2006).

The Panel also pointed out that it was important to investigate the predictors of different criminal career features such as prevalence, frequency, career duration and termination. After reviewing the literature, they concluded that gender and race (like age) were much more predictive of prevalence than of frequency:

> In contrast to the patterns observed in aggregate data on population arrest rates and participation rates, individual frequency rates for active offenders do not vary substantially with the demographic attributes of sex, age or race.
>
> (Blumstein et al 1986, p 76)

For example, while African Americans were more likely than Caucasians to become offenders, African American offenders and Caucasian offenders were rather similar in their individual offending frequencies. In order to prevent onset and continuation after onset and to encourage desistance, it is important to know what are the key risk and protective factors that predict these criminal career features and therefore which factors should be targeted in prevention and intervention programmes (see Farrington 1997, 2007).

Explaining the Growth in Recidivism Probabilities

In an enormously influential longitudinal study of nearly 10,000 boys born in Philadelphia in 1945 and followed up in official records to the 18th birthday, Wolfgang, Figlio, and Sellin (1972, p 162) found that the probability of recidivism increased after each successive offence. For example, it was 0.54 after the first offence, 0.65 after the second offence, 0.72–0.74 after offences 3 to 5, 0.77–0.79 after offences 6 to 7, and subsequently appeared to reach an asymptote of about 0.80–0.83. They also found that 6 per cent of the birth cohort (18 per cent of the offenders), all of whom had committed at least five offences, accounted for the majority (52 per cent) of all crimes. These 6 per cent accounted for even higher proportions of serious crimes: 69 per cent of all aggravated assaults, 71 per cent of homicides, 73 per cent of forcible rapes, and 82 per cent of robberies. The discovery of these 6 per cent, termed 'chronic offenders', led to calls for early identification of these prime targets for intervention, and the application of appropriate methods of prevention and treatment. Several other longitudinal studies, including the Cambridge Study in Delinquent Development in the UK (Farrington and West 1993), also found that about 5–6 per cent of a cohort accounted for over half of all crimes of the cohort.

Blumstein and Moitra (1980) pointed out that Wolfgang et al (1972) identified the chronic offenders retrospectively. Even on the simplest assumption that every offender in the cohort had the same probability p of reoffending after each crime, chance factors alone would result in some of them having more arrests and others fewer. Because of these probabilistic processes, those with the most arrests—defined after the fact as the 'chronics'—would account for a disproportionate fraction of the arrests. This can be illustrated by an example based on throwing a dice. If an unbiased dice was thrown 30 times and the five highest scores were added up, these would account for a disproportionate fraction of the total score obtained in all 30 throws (30 out of 105, on average). In this dice-throwing example, picking the highest scores means that, purely by chance, 16.7 per cent of the throws would account for 28.6 per cent of the total score. In light of this, 18 per cent of offenders accounting for 52 per cent of offences does not seem quite so remarkable.

Blumstein and Moitra (1980) proposed a simple model to explain the growth in recidivism probabilities. They assumed that the probability of a first offence, $p1$, was 0.35, since 35 per cent of the boys were arrested. Similarly, they proposed that $p2 = 0.54$ and $p3 = 0.65$, the observed figures. However, they then proposed that the probability of committing a subsequent offence, p_k, was always 0.72 after every offence from the third onwards, or in other words did not vary with the serial number of the offence k. They showed that they could fit the data (the number of boys committing each number of offences) quite well with this model.

Blumstein and Moitra (1980) divided the cohort into 'innocents' (those with no offences), 'amateurs' (those with 1–3 offences), and 'persisters' (those with more than 3 offences). Because offences are committed at random (with a constant probability of 0.72 after the third onwards), the expected number of offences committed after each offence is also constant and does not vary with the serial number of the offence. Simple mathematics shows that:

$$E = p_k / (1 - p_k) \qquad (1.3)$$

Where E is the expected number of offences.
When p_k=0.72, E=2.57(.72/.28).
Blumstein and Moitra (1980, p 327) concluded:

Thus, if we imprison all persons who have already been arrested three times, we avert 2.57 future arrests per prisoner. If we restrict imprisonment to the 'more chronic' offenders who have already been arrested seven times, we have to deal with fewer prisoners, but we still avert only 2.57 future arrests per prisoner. Thus, more efficient incapacitation cannot be achieved by using a higher value of 'chronicness'.

Blumstein, Farrington and Moitra (1985) then improved on the Blumstein-Moitra (1980) model by a further partitioning of the persisters. They assumed that $p_4 = p_5 = p_6 = 0.72$ and that $p_k = 0.80$ for every offence after the sixth. This model provided a better fit to the observed data. The constant recidivism probability of 0.80 meant that, for every offence from the sixth onwards, the expected number of subsequent offences was 4 (0.80/0.20). Blumstein et al (1985) also showed that a similar model fitted the data from three other longitudinal surveys, including the Cambridge Study.

The problem with this model, however, is that most of the parameters (the probabilities) are set empirically and retrospectively. Blumstein et al (1985) therefore proposed a more parsimonious model by assuming that there were only three categories of boys in the cohort: (1) 'innocents', with a zero probability of arrest, who comprise a fraction β of the cohort; (2) 'desisters', with a low probability of arrest pa, who comprise a fraction α of the offenders; (3) 'persisters', with a high probability of arrest p_r, who comprise a fraction $(1 - \alpha)$ of the offenders. In this model, the persisters and desisters are distinguished by their prospective (a priori) probabilities rather than by their actual numbers of arrests. There will be persisters and desisters with each number of arrests, but as the number of arrests increases the mix of arrestees will be increasingly dominated by persisters.

Blumstein et al (1985) showed that this model fitted the Philadelphia data very well, with the following parameters: β (fraction innocent) = 0.65, p_r (recidivism probability for persisters) = 0.80, p_a (recidivism probability for desisters) = 0.35, α (fraction of first offenders who are desisters) = 0.56. Thus, in a cohort of boys (N = 10,000), 3,500 [$N * (1 - \beta)$] would have at least one offence, and they would comprise 1,960 desisters [3,500 $* \ \alpha$] and 1,540 persisters [3,500 $* (1 - \alpha)$].

Of the 1,960 desisters, 686 [1,960 $* \ pa$] would have a second offence and 240 [686 $* \ p_a$] would have a third offence. Of the 1,540 persisters, 1,232 [1,540 $* \ p_r$] would have a second offence and 986 [1,232 $* \ p_r$] would have a third offence. Of the 3,500 offenders, 1,274 desisters (1,960–686) and 308 persisters (1,540–1,232) would have exactly one arrest, so 80.5 per cent of the 1,582 one-time offenders would be desisters. Blumstein et al (1985, p 210) compared the actual and predicted number of boys with each number of arrests, based on the actual sample size of 9,945 boys. For example, there were 1,613 boys with one arrest, and the model predicted 1,571; there were 344 boys with three arrests, and the model predicted 351; and there were 39 boys with 10 arrests, and the model predicted 41.

A key issue is to what extent the chronic offenders can be predicted in advance, and whether they differ prospectively from the non-chronic offenders in their individual offending frequency. Blumstein et al (1985) investigated this in the Cambridge Study. They used a seven-point scale of variables measured at age 8–10, reflecting child antisocial behaviour, family economic deprivation, convicted parents, low intelligence, and poor parental child-rearing behaviour. Of 55 boys scoring four or more, 15 were chronic offenders (out of 23 chronics altogether), 22 others were convicted, and only 18 were not convicted. Therefore, it was concluded that most of the chronics could have been predicted in advance on the basis of information available at the age of 10. Similar conclusions were drawn in a later analysis (Farrington and West 1993). It is true that only a minority of the high-scoring boys became chronics; however, as will be explained below, the remainder should not all be regarded as 'false positives' or mistakes in prediction.

Blumstein et al (1985) then applied their mathematical model (of innocents, desisters, and persisters) to the Cambridge data. The best fit to the recidivism probabilities in the survey was obtained by assuming that the probability of persisting after each conviction was 0.87 for persisters and 0.57 for desisters. The proportion of first offenders who were persisters was 0.28, while the fraction of the sample who were innocents was 0.67. Persisters and desisters differed in their *a priori* probabilities of persisting, not in their *a posteriori* number of convictions (as chronics did).

Interestingly, the number of empirically predicted chronics among the offenders (37 'high-risk' offenders scoring four or more on the seven-point scale) was similar to the predicted number of persisters (36.7) according to the mathematical model. Remarkably, the individual process of dropping out of crime by the predicted chronics in the empirical data closely matched the aggregate drop-out process for persisters predicted by the mathematical model with parameters estimated from aggregate recidivism data analysis (see Figure 1.1). Therefore, the high-risk offenders might be viewed as the identified persisters. This analysis shows the important distinction between prospective empirical predictions (eg high-risk

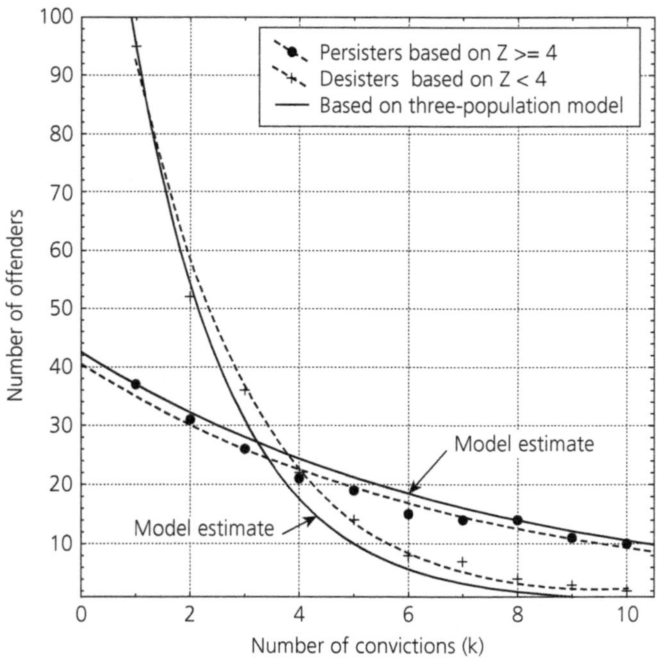

Figure 1.1 Number of persisters and desisters in the London cohort with at least k convictions

Source: Blumstein, Farrington and Moitra (1985)

offenders), true underlying theoretical categories (eg persisters), and retrospectively measured outcomes (eg chronics).

Explaining the Individual Offending Frequency

Barnett and Lofaso (1985) analysed the Philadelphia cohort data collected by Wolfgang et al (1972). Unlike Blumstein and Moitra (1980) and Blumstein et al (1985), they aimed to predict the individual offending frequency rather than the number of offences committed. They assumed that offences were committed probabilistically (at random) over time; technically, this means that offenders accumulate arrests according to a stationary Poisson process (with a constant mean rate). They found that the best predictor of the future individual offending frequency (crimes per year) was the past individual offending frequency.

Barnett and Lofaso (1985) drew attention to the problems caused by truncation of the data at the 18th birthday. Recidivism probabilities for juveniles are often calculated on the assumption that all active offenders desist after their last juvenile arrest. However, especially in the case of a boy who was arrested shortly before the 18th birthday, this 'desistance' might be false, since it is quite likely that he would have a subsequent adult arrest. Assuming that arrests occurred probabilistically according to a Poisson process, they calculated the probability of no arrest occurring between the last juvenile arrest and the 18th birthday, given that the offender was continuing his criminal career and had not truly desisted. Taking account of the past arrest rate and the time at risk between the last arrest and the 18th birthday, Barnett and Lofaso (1985) could not reject the hypothesis that all apparent desistance was false.

Barnett, Blumstein and Farrington (1987) then combined the approaches of Blumstein et al (1985) and Barnett and Lofaso (1985). They analysed conviction data collected in the Cambridge Study, and aimed to predict the number of offences of each person at each age and time intervals between crimes. They tested several mathematical models of criminal careers containing two key parameters: (1) p = the probability that an offender terminates his criminal career after the kth conviction; for any given offender, p is assumed to be constant for all values of k; (2) μ = the individual offending frequency per year, or the annual rate at which the offender sustains convictions while free during his active career.

The individual offending frequency cannot be estimated from aggregate data simply by dividing the number of convictions at each age by the number of offenders at each age, because some active offenders who have embarked on a criminal career may not be convicted at a particular age.

Barnett et al (1987) found that models assuming that all offenders had the same p and μ did not fit the data. They therefore assumed that there were two categories of offenders, 'frequents' and 'occasionals'. Each category had its own values of p and μ, which were assumed to be constant over time. Barnett et al (1987) found that the model that best fitted the data had the following parameters: μF (conviction rate of frequents per year) = 1.14, μO (conviction rate of occasionals per year) = 0.41, pF (termination probability of frequents after each conviction) = 0.10, pO (termination probability of occasionals after each conviction) = 0.33, α (fraction of frequents compared to occasionals) = 0.43. Thus 43 per cent of the offenders were frequents, and the frequents had a higher individual offending frequency and a lower probability of terminating their criminal careers after each conviction. Barnett et al (1987) did not suggest that there were in reality only two categories of offenders, but rather that it was possible to fit the conviction data (convictions of each offender at each age) using a simple model that assumed only two categories.

Barnett, Blumstein, and Farrington (1989) then carried out a test of the predictive validity of their model. The model was developed on conviction data in the Cambridge Study between the 10th and 25th birthdays and tested on conviction data between the 25th and 30th birthdays. The aim was to predict the number of offenders, the number of convictions, and the time intervals between convictions, in this follow-up period. Generally, the model performed well, but more of the frequents were reconvicted than expected, and they had more convictions than expected. The predictions for occasionals were excellent. For example, overall, the model predicted that 29 per cent of all offenders would be reconvicted, and the actual percentage was 33 per cent. For occasionals, the predicted percentage was 29 per cent and the actual percentage was 31 per cent; for frequents, the predicted percentage was 28 per cent but the actual percentage was 36 per cent.

It is illuminating to consider why occasionals and frequents had similar predicted reconviction probabilities. Because pF = 0.10, a frequent who is convicted at age 24 has a 90 per cent chance of continuing in his criminal career at age 25; because $pO = 0.33$, an occasional who is convicted at age 24 has only a 67 per cent chance of continuing in his criminal career at age 25. However, because frequents are convicted at a higher rate than occasionals ($\mu F = 1.14, \mu O = 0.41$), a frequent who was last convicted at age 21 has only a 10 per cent chance of still being an active offender at age 25, whereas an occasional who was last convicted at age 21 has almost a 30 per cent chance of being an active offender at age 25. Because frequents have a higher individual offending frequency, we can be fairly certain that a long conviction-free period indicates that they have terminated their criminal careers. For occasionals, however, because they are convicted at a lower rate, a long conviction-free period does not necessarily indicate that their career has terminated.

Barnett et al (1989) found that the main problem with their predictions was that a few frequents who appeared to have terminated were nevertheless unexpectedly convicted between their 25th and 30th birthdays. They therefore proposed that there might be some intermittency (terminating and later restarting) in criminal careers. A few frequents seemed to cease offending at about age 19 and then were reconvicted after a period of seven to ten years with no convictions. Barnett et al (1989) speculated that this restarting may be connected with life changes such as losing a job or separating from a spouse, in agreement with the observed effects of unemployment (Farrington et al 1986) and separation (Farrington and West 1995) in the Cambridge Study.

The analyses in this book build on the criminal career model of Barnett et al (1987) but go beyond it in a number of ways. First, different categories of offenders are discovered using graphical means. Second, the present analyses are based on very large longitudinal and cross-sectional samples of offenders including comparisons across birth cohorts and time periods. Third, the individual offending frequency and the probability of termination are decoupled, so that two categories of offenders can have the same frequency but different probabilities of termination. Fourth, the current models aim to explain the onset process as well as persistence and desistance in offending. Fifth, attempts are made to explain the criminal careers of less serious offenders. Sixth, we show that the categories identified by our mathematical models have different psychological characteristics. Seventh, the theories are applied to explain a wide range of fundamental and applied criminological topics, including not only criminal career features but also the future prison population.

Objections to Criminal Career Research

In the 1980s, US governmental and funding agencies began to appreciate the enormous importance of criminal career research and longitudinal studies. Major bodies such as the US National Institute of Justice, the US Office of Juvenile Justice and Delinquency Prevention, the US National Institute of Mental Health, and the MacArthur Foundation started devoting significant funding to criminal career and longitudinal research and consequently reduced their funding of the more traditional cross-sectional theory-testing sociological research such as that carried out by Hirschi (1969).

It was perhaps no coincidence, then, that Travis Hirschi and his colleague Michael Gottfredson launched a series of attacks on criminal career and longitudinal research in the 1980s, including the provocatively-titled paper 'The true value of lambda would appear to be zero' (Gottfredson and Hirschi 1986). Their main argument was that individual age–crime curves were the same as the aggregate age–crime curve. Therefore, it was unnecessary to distinguish prevalence and frequency because both varied similarly with age. Between-individual differences in offending depended on a single underlying theoretical construct of self-control (Gottfredson and Hirschi 1990) which persisted from childhood to adulthood. Persons with low self-control had a high prevalence, frequency, and seriousness of offending, an early onset, a late termination, and a long criminal career, so the predictors and correlates of any one of these criminal career features were the same as the predictors and correlates of any other. Gottfredson and Hirschi (1987) also argued that longitudinal research was unnecessary because the causes and correlates of offending (which depended on the stable underlying construct of self-control) were the same at all ages.

Blumstein, Cohen and Farrington (1988a, 1988b) responded to the main criticisms. First, they argued that the predictors and correlates of one criminal career feature (eg prevalence or onset) were different from the predictors of another (eg frequency or desistance). Second, they argued that individual age–crime curves for frequency (which was constant over time for active offenders) were very different from the aggregate age–crime curve. Third, they argued that longitudinal research was needed to test many of

Gottfredson and Hirschi's key hypotheses, such as the stability of self-control from childhood to adulthood. Fourth, they argued that, because of their emphasis on and experience of cross-sectional research, Gottfredson and Hirschi tried to draw conclusions about causes from between-individual differences, but the idea of cause required within-individual change over time, which could only be studied in longitudinal research. Conclusions about causes can be drawn more convincingly in within-individual analyses in longitudinal research, which specify a clear time ordering of events and allow better control of extraneous variables because each person acts as his/her own control (Farrington 1988).

Subsequent research has cast doubt on Gottfredson and Hirschi's arguments. For example, using data from the Cambridge Study, Farrington and Hawkins (1991) found that, in general, participation, early onset, and persistence were predicted by different variables measured in childhood. Similarly, in the Pittsburgh Youth Study, Loeber et al (1991) reported that the correlates of initiation were different from the correlates of escalation but similar to the correlates of persistence versus desistance. After reviewing the literature on this topic, Piquero, Farrington and Blumstein (2003, p 462) concluded that 'it does not appear that correlations are similar for all dimensions, as Gottfredson and Hirschi argued'.

The evidence on the variation with age of individual offending frequency is mixed. The early studies reviewed by Blumstein et al (1986) and Farrington (1986) concluded that the rate of offending by active offenders did not vary with age during the course of criminal careers. However, Loeber and Snyder (1990) found that frequency increased during the juvenile years up to age 16, and Haapanen (1990) discovered that it decreased during the adult years. Farrington and Wikström (1994) systematically compared results in the Cambridge Study in London and in Project Metropolitan in Sweden, and concluded that the individual offending frequency stayed constant in London but peaked in the teenage years (like the aggregate age–crime curve) in Stockholm. In the Seattle Social Development Project, Farrington et al (2003) found that the individual offending frequency increased during the juvenile years according to self-reports but stayed constant according to court referrals. It seems possible that the individual offending frequency may be depressed in official data because it is rare to have more than one court referral in a year, whereas it is common to commit many self-reported acts.

In the last 20 years, there has been an explosive growth of research on offending trajectories, stimulated by the work of Nagin (2005) and reviewed by Piquero (2008). For example, for offending up to age 32 in the Cambridge Study, Nagin, Farrington and Moffitt (1995) found that there were three categories of offenders with different trajectories: an adolescence-limited category whose offending rate increased to a peak at age 16 and then decreased precipitously; a high-level chronic category whose offending rate increased to a peak at about 18 and then decreased gradually; and a low-level chronic category with a very gradual flattened peak between ages 20 and 27. These offending rates are not technically individual offending frequencies because the denominator may include non-offenders (persons who are not in a criminal career between onset and desistance).

Up to age 40, Piquero, Farrington and Blumstein (2007) found that there were four categories of offenders, with the adolescence-limited category of Nagin et al (1995) divided into low adolescence peaked and high adolescence peaked categories. The enormous volume of research on offending trajectories clearly conflicts with Gottfredson and Hirschi's (1990) argument that all individual age–crime curves are the same as the aggregate age–crime curve. As Nagin et al (1995, p 113) point out, 'these results imply that explanations of the age–crime curve at the level of the individual cannot be the same as explanations of average population tendencies'.

Gottfredson and Hirschi's (1990) argument that all criminal career features reflect the underlying theoretical construct of self-control would nowadays be termed a 'persistent heterogeneity' argument. Nagin and Paternoster (1991) were the first researchers to formulate and contrast persistent heterogeneity with state dependence in criminology. Briefly, past offending predicts future offending, and this could be explained either by persistent heterogeneity (the persistence of between-individual differences in some kind of underlying criminal propensity, as Gottfredson and Hirschi propose) or by state dependence (where the act of committing a crime in some way increases the probability of committing future crimes, for example because the offender is labelled or stigmatized).

In the Cambridge Study, Nagin and Farrington (1992b) contrasted persistent heterogeneity and state dependence in explaining the relationship between past and future offending, and Nagin and Farrington (1992a) carried out similar analyses to explain the relationship between early onset and persistent offending. In both studies persistent heterogeneity was more important than state dependence, as it also was in further analyses of the Cambridge Study by Paternoster, Brame, and Farrington (2001). However, a review of the literature by Nagin and Paternoster (2000) concluded that both were important, contrary to Gottfredson and Hirschi (1990). Also, there is a great deal of evidence that offending increases after a conviction, in agreement with labelling theory (eg Bernburg and Krohn 2003; Farrington 1977).

We conclude that Gottfredson and Hirschi's (1986, 1987, 1990) various arguments about criminal career research have generally been proved to be incorrect.

Criminal Career Research in the Last 20 Years

Surprisingly, there has been little effort in the last 20 years to develop and test criminal career theories with quantitative predictions, such as that formulated and tested by Barnett et al (1987, 1989). In this book, we further develop and test quantitative theories of this kind. There has been an enormous amount of criminal career research on other topics, extensively reviewed by Delisi and Piquero (2011), Piquero et al (2003, 2007) and Soothill, Fitzpatrick, and Francis (2009). In the previous section, we reviewed research on trajectory modelling and on persistent heterogeneity versus state dependence. We now briefly review some other criminal career topics.

Most importantly, the enormous investment in longitudinal research since the 1980s has coincided with a huge increase in research on risk and protective factors for offending and on the effects of life events on offending. Coupled with this has been a great emphasis on trying to prevent offending by targeting early risk and protective factors (see Farrington 2007; Farrington and Welsh 2007). This was termed the 'risk factor prevention paradigm' by Farrington (2000) and Piquero et al (2003, p 466) noted that 'there appears to be a paradigm shift away from measurement of criminal career parameters and toward a search for risk and protective factors'. The effects of life events such as getting married have been studied extensively (see eg Theobald and Farrington 2009, 2011).

There has also been a great deal of research on factors influencing desistance (see Kazemian and Farrington 2010; Laub and Sampson 2001). However, there has been little attempt to study career duration or residual career duration (see Francis, Soothill, and Piquero 2007; Kazemian and Farrington 2006). One associated policy issue is: After what period of non-offending do past offenders become similar to non-offenders in their probability of offending? This question is relevant to the issue of how long a criminal record should 'count against' a person. In the US, Kurlychek, Brame, and Bushway (2007) argued that ex-juvenile offenders became similar to non-offenders by about age 23, but in the UK Soothill and Francis (2009) concluded that these two groups did not become similar until about age 30. In the Cambridge Study, Farrington et al (2006) found that, at age 48, 'desisters' (those who were convicted before age 21 but not after) were similar to unconvicted men in various measures of life success. Blumstein and Nakamura (2009) estimated what they called 'redemption times' when the hazard of a new crime had fallen close to that of the general population with no prior record.

Other important criminal career topics that have been addressed recently include specialization (eg Francis, Liu, and Soothill 2010; McGloin, Sullivan, and Piquero 2009), escalation (eg Liu, Francis, and Soothill 2011), co-offending (eg Van Mastrigt and Farrington 2009, 2011), types of offenders (eg Francis, Soothill, and Fligelstone 2004; Soothill, Francis, Ackerley, and Humphreys 2008), and the cost of career criminals (eg Cohen and Piquero 2009; Welsh et al 2008).

Some burning issues of the 1980s are still being addressed. For example, the effectiveness of incapacitation in preventing crimes has continued to be an important topic, as evidenced by the special issue of the Journal of Quantitative Criminology on this topic in December 2007 (see eg Piquero and Blumstein 2007). We address this topic in this book and conclude that incapacitation is ineffective in preventing crimes. Blumstein has continued to address criminal career topics, such as measuring the probability of arrest for different types of crimes (Blumstein et al 2010). We hope that our book will reinvigorate research on simple criminal career theories that make detailed quantitative predictions.

Aims of this Book

In July 2000, John (later Lord) Birt was sent to the Home Office by Prime Minister Tony Blair as his special advisor on crime. Birt was not a criminologist (he was a former Director-General of the BBC) but he asked some fundamental questions about criminal careers, such as:

1. How many offenders are there in the population?
2. How many crimes, on average, do they each commit per year?
3. How long do they keep on offending? (What is the length of their criminal careers?)
4. How many persistent offenders are there in the population, and what fraction of crimes do they account for?

Shockingly, these were very difficult questions for the Home Office to answer at that time, because there had been very little interest in criminal career research since Roger Tarling, the former Head of the Research and Planning Unit, had left. However, two of us (John MacLeod and Peter Grove) were working at the Home Office at that time, and we were asked to address these fundamental questions about criminal careers. This task gave a new impetus to what had previously been considered low-priority theoretical work which up to that time had only been applied to prison population forecasting models (described in Chapter 7). Birt's questions led directly to the further development and testing of the simple quantitative theory that is described in this book, which has been applied to explain a wide range of criminological issues. The theory and some tests were presented in a little-known Home Office Occasional Paper (Grove 2003; MacLeod 2003) but, with some further development and refinement, the theory has now been applied to explain a wide range of criminological topics. We describe the theory and its fundamental and policy applications in this book.

Some other key questions that are addressed in this book include:

1. How many categories of offenders need to be identified in order to explain criminal career findings?
2. How do these categories differ? (eg in individual offending frequency and probability of persistence after each offence)
3. How well can the age–crime curve be explained?
4. How well can ages of onset and termination of offending be explained?
5. How well can criminal career duration be explained?
6. To what extent are results replicable in different birth cohorts?
7. What is the effect of being convicted on offending?

8. What is the effect of imprisonment on offending? Are criminal careers curtailed or just postponed?
9. Does imprisonment have criminogenic, rehabilitative, or incapacitative effects?
10. Do offenders desist because they 'grow out of crime' or because of the effects of the criminal justice system?
11. Can future aggregate crime rates be predicted?
12. Can future numbers of offenders be predicted?
13. Can future prison populations be predicted?
14. Do cautions and warnings reduce the number of persons in a birth cohort who are convicted?

In Chapter 2 we will see that an analysis of about 100,000 detailed criminal careers, of those who have at some time committed a serious offence, indicates the existence of two categories of offenders with constant but different reconviction probabilities. The same kind of analysis looking at the timing of offences indicates two categories with constant but different rates of conviction. The proportions of these categories, in each birth cohort, are essentially constant. In Chapters 3 and 4 we will see how a theory, based on various models with a small number of categories of offenders, can be constructed to explain this, and make successful predictions about independent criminal career data. In Chapter 5 we will also investigate the possibilities of fitting the criminal career information using more intuitive theories assuming that the behaviour of offenders is strongly determined by their age, and that individual age–crime curves are similar to the aggregate age–crime curve. We will discover that such theories are essentially ruled out. In Chapter 6 we will look at the evidence for psychological differences between the categories. Chapter 7 will show how a simplified two category model can be used to make very accurate forecasts of the prison population and the future number of offenders in the DNA database. Finally, in Chapter 8 we explore the policy implications of the theory.

Methodological Notes

Although rooted in the early work of Blumstein and his associates, see Belkin, Blumstein, and Glass (1973), Blumstein et al (1985) and Barnett et al (1987), our models are derived using analytical methods which may be unfamiliar to some of our readers. In our analyses we have been very fortunate in that our datasets are very large and cover a long time period. The information available in the Offenders Index, our primary data source, is relatively limited but is both accurate and complete.[1] In Chapter 2 we describe both the data and our initial analysis in some detail but it may help the reader if we outline here our basic approach.

It is often the case in the physical sciences and engineering that the discovery of mathematical regularity in observations leads directly to mathematical formulae describing the processes generating the data. Graphical representations of the data commonly reveal these mathematical relationships and identify the kind of processes involved. Familiarity with such techniques has guided our analysis and led to the propositions underpinning our theory. In particular we have employed the techniques of survival analysis, leading to the identification of processes very similar to those of radioactive decay and many others observed in the physical world. It is however rare in the social sciences to find strong mathematical or statistical relationships. Relationships which are identified are frequently confounded by multiple potentially causal correlations, making the description of the underlying processes difficult. In our analysis of reconviction data we have been able to identify very strong mathematical relationships and have related them to plausible processes. Carr-Hill and Carr-Hill (1972) employed similar methods in their analysis of reconvictions of released prisoners, resulting in a model with an excellent fit to the data ($Chi^2 = .228$ on $5df$, $p > 0.99$); our models also provide an excellent fit to the data in most of our analyses.

In the Appendix we describe in some detail the mathematical and statistical logic and understanding required for the analysis and model development, and readers may find it useful to refer to the Appendix if it is not clear why we draw specific conclusions from our analysis. In the course of the analysis we also divide the offender population into a variety of different categorizations: high-risk or low-risk, high-rate or low-rate, male or female, serious or less-serious, etc. In each categorization the categories are mutually exclusive but different categorizations may overlap to

[1] We cannot claim that the data is entirely error free but as part of the official ongoing data collection, it was subjected to rigorous validation and consistency checks.

create a new categorization (eg high-risk/high-rate or high-risk/low-rate or low-risk/low-rate) in which case the composite categories are also mutually exclusive as are the constituent categories. The defining property of a categorization, (eg risk, rate, gender, custody, etc); may be inferred (as in risk or rate) or explicit (as in gender or custody) and are properties of the offenders. Categorizations will be defined as appropriate within the text. For clarity of exposition we have reserved the word *category* to refer to our risk and rate categorization. Where categorizations are based on other characteristics, such as custody or assessment scores, we refer to these categories as groups or subsets or simply by the categorization criterion.

We also make extensive use of graphical representations of the data. Notes to the graphs will describe how they were constructed and, if not specifically covered in the text, what can be deduced from them. There are also a number of mathematical equations embedded in the text, many of which relate directly to the graphs. These are included for completeness as it is the inferences which can be drawn from the mathematics that lead to the assumptions of the theory and the development of the models implementing it. Readers who are unfamiliar with the mathematical notation might simply like to accept the mathematics and our interpretation of its implications, safe in the knowledge that the workings are presented for scrutiny by others.

2

An Analysis of the Offenders Index

Sources of Data

In this book we are concerned with criminal careers. In general we will consider only the documented record of a criminal career as seen in formal convictions in an offender's criminal record. The most complete criminal records in England and Wales are held in the Criminal Record Office (CRO) in New Scotland Yard and on the Police National Computer (PNC). However these records are maintained for the police and other agencies in the criminal justice system and are only rarely available for research purposes. The Home Office and Ministry of Justice distribute a 'cut-down' version of the PNC to researchers that excludes vital variables such as co-offenders. It is often unclear, in the distributed version, whether a person found in the PNC search is the same person who was submitted. The uncertainty can only be resolved if the individuals are interviewed.

Also as an operational database the PNC is subject to weeding and periodic reconstruction, and consequently the early cohort samples are incomplete. Offenders who have not offended since May 1995 (when the microfiche collection was discontinued) are not included in the current PNC database unless their offences were very serious. Thus, it is impossible to use the PNC retrospectively for valid criminal career research, although it can be used validly in prospective longitudinal surveys with repeated searches of criminal records over a 40-year period, such as the Cambridge Study in Delinquent Development (Farrington et al 2006).

As an alternative to the PNC, the Research, Development, and Statistics Directorate (RDS) of the Home Office maintained a database of all 'standard list'[1] convictions in England and Wales.

[1] The Offenders Index and the offences included in the Standard List are described in *The Offenders Index: A User's guide* and *The Offenders Index: Codebook* (Home Office 1998a, 1998b).

This database, the Offenders Index (OI), was created in 1963 and is based on records obtained from courts in England and Wales of each court appearance resulting in a conviction for one or more 'standard list offences'. The 'standard list' includes all offences which may be tried at the Crown Court (so called 'indictable' and 'either-way' offences) as well as the more serious summary offences which can only be tried in the magistrates' courts. The definition of standard list has changed during the period covered by the OI, offences being added or more rarely removed from the list, but our analyses are based on the definition used in the early 1990s.

The records of the different convictions of each offender obtained from the courts must be matched to form the OI criminal career record. This is done by a combination of automatic and manual methods. The details on each offender include name, date of birth, gender, and date of conviction. The date of the offence itself is not recorded but there is clearly a relationship between the dates of offence and conviction. Offence classification, sentence and disposal for each conviction are also recorded on the database. The OI was created to facilitate the study of criminal justice interventions and has been the source of data for many statistical and research studies conducted by the Home Office and others over many years. While the CRO and PNC have changed a lot over time (eg from paper to microfiche in 1979, from microfiche to computer in 1995), and many earlier conviction records have been deleted (weeded out) from them, the OI has never changed and is complete from its inception in 1963 to its demise in 2006. The size and completeness of the OI data set allows the extraction of subsets of data conditioned on any of the recorded information.

In extracting the subsets considered in this book, considerable pains (rigorous manual matching) were taken to ensure that all convictions relating to each individual were collated. Although this process can never be perfect, every effort had been made to ensure that there were relatively few cases where the history was incomplete or where two individuals had been erroneously linked together. All but one of the birth cohort samples used in our analysis were extracted from the Offenders Index, in 1992 or 1993, prior to its redevelopment in 1997. As part of this redevelopment the matching system changed to an automatic computerized system. Updated cohort samples were extracted from the OI in 1999 using the new matching rules. The cohorts were updated and Prime, White,

Liriano, and Patel (2001) revised the estimates of criminal career parameters reporting reduced criminality (the proportion of males convicted up to age 46) and increased recidivism after each conviction number when compared with previous estimates. These inconsistencies were reported by Prime et al as due to *improvements* in the data. However, we carried out analyses on the original and updated samples which indicate that the new matching rules may have introduced serious errors into the OI. For example, before the changes the measured recidivism probability of offenders with uncommon names was essentially identical to that of offenders with common names. With the new matching procedures the recidivism of offenders with uncommon names has scarcely changed whereas that for offenders with common names has increased. This suggests that the new matching rules are 'overmatching', that is combining the records of offenders with similar names and dates of birth. In order to extend the follow-up period of the 1953 cohort we disentangled the over matching by collating convictions prior to 1992 between the original and updated samples. The disentangled 1953+ sample provided results consistent with the original sample without the differential recidivism estimates for common and uncommon names. Despite having voiced our concerns at the time and judging from the male criminality estimate (33.2 per cent; much the same as Prime et al, 2001) for the 1953 cohort up to age 52 (Ministry of Justice 2010, p 8), these problems have not been resolved. The use of the OI as an operational research tool has subsequently been phased out in favour of the incomplete and unsatisfactory cut-down version of the PNC database. The cohort samples used in our analyses are available to researchers via the ESRC Data Archive (SN 3935).

Of particular use in the context of modelling the criminal process are the cohort samples drawn from the OI. The cohort samples consist of all records on the database with a date of birth included in one of four sample weeks (spread throughout the year) for each of the cohort years: 1953, 1958, 1963, 1968, and 1973. Because the OI began in 1963, and because the minimum age of conviction is 10, the first birth cohort that could be followed up were children born in 1953. In addition to the automated matching procedures, manual matching of court appearances (using the old matching rules) has also been carried out on these cohort samples to give the maximum possible assurance that they are complete records of unique individuals. In general the ideas to be discussed here were based on analyses of the 1953[2] and 1958 cohorts, which provide the longest follow-up periods and hence capture the most complete criminal careers. The ideas were then tested on the later cohorts, taking at least partial account of the censoring effects.

For the purpose of the analyses, the event considered is conviction for the most serious offence at each court appearance, the 'principal conviction'. There are between one and 25 convictions (different offences) per court appearance with an average of about 1.5. The distribution of convictions per court appearance is highly skewed towards the low values with a little over 70 per cent of court appearances resulting in only one and a little less than 20 per cent resulting in just two convictions. A small proportion of offenders are convicted of a disproportionately large number of offences and it might be reasonably assumed that the allocation of crimes to criminals is similarly skewed. To avoid confusion, throughout this book the words 'conviction' and 'appearance' will be used interchangeably to mean 'a court appearance resulting in conviction for one or more offences'. Thus, one conviction in this book means one occasion of conviction at one court appearance.

Recidivism

We begin with an analysis of recidivism. Figure 2.1 indicates a typical graph of the proportion reconvicted versus the number of previous convictions. The data happens to come from the 1953 cohort but similar graphs are obtained from any data source containing the required information. The main feature of the graph is clear: the recidivism probability starts at about 40 per cent after the first conviction and increases with each subsequent conviction to around 84 per cent after six or seven convictions. A commonsense hypothesis would be that the risk of further offending increases with each conviction. It is important to note that for the 1953 cohort we are effectively seeing the lifetime recidivism probabilities rather than the more usual 'two year' reconviction rate (the proportion reconvicted within two years).

There is a more useful way of looking at this data by following procedures first outlined in Grove, MacLeod, and Godfrey (1998)

[2] In order to extend the follow-up period of the 1953 cohort to the end of 1999 the authors disentangled the overmatching by collating court appearance data to identify where erroneous mergers had taken place.

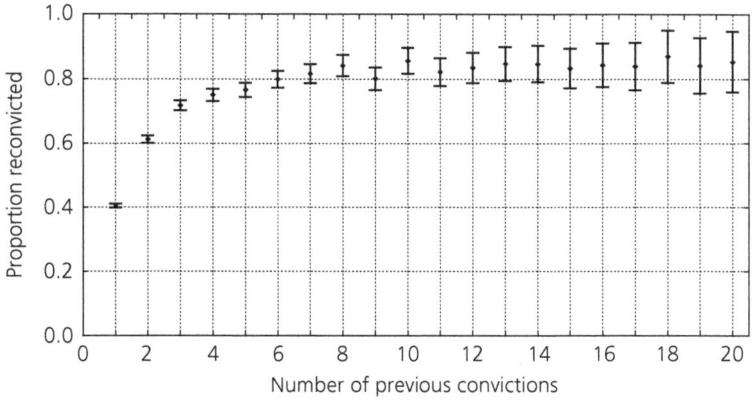

Figure 2.1 Proportion reconvicted for given previous conviction count

Source: 1953 cohort, Offenders Index.
Note: The error bars show ±1 standard deviation about the data points.

and MacLeod (2003). This is a kind of 'survival' curve. Assuming that we had in fact a lifetime recidivism probability of 80 per cent from offence to offence, then starting with the number of offenders with at least one conviction in their lifetime we can plot the number *surviving* (continue to offend and be reconvicted) after each consecutive conviction. If we assume a cohort size of 100 offenders with recidivism probability 'p' then the number of offenders *surviving* to the nth conviction '$y(n)$' is given by:

$$y(n) = 100 * p^{(n-1)} \tag{2.1}$$

With the recidivism probability equal to 80 per cent after each conviction (p = 0.8) the graph would look something like Figure 2.2a.

A logarithmic transformation (base 10) of the y axis results in a straight line graph if there is a constant probability of reconviction. This is shown in Figure 2.2b. The slope of the line is directly related to the recidivism probability and is simply Log(p): the steeper the line the lower the recidivism probability. Because p is a probability and therefore less than one the slope is negative. Figure 2.3 shows what we get if we plot the actual data for the 1953 cohort on such a graph. The '+' symbols represent the number of individuals in the

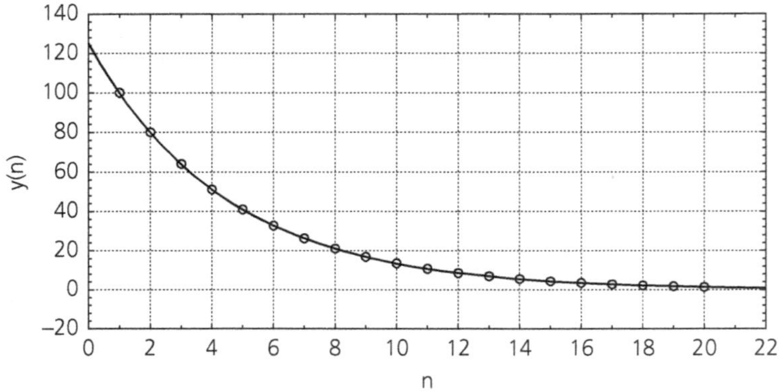

Figure 2.2a Hypothetical number of offenders with at least *n* convictions given 80% recidivism on a linear *y* scale

cohort with at least ***n*** court appearances (convictions). The solid line is the 'best fit' to the data for '$n > 6$', given by the equation:

$$y(n) = 2786 * 0.84^{(n-1)} \quad (2.2)$$

This equation is of the form of Equation 2.1, suggesting that for the higher appearance numbers the probability of reconviction is constant (84 per cent) as illustrated in Figure 2.1.

Let us now project the line, ***y(n)***, back to appearance numbers less than or equal to 6 and in so doing assume that high recidivism offenders form a homogeneous category with a constant recidivism

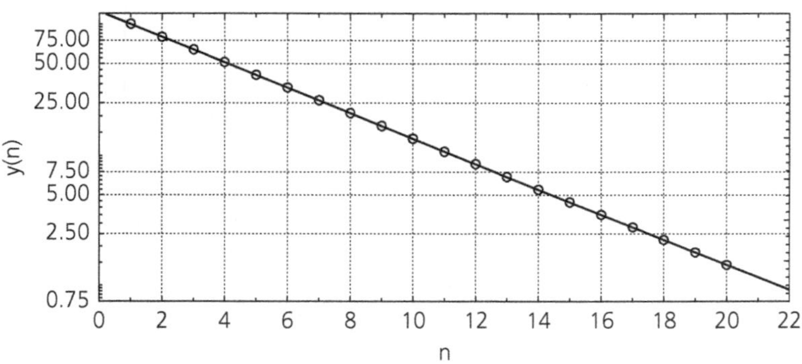

Figure 2.2b Hypothetical number of offenders with at least *n* convictions given 80%recidivism on a logarithmic *y* scale

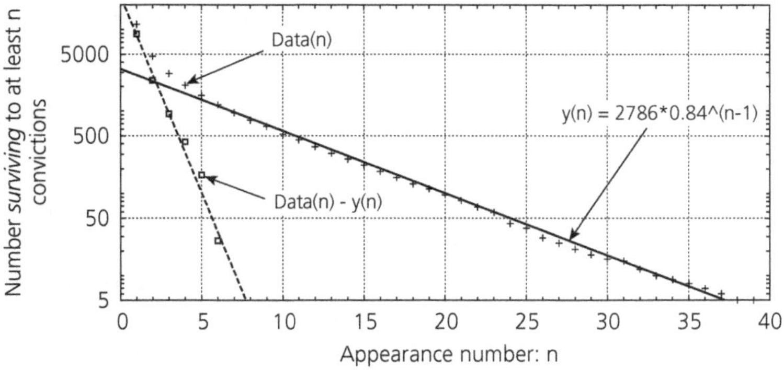

Figure 2.3 Numbers of offenders surviving to at least the number of appearances shown on the *x* axis

Source: 1953 cohort, Offenders Index.

probability from the first conviction onwards. We can now calculate the residuals, by subtracting the value of ***y(n)*** for ***n*** <= 6 from the corresponding data. If we now plot the result we get the 'square' symbols of Figure 2.3. Quite remarkably, these also fall on a straight line given by the equation:

$$y_r(n) * 8884 * 0.313^{(n-1)} \tag{2.3}$$

This suggests that there is a second category of offenders, in addition to those identified above, with a constant probability of recidivism. The probability of reconviction for this second category is much lower at 0.313 (31 per cent) and the category size is much higher at 8884 individuals. Thus, this simple graphical method shows convincingly that the conviction data can be fitted very well by assuming that there are only two *risk* categories of offenders with constant but different recidivism probabilities.

This is the first critical point of our analysis. What at first sight looks like evidence that the recidivism probability for individuals increases in a complicated way depending on the number of previous convictions, can also be explained quite simply, by the existence of two categories of offenders, with each category having its own constant recidivism probability.[3]

[3] In this context, constant probability implies that when members of one of the categories are convicted then a constant proportion will go on to sustain at least one more conviction irrespective of the numbers of previous convictions.

The two fitted equations can be combined into a single equation, *the dual risk recidivism model*, with the general form:

$$Y(n) = A * \left(a * p_1^{(n-1)} + (1-a) * p_2^{(n-1)}\right) \tag{2.4}$$

Where:

'A' is the total number of individuals in the cohort with at least one conviction (11642 in the 1953– cohort),

'a' is the proportion of offenders in the high-risk (of reconviction) category (0.237 in the 1953– cohort),

'p_1' is the high-risk probability of recidivism (0.84 in the 1953– cohort), and

'p_2' is the low-risk probability of recidivism (0.313 in the 1953– cohort).

More technically and arguably more precisely than the graphical approach, the values of the three parameters, 'a', 'p_1', and 'p_2', were obtained using a 'joint iterative maximum likelihood procedure' (see the Appendix). However this is no more than a sophisticated way of carrying out the graphical analysis described above. Figure 2.4 shows the result of the fit of the model to the 1953– cohort data.

The formal statistical properties of the fit of the model to the data are impressive. The model accounted for over 99.9 per cent of the variance in the data with the correlation coefficient $R = 0.9994$; that is, it described almost all the recidivism seen at each conviction.

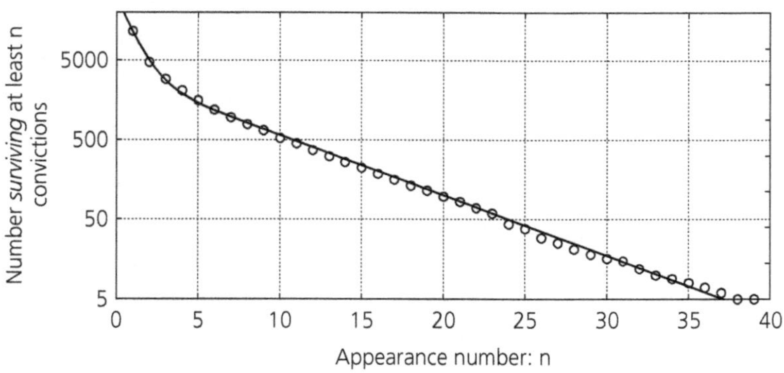

Figure 2.4 Dual-risk recidivism model fit to the 1953 cohort data

Note: The data point at appearance number = 1 corresponds to the total number of convicted offenders in the cohort. The data point at appearance number = 2 is the number of convicted offenders with at least two convictions, etc.

Table 2.1 Parameter estimates for the dual risk recidivism model for all cohorts and the 1997 sentencing sample

	53+ cohort	53 cohort	58 cohort	63 cohort	68 cohort	73 cohort	97 sentencing sample
a	0.237	0.274	0.365	0.452	0.444	0.592	0.217
p_1	0.840	0.822	0.799	0.779	0.771	0.696	0.879
p_2	0.313	0.276	0.238	0.183	0.196	0.068	0.276

Note: 53+ cohort followed up to 1999. 53, 58, 63 cohorts followed up to 1992 and the 68 and 73 cohorts followed up to 1993.

It might be argued that the very high value of R is due the data points not being independent; an individual with n appearances will also have contributed to each of the previous appearance number counts. However, a similar analysis of a sentencing sample,[4] in which the appearance number counts of separate individuals were used, provided similar parameter estimates[5] and an R value of 0.9990. In this sentencing sample all the data points are independent.

Although the 1997 Sentencing sample is essentially cross-sectional, longitudinal information on each of the included offenders is available. Both the appearance number of the current conviction and the time since the previous conviction are known. Indeed, all the longitudinal information on each of the offenders is known back to 1963, the creation date of the Offenders Index, but only current conviction information is used in the cross-sectional analysis. The estimated parameter values for all of the cohort samples and the 1997 Sentencing sample are shown in Table 2.1.

We see the same 'dual risk' characteristics in all the cohorts. Very similar graphs are obtained for the 1958, 1963 and 1968, and 1973 cohorts which all have the same shape, but the slopes are progressively steeper as the cohorts become more recent. This is as expected as we are not seeing lifetime reconviction probabilities but only

[4] The sample consisted of individuals sentenced during the first weeks of alternate months from February to December 1997, six weeks in all. Each individual offender was included only once in the sample. The total sample size was 58,916.

[5] Cohort samples and cross-sectional samples are equivalent if the processes generating them are 'stationary' (that is the same processes operate over the time period under consideration). The similarity of the estimated parameters suggests that this condition held.

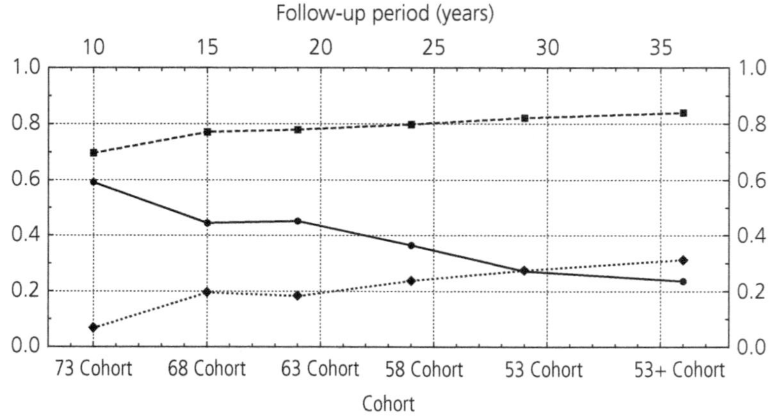

Figure 2.5 Plot of the dual risk recidivism model parameter estimates by OI cohort

Note: (-■-p1,·◆· p2) probability of re-conviction, (—●— a) proportion high-risk

those convictions and reconvictions sustained in the time available for each cohort: 24, 19, 15, and 10 years respectively (from age 10 to 1992/3, the extraction dates of the cohort samples). Fitting the dual risk recidivism model to each of the cohorts generates the parameter values shown in Table 2.1 and plotted in Figure 2.5.

The first thing to note is that although they do differ, the measured p_1 and p_2 vary little from cohort to cohort. In more detail, the parameters p_1 and p_2 both increase and the proportion of high-risk offenders a decreases as the follow-up period increases from 10 to 36 years and we move from the 1973 birth cohort through to the 1953 (followed up to 1992) and 1953+ (followed up to 1999) cohorts. The 1997 Sentencing sample parameter estimates are broadly consistent with the estimates for the longer follow-up periods 1953 cohorts. This suggests that the reconviction probabilities and the proportions of the population in each of the risk categories had in fact changed very little over the time-span of the cohorts. The 1973 cohort parameters deviate from the trend but we might expect this as the follow-up period is dominated by the teenage years when the prevalence of convictions is changing very rapidly. To correct for the effect of the 'censored' offending lifetimes, we need to understand the rate at which offenders are reconvicted which we will investigate in the next section.

The consistency across cohorts provides a strong indication that all offenders fall into one of our two risk categories, a 'high-risk' category and a 'low-risk' category, and that each of these categories is homogeneous with respect to *the probability of* recidivism.

We can use the dual risk recidivism model to calculate the proportion reconvicted for a given number of previous convictions. The proportion is given by:

$$P(n) = Y(n+1) \,/\, Y(n) \qquad \text{For } \boldsymbol{n} >= 1. \tag{2.5}$$

Where $\boldsymbol{n}$ is the number of previous convictions and $\boldsymbol{P(n)}$ is the proportion of offenders convicted for the $\boldsymbol{n}$th time who sustain one or more further convictions. The solid line in Figure 2.6 shows the modelled proportion superimposed on the 1953 cohort data from Figure 2.1. Under the dual risk recidivism model the apparently increasing probability of reconviction is explained by the changing mix of high and low-risk offenders. At the first conviction over 76 per cent of offenders are in the low-risk category and just under 24 per cent are in the high-risk category. The modelled recidivism probability for first offenders is 0.437 compared with 0.405 calculated from the 1953 cohort data. By the second conviction the model predicts that nearly 69 per cent of low-risk offenders will have dropped out (ceased to offend) but only 16 per cent of high-risk offenders will have done so, increasing the modelled recidivism probability at the second conviction to 0.55 compared with 0.61

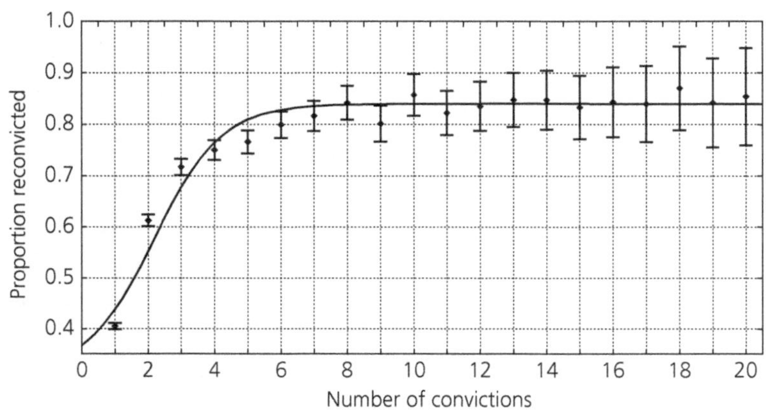

Figure 2.6 The proportion reconvicted by number of convictions

Source: 1953 cohort, Offenders Index.
Note: The error bars show ±1 standard deviation about the data points.

calculated from the data. However by the seventh conviction, less than three in 10,000 low-risk offenders would still be active, giving a combined recidivism probability indistinguishable from the 0.84 of the high-risk category. Above the seventh conviction, all offenders are effectively in the high-risk category (see pp 6–11 for a discussion of similar previous analyses).

In agreement with Blumstein et al (1985), we have shown that the overall reconviction probability changes with the number of previous convictions because the proportions of offenders in our two risk categories change with conviction number and not because the probability of reconviction for any given offender is changing.

Reconviction Rate

Reconviction rates (individual conviction frequencies) can be studied in a similar way to reconviction probabilities. Figure 2.7 shows a graph of data from the 1953+ cohort plotted with a logarithmic scale on the y axis. The graph shows the number of offenders surviving at least the amount of time indicated on the x axis between consecutive convictions. We see that the inter-conviction survival time data falls on a straight line, for times between 7 and 25 years. The equation to that straight line is:

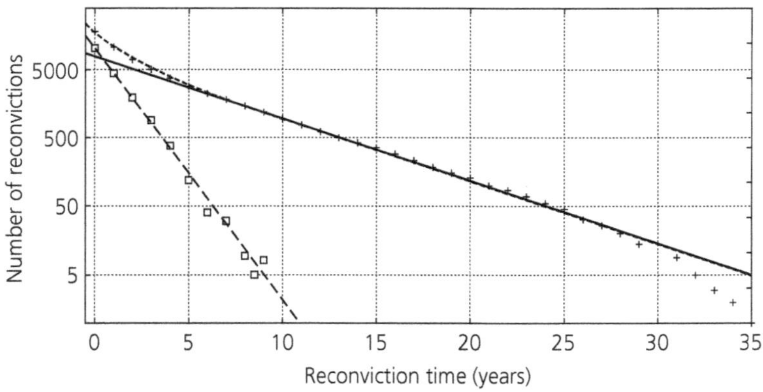

Figure 2.7 Inter-conviction survival time

Source: 1953 cohort, Offenders Index.
Note: The data point at reconviction time = 0 corresponds to the total number of reconvictions sustained by the cohort. The second data point is that total less the number of inter-conviction times less than one year, etc.

$$s(t) = 7782 * e^{-0.21*t} \tag{2.6}$$

Where ***s(t)*** is the number surviving at least ***t*** years between consecutive convictions.

An individual with more than two convictions will have multiple inter-conviction survival times. However, there is no reason to suppose that these multiple measures are not independent samples from the same parent distribution.

On this graph the straight line is characteristic of a Poisson process and indicates that there is a constant rate of reconviction. Here a constant rate means that: the probability of being convicted in a given time period, say one week, is the same whether that time period is now or at some arbitrary time in the future.[6] For very long survival times the data drops below the fitted line. But, given that we are looking at measurements of the 1953+ cohort, individuals in this cohort would have been convicted from the mid-1960s onwards. By the end of 1999 we might well expect that censoring because of potential convictions beyond age 47, or illness, or death, would become important for time periods of 25 years or more.

For survival times less than seven years the slope of the data is somewhat steeper than the straight line from the equation. However, if we assume that, in the straight line modelled by Equation 2.6, we are now seeing a homogeneous *rate* category of offenders who have a constant rate of offending, we can, as before, extend this line backward to lower survival times and calculate the residuals by subtracting the line from the data. If we do this we discover that the residuals (square data points on the graph) fall on a second straight line given by:

$$s_r(t) = 10401 * e^{-0.847*t} \tag{2.7}$$

The simplest explanation of this is that it also indicates a category of offenders who have a constant rate of reconviction, though higher than that of the first category. The equations to these lines can be combined to form a *dual rate survival time model* of the general form:

$$S(t) = B * (b * e^{-\lambda_1 * t} + (1 - b) * e^{-\lambda_2 * t}) \tag{2.8}$$

[6] The Poisson process and what we mean precisely by a constant rate of conviction is described in the Appendix.

Where ***S(t)*** is the number surviving at time ***t*** from the previous conviction, ***B*** is the total number of inter-conviction times in the data, λ_1 and λ_2 are the mean numbers of convictions per year for the high-rate and low-rate categories respectively, and ***b*** is the proportion of inter-conviction times attributed to the high-rate category.

As before, the parameters in Equations 2.6 and 2.7 can be more precisely jointly estimated using a 'least squares iterative procedure', formalizing the graphical method used above, resulting in a correlation coefficient of $R = 0.9999$ between the model and the data, indicating that the model describes almost all the shape of the graph. The fitted function ***S(t)*** is shown as a dotted line in Figure 2.7. The dotted line is coincident with the solid line for survival times greater than six years.

The same *dual rate survival time model* structure is seen in all the OI cohorts. However, in the later cohorts there are, necessarily, fewer long inter-conviction intervals simply because of the shorter follow-up periods, and the consequent censoring effects are increasingly apparent. Table 2.2 and Figure 2.8 show how the best fit parameter values change with the cohort samples. The data are taken from the 1953 to 1973 cohorts and the updated 1953+ cohort.

Again the most important point to notice is the trend in parameter values as the follow-up period increases, from the 1968 cohort to the 1953 cohort.

As expected the mean conviction rates, λ_1 and λ_2, for the high and low-rate categories respectively, tend to reduce as the follow-up period increases. Also, as the follow-up period increases the proportion ***b*** of high-rate inter-conviction survival times initially

Table 2.2 Parameter values for the dual rate survival time model by OI cohort

	b	λ_1	λ_2
1973 cohort	0.992	1.235	0.163
1968 cohort	0.679	1.026	0.467
1963 cohort	0.519	1.035	0.413
1958 cohort	0.542	0.956	0.315
1953 cohort	0.531	0.911	0.248
1953+ cohort	0.565	0.859	0.212

Note: ***b*** = proportion high-rate; λ_1=high-rate; λ_2=low-rate (convictions per year)

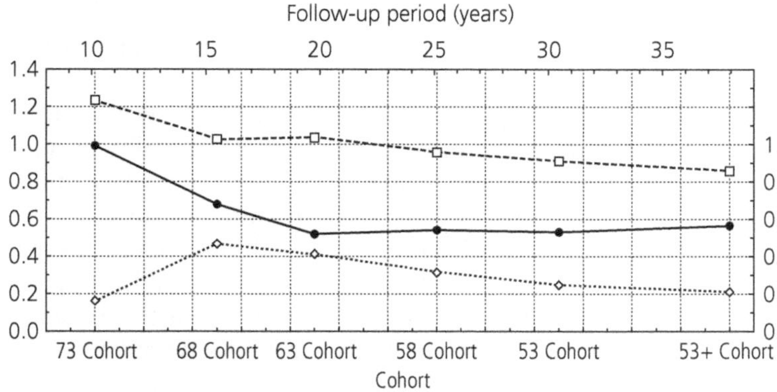

Figure 2.8 Parameter values for the dual rate survival time model by OI cohort

Note: (-□- λ_1, ··◇·· λ_2) mean convictions per year (—●— b) proportion high-rate

reduces, from close to 100 per cent in the 1973 cohort to 52 per cent in the 1963 cohort and it then increases slowly to 56.5 per cent in the updated 1953+ cohort. Again the 1973 cohort parameters deviate from the trend, due mainly to the rapidly changing prevalence of convictions during the teenage years and the very short follow-up period for most of the offenders. In particular the low-rate offenders, who have more than one conviction before age 20, would have inter-conviction times similar to the high-rate offenders with the consequent difficulty of separating the categories.

There is, however, a consistent pattern in the trends of both the recidivism probabilities and rate parameter values. What we would expect given the different follow-up periods of the various cohort samples is that, for later cohorts, our measured recidivism probabilities would be lower than for earlier cohorts and the rates of offending would be higher. This is precisely what the slopes of the risk and rate parameter value plots indicate in Figures 2.5 and 2.8 respectively.

We may therefore conclude from these graphs that offenders from each birth cohort can be split into two *rate* categories, each with a constant rate of conviction, as well as two *risk* categories, each with constant lifetime probabilities of recidivism. As well as being constant over time for each member of a cohort, the parameters also seem essentially constant from cohort to cohort. The best estimates that we have for the lifetime recidivism probability and rate parameters are given by the cohort with longest follow-up period, the updated 1953+ cohort, which we will now refer to simply as the 1953 cohort.

The rate analysis above has been conducted using survival curves in which each point represents the number of individuals surviving for at least the time indicated on the x axis. Thus successive points on the curve are not independent, since the number surviving for any given time period have also survived in all times less than that given period. However, the survival curves have the advantage of clarifying the structure of the data by averaging out the expected random variations. The fitted survival equations have a direct relationship with the distribution of independent inter-conviction times; this relationship is given by Equation 2.9:

$$-\frac{dS}{dt} = B*\left(b*\lambda_1 *e^{-\lambda_1 *t} + (1-b)*\lambda_2 *e^{-\lambda_2 *t}\right) \qquad (2.9)$$

The curve for Equation 2.9 is plotted in Figure 2.9. The parameter values for $\boldsymbol{\lambda_1}$, $\boldsymbol{\lambda_2}$ and $\boldsymbol{b}$, are those estimated above for the survival Equation 2.8. Inter-conviction time frequency data from the 1953 cohort is also plotted in Figure 2.9. The frequency counts are for inter-conviction times falling in three-monthly intervals from zero to 35 years. The dotted curves are the $\pm 2\sigma$ (two

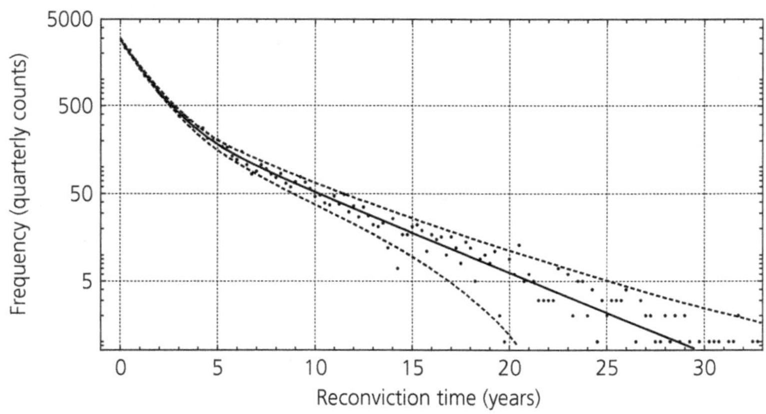

Figure 2.9 frequency of time to reconviction

Source: 1953 cohort, Offenders Index.
Note: Each data point represents the number of reconvictions occurring in a 3-month time interval.

standard deviations) expected variation bounds assuming a Poisson distribution about the expected count in each of the intervals, approximately equivalent to the 95 per cent confidence interval. It can be seen that only seven data points, 5 per cent of the total 140 intervals, fall outside the $\pm 2\sigma$ region, which is exactly as expected.

Reconciling the Risk and Rate Categories

We have identified two categorizations of offenders from the OI cohorts. The obvious question to ask next is: are the high-risk recidivists (where risk = recidivism probability) the same as the high-rate offenders, and are the low-risk recidivists the same as the low-rate offenders? The dual risk recidivism model, Equation 2.4, enables us to calculate the expected number of reconvictions for both the high and low-risk categories in the 1953 cohort (see the Appendix for details). The estimate for the total number of reconvictions is within 2 per cent of the observed value, but the estimates for high and low-risk categories do not correspond with the numbers derived from the high and low-rate elements of the fitted dual rate survival model. There are many more low-rate reconvictions than can be accounted for by the low-risk recidivists, which implies that some of the high-risk recidivists are convicted at the low-rate. The risk and rate categories overlap but are not coincident. Table 2.3 shows the proportion of offenders in the 1953 cohort allocated to each of the composite categories.

In total, 7 per cent of offenders have been allocated to a low-rate/high-risk of recidivism category.

Although the above analysis indicates the existence of homogeneous categories of offenders, with each offender having the particular recidivism and rate characteristics of his or her category,

Table 2.3 Allocation of offenders between the categories for the 1953 cohort

	Offenders		Total
	High-risk of recidivism	Low-risk of recidivism	Offenders
High-rate of conviction	17%	0%	17%
Low-rate of conviction	7%	76%	83%
Total	24%	76%	100%

allocating individual offenders to the categories suggested by Table 2.3, purely on their conviction statistics, is problematic. Knowing the number of offences committed and the inter-conviction times for an individual does not permit unequivocal allocation to a specific category. For example some 16 per cent of high-risk offenders will have only one conviction and could be allocated to any one of the categories. Similarly an offender with more than six convictions spread over say 10 to 15 years could be allocated to either of the high-risk categories but would be very unlikely to be a member of the low-risk category. In Chapter 6 we investigate whether the psychological characteristics of an offender can be used to help make the allocation to risk/rate categories. From the above analysis there is no evidence of the existence of a low-risk/ high-rate category. It is also the case that subsets of offenders, conditioned on characteristics like gender, custody, or a specific offence type, will retain the structure of the risk and rate distributions but may have different parameter values. The effects of gender are discussed below and the subset of offenders given custodial sentences is analysed in Chapter 4.

In the analysis above we have been concerned with those offenders who are eventually reconvicted rather than those who are not. At the time of a conviction, although within each category the probability of each outcome is known, it is difficult to predict whether a particular individual will recidivate or desist. However, as time progresses, for an individual who has not been reconvicted, the probability that he or she has in fact desisted increases. From the mathematical properties of the survival processes evident in the OI cohort data, we can calculate this probability for any time since the previous conviction. Equation 2.10 uses the recidivism probability and the survival time function to make the calculation.

$$p_{desisted}(t) = 1 - p * e^{-\lambda * t} \quad (2.10)$$

Where t is the time since the previous conviction, and p and λ are the recidivism and rate parameters for the category in question.

Gender

Repeating the recidivism analysis of the 1953 cohort data for male and female offenders separately yields parameter values for the

Table 2.4 Dual risk recidivism model parameter estimates for male and female data from the 1953 cohort

	A	*a*	p_1	p_2
Male	9399	0.269	0.84	0.35
Female	2243	0.087	0.81	0.19

Note: ***A*** = No of offenders, ***a*** = fraction with high recidivism probability, p_1 and p_2 = high- and low-recidivism probabilities respectively.

dual risk recidivism model (Equation 2.4), which are given in Table 2.4 and the plots and fitted curves are shown in Figure 2.10.

The first point to note is the difference in the offender cohort size between males and females, *A* in Table 2.4. Less than 20 per cent of offenders in the 1953 cohort are female, comprising approximately 9 per cent of the total number of females in the birth cohort. Male offenders, on the other hand, comprise over 37 per cent of males in the birth cohort and 80 per cent of the offenders. This result is not too surprising. In self-reports from the 1998–99 Youth Lifestyle Survey (Flood-Page et al 2000), 57 per cent of males and 37 per cent of females, between the ages of 12 and 30, admitted to having committed at least one of the offences asked about. In the Cambridge Study, 40 per cent of the males (born mostly in 1953) were convicted up to age 50 (Farrington et al 2006).

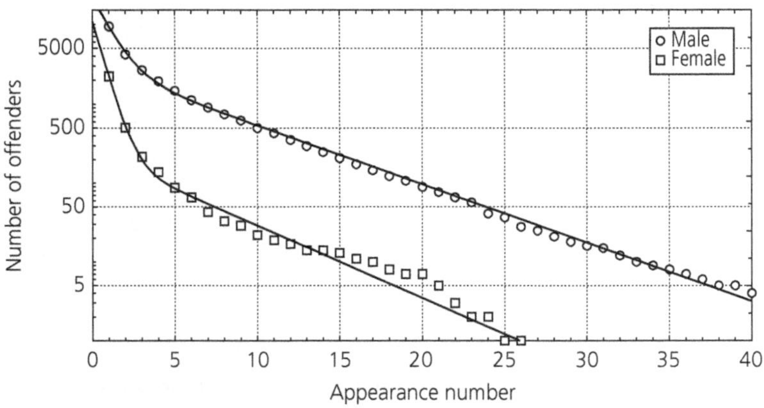

Figure 2.10 Male and female recidivism plots

Source: 1953 cohort, Offenders Index.

Note: The data points represent the number of offenders with at least the number of appearances (resulting in conviction) shown on the *x* axis.

Table 2.5 Dual-rate survival time model parameter estimates for male and female data from the 1953 cohort

	B	***b***	λ_1	λ_2
Male	16,904	0.564	0.854	0.212
Female	1279	0.544	0.971	0.231

Note: ***B*** = No of reconvictions, ***b*** = proportion high-rate, λ_1, λ_2 = high and low-reconviction rates respectively (convictions per year).

Of greater significance, perhaps, is the difference in value of the parameter ***a***. Fewer than 9 per cent of female offenders, compared with almost 27 per cent of male offenders, fall into the high-risk of recidivism category. Not only are females very much less likely to be criminal but, of those who are, a much smaller proportion are in the high-risk category. Interestingly the recidivism probability of high-risk females is very close to that of their male counterparts, 0.81 and 0.84 respectively. The vast majority of female offenders are in the low-risk category and their probability of recidivism is even lower than that for males, 0.19 and 0.35 respectively. Again for both males and females the goodness of fit of the dual risk recidivism model is extremely high with over 99.9 per cent of variation in the data accounted for.

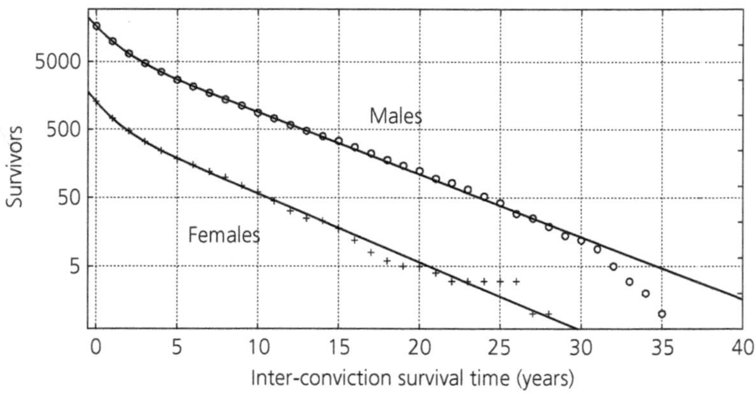

Figure 2.11 Male and female reconviction survival time plots and fitted curves

Source: 1953 cohort, Offenders Index.
Note: The data points at Inter-conviction survival time = 0 represents the total number of reconvictions sustained by the offenders in the cohort. The subsequent points represent the number of reconviction times longer than the time indicated on the *x* axis.

Repeating the inter-conviction survival time analysis of the 1953 cohort data for males and females separately produces parameter estimates for the dual rate survival time model, Equation 2.8, given in Table 2.5, and the plots and fitted curves in Figure 2.11. As expected from the recidivism analysis above, the number of reconvictions sustained by female offenders is very much smaller than the number sustained by male offenders, 1,279 and 16,904 respectively. However, the proportion high-rate b parameters for males and females are not significantly different from each other. The rate parameters, λ_1 and λ_2, are also similar for males and females but the female offenders who do reoffend would appear to do so slightly more quickly than their male counterparts.

Finally we can divide the male and female offenders into the risk/rate categories identified earlier. Table 2.6 replicates Table 2.3 but with each cell broken down by gender.

Is Criminality Constant over the Cohorts?

We have seen from the analysis of risk and rate across the cohorts that the estimated parameter values are similar and follow a consistent trend with increasing follow-up period. Longer follow-ups tend to increase both recidivism probabilities and mean survival times. The observed trends are consistent with our expectations of the effects of increasing censorship of the data in the more recent cohort samples. This censorship, however, also creates problems in estimating the lifetime prevalence of conviction for standard list offences in the cohorts. To resolve these difficulties fully we need to be able to explain and model the age–crime curve and in particular the distribution of age at first conviction.

In Chapter 3 we will develop a theory of crime and conviction, based on the risk/rate analysis above, which enables us to fit a model to the age at first conviction data from the 1953+ cohort. In particular the model enables us to estimate the number of offenders surviving to a given age prior to their first conviction. The 36-year follow-up period of this cohort (to 1999) ensures that most offenders (an estimated 97.2 per cent of the individuals who will receive a conviction in their lifetime, based on the age at first conviction model of Chapter 3) will have been convicted by age 46. If we assume that the age at first conviction model, and in particular the parameter values estimated from the 1953 cohort data, are valid

Table 2.6 Proportions of male and female offenders allocated to the risk/rate categories

	Offenders						Total		
	High-risk of recidivism			Low-risk of recidivism			Offenders		
	Male	Female	Both	Male	Female	Both	Male	Female	Both
High rate of conviction	19%	7%	17%	0%	0%	0%	19%	7%	17%
Low rate of conviction	8%	1.5%	7%	73%	91.5%	76%	81%	93%	83%
Totals	27%	8.5%	24%	73%	91.5%	76%	100%	100%	100%

Table 2.7 Cohort criminality *q*

Cohort	1953	1958	1963	1968	1973
Criminality	22.5%	24.3%	24.6%	22.3%	20.4%

Note: Criminality = Cumulative lifetime prevalence of convictions.

for all cohorts, then we can estimate the lifetime prevalence of conviction in all of the cohorts. Table 2.7 shows the estimated proportion of each of the birth cohorts expected to receive at least one standard list conviction in their lifetime, defined as the cohort criminality '*q*'.

The criminality estimates are all quite close but spread over a wider range than random variation would suggest. The mean of the estimates is 23 per cent with a 2σ (~95 per cent) confidence interval of ±3.4 per cent, as opposed to the expected random 2σ variation, based on the mean cohort size, of ±0.4 per cent. However in making these estimates we have assumed no errors in the estimation process and that nothing has changed over the 30 year period covered by the cohort data. Inspection of the age–crime curves for the individual cohorts suggests that there have been significant changes in convictions for juveniles over the period, which is particularly noticeable in the 1973 cohort. We will return to these changes and their implications in Chapter 3.

Over the period of the cohorts there have also been significant changes in social conditions, lifestyles, education, and employment, all of which might impact on an individual's decision to engage in crime. The nature and perception of crime has also changed over the period as have policies to deal with it. Another possible explanation is that the cohort size has an amplification effect on criminality (see Maxim 1986). The cohort size (number born) in 1963 was nearly 25 per cent higher than in 1953 and the criminality increased from 22.5 per cent in the 1953 cohort to 24.6 per cent in the 1963 cohort. Over the next decade the cohort size decreased and by 1973 it was 1.2 per cent less than in 1953, while the criminality estimates reduced to 22.3 per cent in the 1968 cohort and 20.4 per cent in 1973 cohort. It could be that, while the young population is increasing, community resources[7] are put under greater strain, creating a more criminogenic environment.

[7] Health, social work, education, police and employment.

Community resources would increase to cope with the increasing demand but would lag behind until the population trend stabilized or reversed. When the young population is in decline the process would be reversed with less strain on community resources, perhaps leading to greater social cohesion and control.

The above may provide explanations for the small variations in criminality observed across the cohorts but we still require an explanation for the relative stability of criminality over time. Criminality, as measured by the proportion of the population with one or more convictions in their lifetime, has barely changed since the 1960s. Thus, at this stage of the argument, we suggest that criminality is broadly constant over the cohorts.

In summary the results of the risk/rate analysis are:

- The data on lifetime reconviction probabilities suggests that there are two categories of offenders each with a constant risk of reconviction after each conviction.
- The data on inter-conviction times suggests that there are two categories of offenders each with a rate of reconviction (convictions per year) which is constant over time.
- The proportion of offenders in a cohort is essentially constant.
- The risk and rate parameters are essentially constant over the different cohorts.
- There is a strong correlation between the high-rate offenders and the high-risk offenders. However the number of high-risk offenders is significantly greater than the number of high-rate offenders, which suggests the existence of a high-risk/low-rate category of offenders. The characteristics of this category will be explored later.
- There is no evidence for a low-risk/high-rate category.
- The proportions of offenders in each of the risk/rate categories is substantially constant across the cohorts.

Because our theory, described in Chapter 3, is derived from these results it will automatically reproduce them. The interesting question is: what other unrelated or more detailed results can we explain? Conversely, no theory or model that cannot reproduce these results is a candidate to describe the large scale structure of criminal careers. We will also discover in Chapter 5 that the assumptions underlying some commonly held views of criminal career analysts cannot reproduce these results.

3

The Theory and a Simple Model

Orientation

In Chapter 2 we have seen that an analysis of a large number of detailed criminal careers of those who have at some time been convicted of a serious (standard list) offence indicates the existence of two categories of offender with constant but different reconviction probabilities. The same kind of analysis looking at the timing of offences indicates two categories of offender with constant but different rates of conviction. These categories were revealed by plotting graphs. The proportion of the population in each of these categories is essentially constant across birth cohorts. In this chapter we will describe our theory which explains these results and we will construct a three category model to predict independent criminal history data.

Introduction

Having looked at the Offenders Index (OI) we will now construct a theory which will explain the observed regularities. The theory will be 'large scale', in that it does not consider the psychological, social and economic causes of general offending behaviour and also in that there are almost certainly other special groups and subgroups of offenders beyond those we have discovered from our aggregate level examination of the OI.

Commonly, it has been believed that sex offenders would form one such group, generally characterized by a much greater degree of specialization than more typical offenders, although empirical evidence suggests this may be an over-simplification (Zimring, Jennings, Piquero, and Hays 2009).

A more definitive group consists of around half of life sentence prisoners who have very low probabilities of recidivism. There is also likely to be some variation in the parameters for the recidivism probability and the rate of conviction for subsets of offenders within each category, as we saw with male and female subsets in Chapter 2. However this variation is much less than the differences in parameters between the categories.

The utility of our theory might be questioned because it does not consider individual motivations leading to crime and therefore gives us little idea how to intervene. We take the opposite view. It seems to us that without a large scale theory one cannot begin to understand the features of general criminality which need in turn to be explained by psychological, sociological, and economic criminological theories. We would have no idea of the basic parameters we were trying to measure or how they were interrelated in actual measurements. For example the often used two-year reconviction 'rate' (actually a probability) depends on both reconviction probabilities and offending rates. Also, different descriptions may be appropriate for differently defined categories. We shall see in Chapter 6 that in one of our categorizations offenders can be divided into those who are unusually impulsive and those who seem to have otherwise quite normal psychological features. This in turn implies the need for different interventions to reduce offending.

Another objection to our 'large scale' approach is that it will ignore a great deal of important detail, and we agree. However, without understanding the large scale framework one will never understand the small scale detail. A similar objection may also come from those who would argue that we are ignoring 'statistically significant' information and making too much use of our own judgement of what is important. We would respond by pointing out that no analysis is judgement-free and in what follows we will make our judgements explicit rather than hiding them in the underlying assumptions of particular statistical techniques.

The paradigm that we believe is most useful for developing an understanding of criminal careers is similar to that of the historical understanding of planetary motion (which is indeed the paradigm of most successful scientific research). By the time of the Renaissance it had become clear that the Ptolemaic geocentric description of planetary motion, although still empirically very effective, was philosophically unacceptable. The rival Copernican system, though superior philosophically, in its simplest form (as championed famously by Galileo) simply did not work. To make his system work, Copernicus had shown that it was necessary to build in so many epicycles that, on grounds of simplicity, it was considerably less acceptable than the Ptolemaic approach. The answer was found by Kepler, who realized that Galileo's simple picture of planets orbiting the sun could be made to work as accurately as Ptolemy's by replacing the perfect circles with ellipses. In turn the attempt to explain Kepler's ellipses led to Newton's idea of gravity. This in turn predicted that the gravitational interaction of the planets would make them follow non-elliptical orbits, leading to the discovery of Uranus, Neptune, and Pluto. The discrepancy between the actual orbit of Mercury and that predicted by Newtonian theory led to the discovery by Einstein of General Relativity which describes the motion of the Universe. At an even smaller scale we know that the orbits of the planets are in fact chaotic and not predictable at all.

We thus have a hierarchy of descriptions, beginning with circular orbits which are still suitable for qualitative description (Galileo). These lead to slightly elliptical orbits (Kepler). In turn these lead to perturbed elliptical orbits and finally to chaotic orbits. In each case the larger scale description provides the arena within which the smaller scale structure can be identified and then understood.

Our theory is a large scale description of the process of offending, capture, conviction and eventually desistance. We fully acknowledge that it ignores many important features of offenders, offending, motivation, and criminal justice system responses. But we hope that the theory and the models can provide a framework within which these features and their associated mechanisms can be understood.

The Assumptions of our Theory

In Chapter 2 we conducted a detailed analysis of the recidivism characteristics of the (1953, 1958, 1963, 1968, and 1973) cohort samples and the 1997 sentencing sample from the Offenders Index. The statistical models fitted to the distributions of both conviction-number and inter-conviction times resulted in very high values of the correlation coefficients and were highly suggestive that the first four assumptions of our theory are correct.

The basic assumptions of the theory are:

1. The population at large can be categorized into one non-criminal and a small number of criminal categories. The criminal categories consist of individuals who will commit relatively serious criminal offences and be convicted of one or more of these offences within their lifetimes.

2. Criminality is constant: the proportion of the population in the criminal categories is approximately constant[1] across cohorts.

   Within each of the criminal categories:

3. Recidivism is constant: immediately after each conviction the probability of an individual being reconvicted of one or more further offences at some time in the future is constant.
4. Rate of offending is constant: whilst active, the probability of an offender committing an offence in a given time period is constant whether that time period is now or at some arbitrary point in the future.

For individuals in the largest 'non-criminal' category we assume that the rate of (relatively serious) offending is very close to zero and, as they are never convicted for standard list offences, their recidivism probability is zero. This raises the possibility that there are individuals in the non-criminal category who do commit relatively serious offences; however, we believe that their numbers and the proportion of serious crime for which they are responsible is small.

These assumptions ensure that our theory will reproduce the results of Chapter 2 on recidivist behaviour as observed in the Offenders Index. It is easy to show however that alone they do not provide any hope of explaining the most well known result on offending, namely the 'age–crime' curve, or more accurately, in the context of the Offenders Index analysis, the 'age–conviction' curve.

Explaining the Age–Crime Curve

The age–crime curve is a histogram of the numbers of convictions at each age. The curve can be constructed using data from either a cohort or a cross-sectional sample. Figure 3.1 shows the age–crime curve for the 1997 sentencing sample.[2] The graph shows the count of court appearances, resulting in one or more convictions during

[1] There will be some variation in measured criminality over time due to changes in prosecution policy concerning cautions/warnings etc and offence classifications.

[2] Sentencing samples were drawn from the Offenders Index at regular intervals to investigate the impact of sentencing policy on reconvictions. The 1997 sentencing sample consists of the complete (OI) criminal histories of all offenders convicted of one or more offences at court appearances during the first weeks of alternate months from February through December 1997, including all reconvictions up to 01/01/2002.

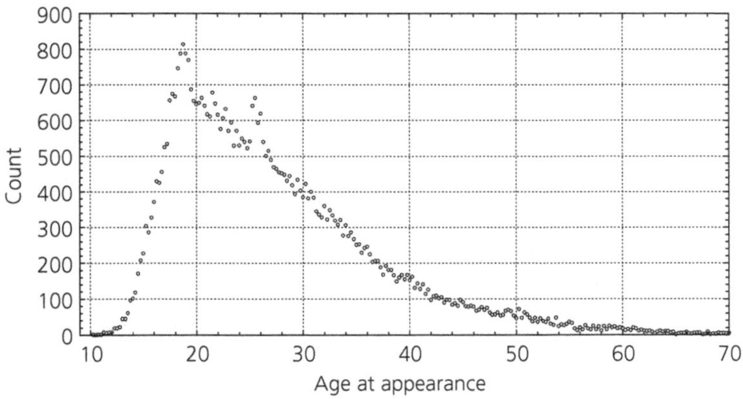

Figure 3.1 Age–crime curve

Source: 1997 sentencing sample, Offenders Index.
Note: Each data point represents the number of offenders in the sample convicted at the age shown on the *x* axis in three-month increments of age.

the sample weeks, for individuals at the age indicated on the *x* axis, in age increments of three months. The data has been age-weighted to standardize the graph to a constant number of individuals at each age in the community.

The graph starts at age 10, the age of criminal responsibility, which is the first age at which an individual can be convicted of a criminal offence in England and Wales. As age increases the count of convictions increases until typically 17–18 years of age, and after this there is a slow decline. The small secondary peak at age 25 reflects individuals of unknown age who are coded by the courts as age 25 (with date of birth coded 01/01/1972 in the 1997 sample). This secondary peak disappears completely if offenders with a recorded date of birth of 01/01/1972 are excluded from the sample.

The assumptions we have written down so far imply that offenders appear at the age of criminal responsibility, offend and are then convicted, at which stage some drop out. The remainder then go on to be convicted again after which some drop out and so on. This would lead to an age–crime curve similar to Figure 3.2.

We can see that the fall off with age above age 20 is reproduced but not the rise until age 17–18. However, Figure 3.2 is consistent with other graphs of antisocial behaviour against age. For example we may consider the results of Nagin and Tremblay (1999) who

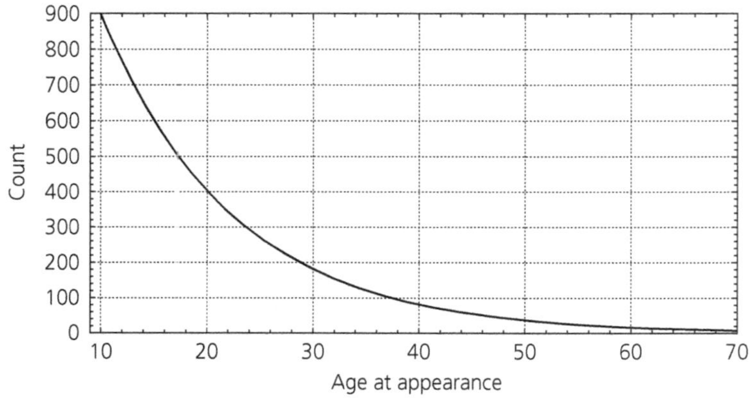

Figure 3.2 Hypothetical age–crime curve from Assumptions (1) to (4).

measured the antisocial behaviour of over 1,000 boys in Montreal from age six to age 15. Three types of antisocial behaviour were considered: physical aggression, opposition, and hyperactivity. Four trajectories of externalizing behaviour problems with age were identified for each of the types of behaviour. Figure 3.3 shows the fitted trajectories for physically aggressive antisocial behaviour at age six and then annually from age 10 to 15. Very similar trajectories were found for the other two antisocial behaviours; but the

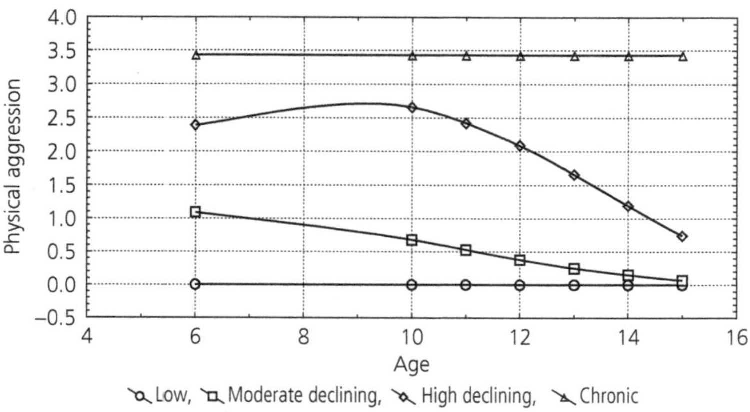

Figure 3.3 Trajectories of physical aggression, Montreal longitudinal experimental study of boys.

Source: Nagin & Tremblay (1999).

groups of individuals following similar trajectories for different behaviours, although overlapping, were by no means coincident. What is important however is that none of the trajectories show antisocial behaviour increasing up to age 15. They actually show such behaviour staying constant or decreasing. There are also no late onset groups identified for any of the behaviours among the study boys (p 1189). Nagin and Tremblay (1999, p 1192) also remark that childhood physical aggression is a distinct predictor of violence and serious delinquency in adolescence and that these findings (including the non-increasing rates) are replicated in five other longitudinal data sets from around the world.

What then is the cause of the disparity between other measures of antisocial behaviour and convictions in England and Wales? There are two simple explanations. The first is society's attitude to certain behaviours at different ages: from a legal standpoint, in England and Wales, the age of criminal responsibility precludes formal criminal conviction of children under the age of 10 (at the time of the offence). At ages just above 10, if one child hits another in the school playground or is caught stealing, these events are unlikely to result in any more than a telling-off. If juveniles are caught shoplifting, damaging property, or fighting, this will probably be dealt with within the school, by parents or informally by the police. Even if the incident is serious, there will be a high probability of the use of a formal reprimand, final warning, or formal caution by the police for younger offenders. However, if one young adult hits another young adult in a public place or steals a car, this is much more likely to lead to prosecution and conviction in the courts. The second explanation is the individual's capacity to commit criminal acts. For example, Farrington (1997) reminds us that children must have reached a certain size before they can reach the controls of a car, and are thus incapable of stealing one. Physical aggression by children is unlikely to result in serious injury unless weapons are involved and children are unlikely to be able to purchase goods in shops with forged cheques or credit cards.

These explanations combine to give our fifth assumption:

5. The probability that similar *criminal* behaviours will result in conviction increases with age from age 10 to age 17.

Unless the details of informal sanctions are well understood, there are serious empirical difficulties in measuring criminality. Most studies using official records of arrest or conviction report male participation rates between 20 per cent and 40 per cent; however, Farrington (2002) found that, although 40 per cent of his Cambridge Study male cohort had official convictions up to age 40, 96 per cent admitted to committing at least one equivalent criminal act up to age 32 in self-reports. The criminal categories defined in assumption (1) do not include any individuals who cease to offend following informal sanctions, police reprimands, warnings or cautions. Criminality as defined in assumption 2 may therefore vary between cohorts because of changes in prosecution policy.

We now need just one further assumption to enable us to model the age–crime curve:

6. The probability of capture and conviction for similar offences increases after the offender is known to the police.

Assumption 6 is necessary to resolve an inconsistency between the survival time distributions of time to first conviction and interconviction time. The statistical details are explained below, but the assumption is intuitively plausible *a priori*.

The inconsistency becomes apparent if we construct a survival curve for time to first conviction for the 1953 cohort and compare the slope of the straight line section of the curve, Figure 3.4, with that of the reconviction survival time curve of Figure 2.7.

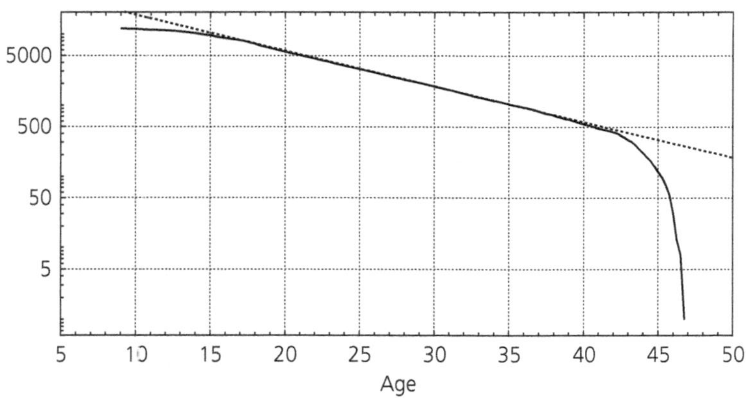

Figure 3.4 Survival time to first conviction

Source: 1953 cohort, Offenders Index.
Note: The *y* axis is on a logarithmic scale. The solid curve on the graph shows the number of offenders in the cohort sample who remain conviction free up to the age shown on the *x* axis. The data is plotted at monthly intervals. The overlaid dotted straight line is the exponential fit to the curve between ages 18 and 40.

The equation to the straight line in Figure 3.4 is:

$$y = A * e^{-0.115*t} \tag{3.1}$$

Equation 3.1 gives a mean time to first conviction, for unconvicted offenders over the age of 18, of 8 years and 9 months.[3] This can be compared with a mean time to reconviction of 4 years and 9 months derived from Equation 2.6. As we show in the Appendix, a random sample from a stream of random events, with a mean inter-event time T, results in a stream of random events with a mean inter-event time T/p where p is the sampling probability. We can apply this result to the inconsistency between first and subsequent convictions by letting p equal the ratio of the mean time to the next conviction to the mean time to the first conviction. As a first approximation this gives the relative[4] probability, p, of a first conviction compared with subsequent convictions of 0.55.

A second inconsistency between the survival to first conviction and the survival to reconviction curves is the slope of the curves prior to the straight line sections; age less than 17 in Figure 3.4 and reconviction time less than five years in Figure 2.7. In the former, as a direct result of assumption 5, which has the effect of slowing down the rate of first conviction, the initial slope is less than that of the straight line section. In the latter, due to the rapid reconviction of the high-rate offenders, the initial slope is greater. In the survival (age) to first conviction curve the effect of the high-rate offender category is completely masked by the effect of assumption 5 and the preponderance of low-rate offenders in the criminal categories. At least 85 per cent of offenders are low-rate (see Table 2.2).

Both first conviction and reconviction curves exhibit the rounding down in the tail of the curve due to censorship of the data at age 46. This rounding down can be successfully modelled by the subtraction of a constant from the right hand side of the survival

[3] For the exponential survival time distribution the mean time to failure applies from any time during the process. For example at age 18 the expected (mean) time to first conviction is 8 years 9 months $\left(\frac{1}{0.115}\, years\right)$. For all those surviving to age 25, or indeed to any other age greater than 18, the expected time to first conviction is also 8 years and 9 months.

[4] If the probability of reconviction given a crime is q then the probability of first conviction given a crime is $p*q$; ie p is the relative, or effective sampling, probability.

equations, or alternatively by adding the same constant to all of the data points. This constant represents the number of offenders who will be convicted for the first time after the age of 46. We are now almost in a position to convert our descriptive statement of the assumptions into empirically measurable parameters. But first we need to expand on assumption 5.

The Rise in Crime from 10 to 17 Years of Age

There is very little empirical evidence relating society's response to similar behaviours at different offender ages except that children under the age of 10 in England and Wales are deemed not criminally responsible. Intuitively we would not expect society's response to be very different at 10 years and one month compared with 9 years and 11 months. We would also expect the transition from all acts being non-criminal to individuals being fully responsible, as in assumption 5, to be smooth, ie a small increment in age would not result in a large change in response. As an indicator of these changing responses we can look at police use of reprimands, final warnings, and cautions. Each of these police disposals is recorded on the Police National Computer (since May 1995) but are not criminal convictions. Reprimands and final warnings are given to those under 18 and cautions to those over 18; we will refer to all these disposals as cautions. Each of these disposals requires that there is evidence linking the offender to the offence and that the offender admits his/her guilt. These informal disposals may also involve reparative, rehabilitative and/or punitive elements. Figure 3.5(a, b, c, and d) shows the use police made of these cautions for offenders aged 10 to 20 in the second quarter of 2004, in age bands of three months.

Figure 3.5a shows the number convicted and the number cautioned on their first recorded police contact and Figure 3.5c shows the number convicted and cautioned on their second or subsequent contacts. Figures 3.5b and d show the proportions convicted for first and subsequent contacts respectively.

It can be seen that on their first police contact the overwhelming majority of offenders are dealt with outside the court system. Prior to age 14, less than 6.25 per cent of offenders are charged and convicted, although the number of offenders steadily increases, from around 125 per three-month age increment at age 11 and under, to a peak of over 1,100 at age 16. The proportion convicted at

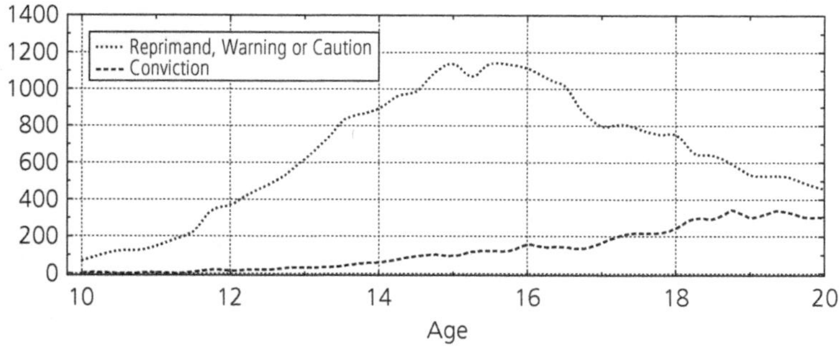

Figure 3.5a Recorded outcome of first police contact.

Source: PNC April 2004 sample.
Note: The *y* axis shows the number of offenders cautioned or convicted at the age shown on the *x* axis in age increments of three months.

age 16 exceeds 10 per cent for the first time and continues to increase to 40 per cent at age 20, as shown in Figure 3.5b.

The pattern is entirely different for second and subsequent police contacts. The total number of offenders with more than one recorded police contact at or below age 12 is less than 360, and the proportion convicted is 55 per cent. This proportion steadily increases to 87 per cent at age 20 (see Figure 3.5d). The increase in the proportion of offenders convicted as age increases provides some support for assumption 5 and the differences in disposals between first and subsequent police contacts provide support for assumption 6.

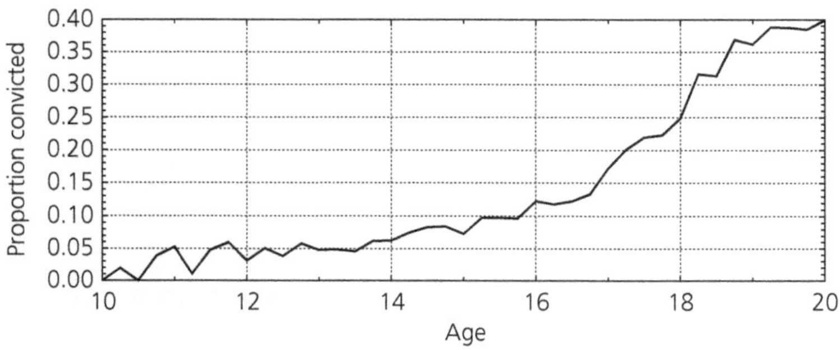

Figure 3.5b Proportion convicted on first police contact

Source: PNC April 2004 sample.

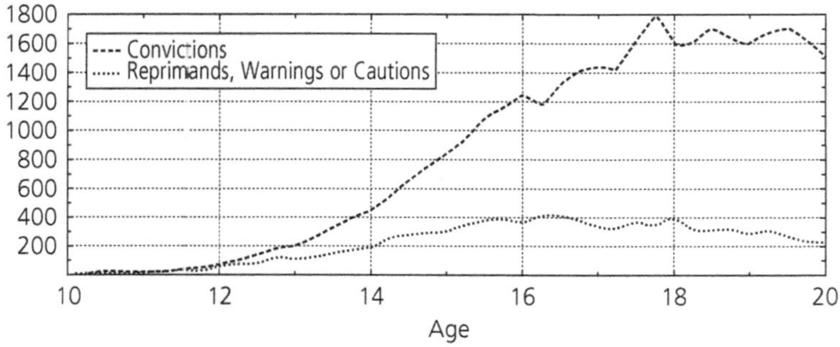

Figure 3.5c Recorded outcome of second and subsequent police contacts

Source: PNC April 2004 sample.
Note: The *y* axis shows the number of offenders cautioned or convicted at the age shown on the *x* axis in age increments of three months.

The evidence in Figure 3.5(a–d) does not provide the complete picture concerning changes in society's response to criminal behaviour as age increases, only the official response after all informal actions have been exhausted. In order to model the early part of the age–crime curve we need a function which reflects society's view, both formal and informal, of what is or is not criminal as age increases. At age 10 the probability of conviction, given a criminal act, should be close to zero. It should then increase, at first slowly but accelerating and increasing most rapidly in early to mid-teens

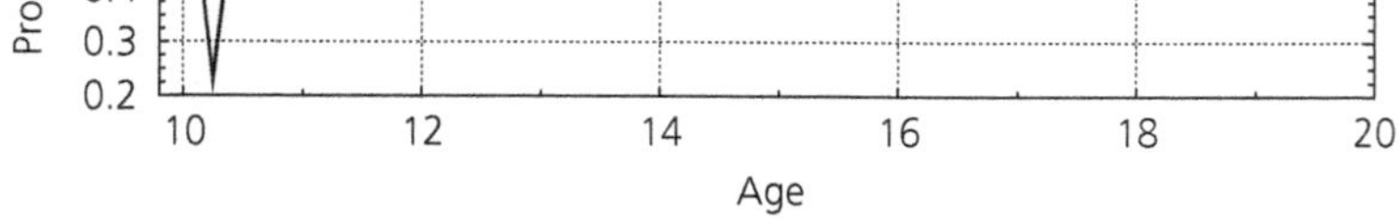

Figure 3.5d Proportion convicted on second and subsequent police contacts

Source: PNC April 2004 sample.
Note: The large fluctuations between ages 10 and 12 are due to very small numbers of offenders with more than one police contact at these ages.

then slowing and levelling off at a probability of one in late teenage. Such a function is given in Equation 3.2:

$$P(convicted \mid age = t) = 1 - \frac{1}{1 + e^{\alpha*(t-c)}} \tag{3.2}$$

Where:

α Controls the slope of the transition (small values of α give a shallow slope and large values >1 give increasingly steep transitions)

c is the age at which the probability P is ½ (as $e^{o}=1$).

The function is arbitrary but provides a plausible shape, which is theoretically defensible, with flexibility in the parameters to enable the initial portion of the age at first conviction curve to be modelled in a mathematically tractable way.

There are of course other functions which can be used to model this phase of the age–crime curve. Farrington (1986, pp 240–243) explores several distributions and functions describing the association between age and crime, the most successful of which used a term of the form $a*x^b$ to approximate the rise in crime in the early teens which is then counteracted by a negative exponential, e^{-c*x}, which becomes dominant beyond the peak age of offending. This was offered as an empirical fit to the curve but, as Farrington points out, the Gamma distribution function is of this general form and, as we shall see in Chapter 4, the gamma distribution can be applied as a theoretically defensible approximation.

Modelling the Age–Crime Curve

Returning to the survival time to first conviction graph of Figure 3.4, the straight line section, between ages 18 and 42, is characteristic of a proportional hazard survival process in which the number failing (that is being convicted) at a given age is a constant proportion of the number surviving to that age. This is consistent with the high- and low-rate reconviction survival processes described in Chapter 2 and with assumption 6 which asserts that the underlying survival processes are the same but with the initial failure rate reduced by the relative probability[5] of a first conviction. In addition, over the

[5] We use the term relative probability because we assume: that the rate of criminal behaviour is the same while offenders are active, both before and after the first conviction; and that the probability of conviction given a crime is lower for first

early part of the curve, ages 10 to 20, the failure rate is also multiplied by the right hand side of Equation 3.2.

We can describe these processes mathematically as follows. Within each of the homogeneous rate categories, the 'survival to first conviction' process can be described by the solution to the following differential equation:

$$\frac{d}{dt}S_f(t) = -P_f * \lambda * S_f(t) * \left(1 - \frac{1}{1 + e^{\alpha * (t-c)}}\right) \tag{3.3}$$

Giving the survival function:

$$S_f(t) = C * \left(1 + e^{\alpha * (t-c)}\right)^{-\frac{P_f * \lambda}{\alpha}} \tag{3.4}$$

Where:

$S_f(t)$ is the number of offenders surviving (without conviction) to age (***t***),

P_f is the relative probability of first conviction,

λ is the rate parameter for reconvictions,

C is the number of offenders in the rate category who will be convicted in their lifetime.

In order to model and fit the survival curve of Figure 3.4 we need to sum the survival functions (the right hand side of Equation 3.4) for both high- and low-rate offenders with parameter values as estimated for the 1953 cohort in Chapter 2 and listed in Table 3.1.

In Table 3.1 the numbers of offenders has been increased by 33 for the high-rate and 113 for the low-rate categories to adjust the initial value at age 9.[6] In addition, to compensate for censorship, 310 has been added to the low-rate offender total to represent offenders who will be convicted for the first time after age 46, the limit of the observation period. The remaining parameters, P_f, α and *c*, were estimated by fitting the combined survival function to the survival time data of Figure 3.4, with 310 added to each of the

convictions than for subsequent convictions. The alternative assumption is that the rate of criminal behaviour increases as a direct result of the first conviction.

[6] In Figure 3.6 (a and b) it can be seen that there is a data point at age 9. When the Offenders Index was first created in 1963 the age of criminal responsibility was 8 years but was increased to 10 in the 1963 Children and Young Persons Act. The revised age of criminal responsibility (which took effect on 01/02/64) was not effective during 1963 with the result that 99 individuals in the 1953 cohort received convictions before their tenth birthday.

Table 3.1 Parameter values for 1953 cohort

	Number of offenders: **C**	Rate parameter: λ
High-Rate	1507 + 33	0.86
Low-Rate	10137 + 310 + 113	0.211

data points. A least squares iterative fitting procedure was used, and over 99.9 per cent of the variance in the data was accounted for by the model. The parameter estimates were: $P_f = 0.51$, $\alpha = 0.56$ and $c = 14.45$. Figures 3.6a and 3.6b show the fitted curve and data points with linear and logarithmic (to base 10) y axis scales respectively.

Equation 3.4 can be differentiated to give an expression for the age at first conviction curve for each of the rate categories.

$$y_1(t) = C * \left(1 + e^{\alpha*(t-c)}\right)^{-\frac{P_f*\lambda}{\alpha}} * P_f * \lambda * e^{\alpha*(t-c)} \qquad (3.5)$$

Figure 3.7 shows the onset age–crime curve derived from the above survival analysis based on the sum of the high and low-rate versions of Equation 3.5. All the parameter values are the same as those for the survival analysis which generated Figures 3.6a and b.

The dotted lines above and below the fitted curve in Figure 3.7 are the ±2 standard deviation (95 per cent) confidence limits assuming a Poisson distribution of convictions in each three-month interval of age. A feature of Figure 3.7 that requires some explanation is the group of convictions between age 15 and a half and 17 which fall below the -2σ line and a second group between the ages of

Figure 3.6a Survival to first conviction (linear *y* axis)

Figure 3.6b Survival to first conviction (logarithmic *y* axis)

Source: 1953 cohort, Offenders Index.
Note: The data plotted on these graphs is the same as that used in Figure 3.4 above, but plotted at annual increments and with 310 added to each data point.

17 and 18-and-a-half which fall above the $+2\sigma$ line. In 1968 the Metropolitan Police introduced formal cautioning as an alternative to prosecution, which had the effect of diverting many juveniles away from court and reducing the numbers convicted prior to age 17. However on reaching the age of 17 (the minimum age for adult court at that time), cautioning was much less likely and individuals who offended at age 17 were more likely to be convicted. It may even have been the case that prosecutions were delayed to ensure that adult sentences were imposed. Thus the introduction of

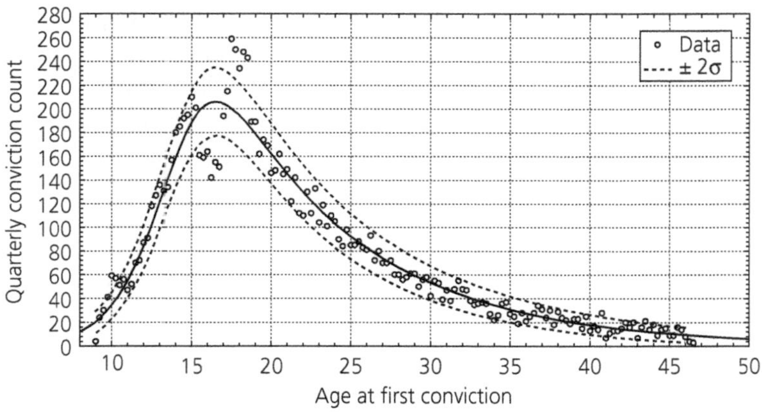

Figure 3.7 Age at first conviction for the 1953 cohort.

Source: Offenders Index.
Note: The points on the graph show the number of offenders with their first conviction at the age shown on the *x* axis, in age increments of three months.

cautioning postponed some first convictions from 1968 to 1979 (see also Farrington 1990; Farrington and Bennett 1981; Farrington and Maughan 1999). These two groups of outliers counterbalance each other making a *suppressed-demand* kind of explanation plausible and suggests that cautioning was less successful than hoped for. A similar, but much smaller, fluctuation in conviction numbers is apparent in the 1958 (see Figure 3.8), 1963 and 1968 cohorts.

Repeating the *survival to first conviction* analysis on the 1958 cohort data yields parameter values of: $P_f = 0.72$, $\alpha = 0.64$ and $c = 15.01$. Here the transition slope α is greater (steeper) than the 1953 cohort value and the middle age of the transition is six months later. The high- and low-rate parameters used were those estimated for the 1953 cohort. The fit to the age at first conviction curve for the 1958 cohort is shown in Figure 3.8. The suppressed demand effect around age 17 is in evidence in the data, but only the third quarter of age 16 falls outside the $\pm 2\sigma$ bounds. A suppressed demand effect could also account for the small number of above 2σ outliers in the age range 10 to 11 as the most troublesome children become eligible for prosecution. The same basic structure is seen in the remaining cohort samples but the parameter values for P_f, α and c vary between cohorts. In particular the slope α and the mid-transition age c both increase as the cohorts become more recent. These parameter changes reflect the increasing use over time of police cautions for young offenders.

Figure 3.8 Age at first conviction for the 1958 cohort

Source: Offenders Index.

To illustrate the consistency of the basic structure of the data over time, the survival function was also fitted to data from a sub-sample of the 1997 sentencing sample. The sub-sample was created by selecting target conviction records that were *first convictions*. Also, individuals with a 'coded' date of birth of 01/01/1972 were omitted from the sample, completely removing the spurious peak at age 25 that was observed in Figure 3.1. The rate parameters, $\lambda 1$ and $\lambda 2$, estimated for the 1953 cohort were used for the fit and the proportion of high-rate offenders was estimated from the sentencing sample. P_f, α and c were estimated using a least squares procedure as before. The derived age at first conviction profile is plotted in Figure 3.9.

The fit to the sentencing sample data includes first convictions up to age 70 and overall just 13 data points lie outside the $\pm 2\sigma$ confidence limits, whereas statistical theory predicts 12. Virtually all variation in the data, in all three data sets, is explained by the statistical model. However, it should be stressed that at the individual offender level there will, no doubt, be causal explanatory factors which influence their offending behaviour. However, these individual explanations aggregate in such a way as to be consistent with our large scale theory.

The parameter estimates used to fit the age at first conviction curves for the 1953 and 1958 cohorts and the 1997 sentencing sample data are presented in Table 3.2. The relative probability of

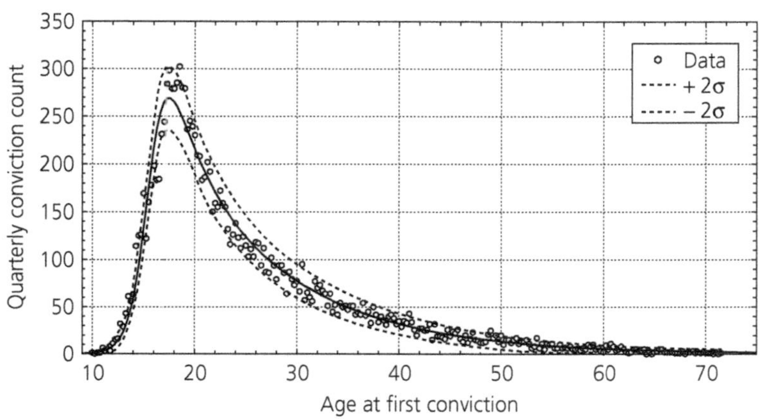

Figure 3.9 Age profile for first convictions during 1997

Source: 1997 sentencing sample, Offenders Index.

Table 3.2 Parameter values for age at first conviction fitted curves

Data source	Number of offenders	Proportion high-rate	λ_h	λ_l	P_f	α	c
1953 cohort	12,127	0.161	0.86	0.211	0.51	0.54	14.68
1958 cohort	13,006	0.159	0.86	0.211	0.76	0.61	15.37
1997 sentencing sample	14,090	0.160	0.86	0.211	0.406	1.00	15.82

Note: λ_h and λ_l are the high and low-rate parameters from Table 3.1 and P_f, α and c are the values obtained by fitting the combined high and low-rate first conviction survival functions (Equation 3.4) to the specified data source.

a first conviction is subject to greater variation than the other parameters, although changes in cautioning policy for older offenders could explain this variation. In addition, the 'probability of conviction given age' parameter values, α and c, display a progressively increasing trend as the data becomes more recent. This trend is consistent with known policy changes; the diversion of young offenders away from formal conviction has resulted in a progressive and significant increase in the use of cautioning for juveniles. The effect of this has been that peak age of onset has been delayed slightly and the rise to that peak has become much steeper in the more recent data.

The proportions of offenders who are high-rate,[7] estimated independently for each sample, are remarkably consistent at around 16 per cent. Although we have seen significant changes, over time, in the parameter values describing the onset phase of the criminal career, the basic structure of the model has not changed. In particular the parameters describing the ongoing criminal behaviour appear to have remained substantially constant over the 40 years covered by the available data.

The mathematical models derived above specifically describe the numbers of offenders convicted for the first time at each age (the age of onset). The full age–crime curve includes all subsequent convictions, second, third, etc. We now derive a model for the age–crime curve for each subsequent conviction number. Our theory

[7] The proportion of offenders who are high-rate differs from the estimate given in Chapter 2 for the 1953 cohort because the estimated number of offenders yet to offend has been included in the calculations here.

predicts that, within a risk/rate category, at any given age the number of offenders convicted is proportional to the size of the active offender population at that age. This relationship also holds for the subset of the active offender population at the given age with just i previous convictions. A proportion p of this subset will be reconvicted at rate λ moving them into the subset of the offender population aged t with $i + 1$ previous convictions. At the same time some of this latter subset will themselves be convicted at rate λ and leave the subset. This process is described mathematically by Equation 3.6:

$$\tfrac{d}{dt}(y_{i+1}(t)) = p * \lambda * y_i(t) - \lambda * y_{i+1}(t) \tag{3.6}$$

for $i > 0$

Starting with $i = 1$ and solving Equation 3.6 for each of the risk/rate categories and successive values of i, gives us the size of the offender population in each category with just i previous convictions at age t. Substituting back into Equation 3.6 and summing the results over the three risk/rate categories generates the age–conviction curve for each conviction number. This series of equations was solved numerically as no simple analytic solution exists. Over 90 per cent of data points for the number of convictions in three-monthly age increments at each previous conviction count fell within the $\pm 2\sigma$ confidence limits for the 1953 cohort.

We can generate the age profile for all reconvictions within each risk/rate category by lumping all active offenders together into a single active convicted offender pool. A proportion $1 - p$ leave the pool after each conviction (convictions occur at rate λ in direct proportion to the size of the active convicted offender pool $Y(t)$) modifying Equation 3.6 as shown in Equation 3.7:

$$\tfrac{d}{dt}Y(t) = p * \lambda * y_1(t) - (1 - p) * \lambda * Y(t) \tag{3.7}$$

Where:

p is the reconviction probability,

$Y(t)$ is the size of the active convicted offender pool.

Equation 3.7 was again solved numerically for each of the risk/rate categories, but with the high-risk probability increased from 0.840 to 0.855 to compensate for censorship at age 46 in the 1953 cohort and to provide a better fit to the data. To justify this change, see the graph in Figure 2.5 which shows an increasing trend in recidivism probability estimates with the length of follow-up in the cohorts. Ideally the parameter values used in constructing the theoretical age–crime curve should be 'whole life' values rather than estimates determined from censored data sets.

The size of the active convicted offender pool for all convictions in each risk/rate category at age $\boldsymbol{t}$ is given by:

$$Y_{tot}(t) = y_1(t) + Y(t) \tag{3.8}$$

The overall age–crime curve is given by substituting back into Equation 3.7 and summing over the three categories, high-risk/high-rate, high-risk/low-rate and low-risk/low-rate. Figure 3.10 shows the fitted theoretical age–conviction curve with the $\pm 2\sigma$ confidence limits and the 1953 cohort data. With the exception of the outliers around age 17, explained above as a policy-induced period effect, the majority of data points fall within the $\pm 2\sigma$ (95 per cent confidence interval) of the model.

With suitable adjustment for juvenile cautioning policy (see Table 3.2 for the 1958 cohort and 1997 sentencing sample parameters) the model fits the *all convictions* age-crime data from the remaining cohort samples, 1958, 1963, 1968, and 1973, and the 1997 sentencing sample.

Assumptions 1 to 6 above and their mathematical representation are thus sufficient to accurately model the age–crime (conviction)

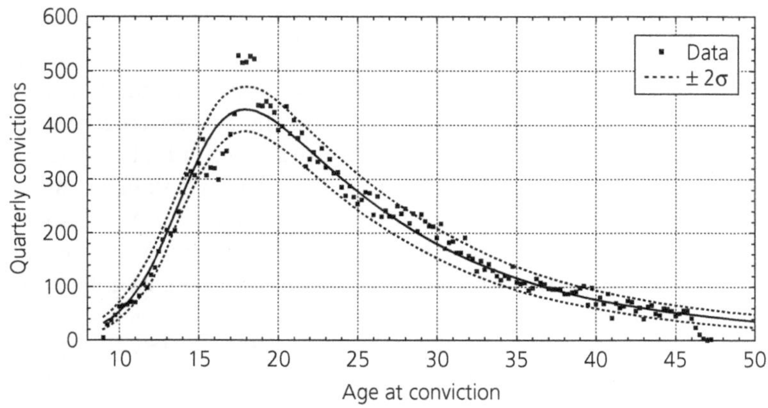

Figure 3.10 Age–crime curve for all convictions

Source: 1953 cohort, Offenders Index.

curve, for first convictions (onset), all subsequent convictions, second, third, fourth, etc, and overall. This is not just an exercise in curve fitting, since the equations follow directly from the assumptions and the parameters have real world interpretations relating to the process of offending and conviction.

As with any theory, it is not sufficient just to explain the observations but the theory must also be capable of making verifiable predictions and the premises of the theory must be credible and acceptable. We have already seen that the structure and parameters of the age-crime model are consistent across cohorts and even cross-sections and in Chapter 7 we will show how the theory can accurately predict the prison population for given sentencing policies. The premise of the theory is that: *for individuals with a propensity for crime, criminal acts will occur at random, the convolution of inclination and opportunity. These individuals will continue to (re-)offend until they are caught and convicted at which point a life-choice decision is made either to continue as before or to modify their behaviour to avoid further conflict with the law.* In this premise we have assumed that offences are committed at random, according to a Poisson process. In the Appendix we show that a random sample of events from a Poisson process is itself a Poisson process. Our analysis has shown that convictions display the characteristics of a Poisson process which in turn implies that they are a random sample of offences committed at random according to a Poisson process.

The 100,000 Active Prolific Offenders

One result of our theory became quite influential[8] in the first few years of the twenty-first century. Among the risk/rate categories identified in the theory the high-risk/high-rate individuals are likely to have the highest number of convictions, to start their criminal careers earliest, and to commit the most crimes. Because the model separates the categories we can calculate the expected number of convictions in a year for members of this particular category. This is achieved using numerical solutions to Equation 3.6 for each conviction number with the parameters derived for the 1997 sentencing sample (Table 3.2). Summing over all conviction numbers results in some 180,000 convictions in 1997 which can be attributed

[8] *Criminal Justice: The Way Ahead* (Home Office 2001).

to high-risk/high-rate offenders. Not all of these offenders will become persistent, in the sense that they will accrue four or more convictions during their criminal career.

The number of high-risk/high-rate offenders who receive their fourth or higher conviction during a year can be calculated by summing over conviction numbers greater than 3. From the theory we would expect some 18 per cent of the convictions (fourth or higher) to be attributable to individuals convicted more than once during the year, but also that only 78 per cent of these active prolific offenders will actually be convicted during a 12-month period. The estimated number of four-plus convictions is 98,000, the number of convicted active prolific offenders is 98,000 * 0.82 = 80,360 and the total number of active prolific offenders is therefore 80,360 / 0.78 = 103,000. This number will of course be subject to both demographic and random variation and is therefore rounded down to a ballpark estimate of 100,000. It is also implicit in the theory that this number is relatively stable over time. As individual offenders give up crime, up to 18 per cent after each conviction, the same number of high-rate offenders graduate into the active prolific offender group by being convicted for the fourth time.

Under this definition of a prolific offender, we would expect around 2 per cent of the population to become prolific offenders at some time between the ages of 10 and 35. Of these, 90 per cent will have joined the group by the age of 26 and 56 per cent will already have left by that age. Less than 5 per cent will still be active at the age of 40. The peak age for membership of the active prolific offender group is 24 when 40 per cent will be active at that age.

It is important to note that different definitions, and different models, will give rise to different numbers and that this particular calculation is only intended to provide an insight into the transient nature of the criminal population. This group of active persistent offenders has been highlighted because they are responsible for a disproportionate number of criminal convictions and, by inference, of crimes. The underlying theory suggests that the behaviour patterns that lead to conviction are consistent throughout the criminal career and predate the first conviction. Thus, for example, falling within the Home Office active persistent offender definition, by sustaining a fourth conviction, does not mark an increase in anti-social and criminal behaviour but simply confirms the status. Indeed, for about 18 per cent of these offenders, confirmation of the active persistent status marks the end of their criminal career as they modify their behaviour to avoid criminal convictions in the future.

Corollaries and Comments

In many respects the theory proposed here is counter-intuitive. Crime is perceived by many as a youthful phenomenon. Certainly the peak age of offending would appear to support that contention, yet in the 1953 cohort over 50 per cent of offenders were convicted for the first time over age 19 and 50 per cent of convictions occurred over the age of 22. Our theory accurately predicts quarterly first conviction rates up to age 70 and beyond in the 1997 sentencing sample and almost 50 per cent of offenders convicted in that sample were over the age of 25.

In many theories of crime, maturation or simply getting older is thought to have a causal influence on desistance. Although the fact that crime diminishes in older generations is beyond dispute, our theory suggests that age itself is not a causal factor. More recent desistance research variously ascribe desistance to 'turning points' in the life course (marriage, employment, military service: Sampson and Laub 2003), developmental taxonomies (adolescent limited, life course persistent: Moffitt 1993), and the identification of life course trajectories modelled using cubic polynomials (Nagin 1999; Sampson and Laub 2003, 2005). Bottoms et al (2004, p 372) set out a list of concepts needed for the study of desistance, these were: 'programmed potential; (social) structures; culture and habitus; situational context; and agency'. Changes in individual circumstances related to these concepts being instrumental in causing desistance. Although most of the desistance studies have found correlations between life events or personal circumstances and desistance or reductions in offending as part of the process of desistance, it is not clear whether these factors are in fact causal. As Kazemian and Farrington (2010, p 42) observed: 'Since turning points and life events are not randomly assigned among individuals, it is difficult to assess whether these events are causes or correlates of desistance.'

In the analysis leading to the generation of our theory and in the mathematical models implementing it, we have identified strong evidence that both first convictions and reconvictions are governed by a proportional hazard survival process. These survival processes are characterized by the negative exponential inter-conviction survival time distributions. The hazard operates on the individuals at risk of conviction, that is the active offenders. Within our risk/rate categories, after each conviction, the same proportion (*p*) of offenders are reconvicted and the same proportion (1 – *p*) are never convicted again. If the offenders who were not reconvicted had continued to offend but desisted after some life event turning point at some random time after conviction, we would not expect to see the negative exponential inter-conviction survival time distribution. Unless, that is, the turning point events of the desisters occurred at precisely the right time to prevent their next conviction. In addition this precise timing would need to occur in both the high and low-rate categories and consistently across the whole life course.

A simpler and, we believe more plausible, explanation is that the proportion (1 – *p*) of offenders do truly desist and that for them *the turning point is conviction*. Burnett and Maruna (2004), who interviewed prisoners just prior to release from prison, identified 'hope' (effectively the desire and will to desist) as a strong correlate of desistance in a ten-year follow-up. However, even among the most hopeful, social difficulties undermined their resolve and 82 per cent of the sample were reconvicted one or more times in the ten-year follow-up period. The decision to desist seems to have been made prior to release and, much as we would predict, 18 per cent managed to stick with it for at least ten years.

In our theory both desistance and the age–crime relationship are a by-product of the processes of offending, capture and conviction. We therefore suggest that *the cumulative effect of the criminal justice system is the major cause of desistance*. We return to this issue in Chapter 5 where we demonstrate that age-based theories are inconsistent with the evidence from the Offenders Index.

Conventional theories also suggest that the rate of offending slows down as individual offenders get older (Gottfredson and Hirschi 1990; Haapanen 1990) or that the rates of offending reduce as part of the process of desistance (Bushway et al 2001; Bushway, Thornberry, and Krohn 2003). This slowing down is apparent because samples of offenders convicted in increasing age-bands show lengthening inter-conviction times. Like Barnett et al (1989, p 347), our theory attributes this effect to the increasing proportion of low-rate offenders in the older age groups as more of the high-rate offenders have had the opportunity to desist after repeated convictions. For an individual, the rate of offending or conviction remains constant throughout the criminal career; see Blumstein et al (1986) and Farrington (1986).

The most consistent predictor of reoffending is the number of previous convictions: the higher that number, the more likely is a reconviction. Our theory explains this apparently increasing probability as the effect of the reducing proportion of low-risk offenders with higher numbers of previous convictions. If for an individual the category membership were known, the *a priori* probability of reconviction is constant and independent of his or her conviction history. We return to this issue in Chapter 6 in our discussion of the identification of risk/rate categories from psychological characteristics of offenders.

Although sentencing policy did change in the period between 1970 and 1992, the consistency of parameter estimates across cohorts indicates that these changes had little or no impact on either the rate of offending or recidivism. Further we shall see from the prison population forecasting work, discussed in Chapter 7, that after 1993, when there were major increases in the use of custody, continuing to assume no change in the recidivism probability or the offending rate accurately predicts the prison population. Thus, the hypothesis suggests that any changes in sentencing (tried on a major scale) between 1970 and the recent past, in particular the increased use of custodial rather than non-custodial sentences, were not effective in reducing conviction rates or recidivism probabilities. It might be argued that the consistency in parameter estimates simply reflects the capacity of the CJS to process offenders, but in our analysis the main driver of convictions would appear to be demographics. As we shall see in Chapter 7 demographics together with sentencing policy are sufficient to accurately model the prison population between 1970 and 1997.

As we shall see in Chapter 5, custody does not reduce recidivism probabilities compared with supervisory sentences and, in line with our theory, the rate of conviction for recidivist offenders remains the same over the entire career. Together these results imply that there is no incapacitative effect of shorter prison sentences. Custody does not reduce overall offending as crimes are effectively saved-up rather than averted whilst an offender is in prison. This is because, for active offenders in the same risk/rate category, the expected residual career length of an *active* released prisoner is the same as that of an *active* offender following a non-custodial sentence.

As has been discussed the theory does not pretend to be a complete theory. It does not begin to consider many aspects of offending or conviction. However, we show that it fits many of the known facts and is not known to contradict any particular large scale empirical finding in a way which cannot be reasonably explained by, for example, some kind of selection effect. An example of this would be when a group of offenders is selected on the basis of having committed only very serious offences, such as murder or large scale corporate fraud, which would lead to non-typical mixtures of the various offending categories. We will discover in Chapter 6 that the main offending categories identified in our theory can in part be distinguished on the basis of certain kinds of psychological information.

We know that some treatment programmes for offenders do reduce recidivism (see for example Goldblatt and Lewis 1998; Tong and Farrington 2006). These had not been used in the period of the analysis presented here (ie before 1998) to the extent required to make a significant impact on the overall rate of recidivism. However, we will show how to calculate their effects in Chapter 8 and also in more detail in the Appendix.

It may be true that improving education[9] and employment would decrease criminality. However, any changes in these over the last 30 years of the twentieth century have not shown up as effects in our analysis, the risk and rate parameters having remained substantially constant over the entire period.

Conclusion

In this chapter we have shown how the results on recidivism probability and rate of offending obtained from the Offenders Index can be explained by a theory with four easily stated basic assumptions. With the addition of two further assumptions, a fifth concerning the transition from the universal informal sanctioning of

[9] For example, it is known that the educational achievement of prisoners is typically lower than the national average (National Prison Survey, Main Findings, Home Office 1991). Of course one should not assume that improving educational standards would reduce offending from such a correlation. Low educational achievement may be a symptom of an underlying antisocial personality rather than a cause of offending.

young children to the near universal formal sanctioning of adults, and a sixth, concerning the relative probability of a first conviction, we have shown that we can explain the shape of the well known 'age–crime', or more correctly, 'age–conviction' curve. This is remarkable as the behaviour of offenders is assumed to remain the same throughout their active offending careers until such point as they decide, following a conviction, to cease offending. The rise of (recorded) offending between the age of criminal responsibility (10) and 17–18 years of age can be simply explained in terms of the increased use of formal sanctions as offenders become legally classified as adults. Additional factors may be that offenders have increased capacity for harm as they get older, and that society has run out of patience with those repeat offenders who return over and over again after informal sanctions. The decline in offending with age from 19–20 years onwards is explained by offenders being convicted and a proportion then ceasing to offend; it is not caused by an intrinsic reduction in the predilection for criminal activity with age.

4

Criminal Careers of Serious, Less Serious, and Trivial Offenders

Orientation

In Chapter 2, we proposed a theory that there are three categories of offenders: high-risk/high-rate, high-risk/low-rate, and low-risk/low-rate. Both the risk of reconviction and the rate of offending are constant over age. In Chapter 3 we applied this theory to predict independent criminal career data, including the age–crime curve. In order to explain the increase in the aggregate offending rate before the peak age of offending, we postulated that the probability of being charged and convicted after being caught increased with age during the juvenile years. We also estimated that there were about 100,000 prolific offenders in England and Wales at any one time.

In this chapter we investigate more serious offending, offences leading to custodial sentences, and the criminal careers of *serious offenders*. We show how an approximate two category model adequately explains particularly serious offences and approximately fits all offences. We then explore the offending patterns of *serious offenders*, those with at least one custodial sentence in their careers, and compare them with the offending patterns of *less serious offenders*, those without any custodial sentences in their criminal careers. We then look briefly at offenders who commit mainly summary offences, ranging from regulatory offences, vagrancy, and drunkenness to offences against the bird protection act and of course minor motoring offences.

Introduction

Examining serious offences first raises the question of what constitutes a serious offence. The data from the Offenders Index (OI) that we have examined so far includes all convictions for standard list offences. In the main these are offences which are potentially triable in the Crown Court, although some ('either way') offences may be tried in the magistrates' court with the agreement of the defendant. There are also a small number of the more serious summary offences included in the standard list. Offences in the standard list range from minor assaults to murder and from petty theft and shoplifting to armed robbery. We clearly need to distinguish between petty offenders and serious criminals. One measure of seriousness could be the imposition of a custodial sentence. But even here, for the same offence seriousness, offenders with several previous convictions are more likely to receive custody than offenders with a short or no criminal history. To control for this we first looked at a subset of offenders who received a custodial sentence at their first court appearance and then at the subset of *serious offenders*[1] with at least one custodial sentence in their careers.

Offenders with Custody at First Court Appearance

For this analysis we used the 1958 cohort sample from the Offenders Index, which is the largest of the cohort samples and includes offenders up to age 35. In this sample some 20 per cent of male offenders receive a custodial sentence at some point in their criminal career, but less than 5 per cent of male offenders fall into the subset of offenders with a custodial sentence at the first court appearance. In the *custody at first appearance* subset we can be reasonably sure that the level of minimum seriousness for the offence is set at the higher end of the seriousness spectrum.

Repeating the risk/rate analysis of Chapter 2 on this subset provided goodness of fit statistics comparable to those obtained for the whole male sample data. Table 4.1 shows the parameter estimates obtained for both the whole sample and the *custody at first appearance* subset.

It can be seen from Table 4.1 that the parameter estimates for the subset are very close to those for the whole sample. There are some differences. A smaller proportion of offenders in the *custody at first appearance* subset are at high-risk of recidivism, 38 per cent compared to 42 per cent in the whole sample. In part, this is because

[1] Throughout this chapter the use of italics for *serious offenders*, *less serious offenders*, *custody at first appearance*, and *other offenders* refers to subsets of offenders as defined in the text where the italics are first used.

Table 4.1 Comparison of parameter estimates for the risk and rate models for male offenders in the 1958 cohort, whole sample and *custody at first appearance subsets*

1958 cohort	***N***	***a***	p_h	p_l	***B***	***b***	λ_h	λ_l
All male offenders	10,077	0.42	0.80	0.25	19049	0.52 ± 0.02	1.01 ± 0.03	0.33 ± 0.01
Male offenders with custody at first court appearance	465	0.38	0.80	0.17	766	0.55 ± 0.08	0.96 ± 0.08	0.37 ± 0.03

Where:
'***N***' is the total number of male offenders in the cohort with at least one conviction,
'***a***' is the proportion of offenders in the high-risk (of reconviction) category,
'p_h' is the high-risk probability and
'p_l' is the low-risk probability.
'***B***' is the total number of inter-conviction times in the data,
'λ_h'and 'λ_l' are the mean numbers of convictions per year for the high-rate and low-rate categories respectively and
'***b***' is the proportion of inter-conviction times attributed to the high-rate category.

high-risk offenders are more likely to be convicted at an early age and hence receive more lenient treatment at their first appearance, despite the seriousness of the offence. The probability of recidivism in the low-risk category is lower in the subset than in the whole sample, 0.17 compared with 0.25, so perhaps custody is a greater deterrent for offenders in the low-risk category. The rate parameters are even closer with two of the three having overlapping confidence intervals and the third parameter's confidence intervals touching. From this evidence it would be hard to argue that these characteristics are meaningfully different between the whole sample and the *custody at first appearance* subset.

From the risk/rate analysis we can calculate the numbers of offenders in each of the risk/rate categories (see the Appendix which reconciles the risk/rate categories). Table 4.2 shows the allocation of offenders to the categories, for both the whole sample and the *custody at first appearance* subset. With a null hypothesis that these serious first offenders occur randomly among the offender categories, we can test the 3 by 2 contingency table, highlighted in Table 4.2, for random (in proportion to the marginal totals) allocation of offenders to the risk/rate categories.

Table 4.2 Allocation of offenders to the risk/rate categories

1958 cohort male offenders	*N*	High-risk/ high-rate	High-risk/ low-rate	Low-risk/ low-rate
Whole sample	10077	**2479**	**1753**	**5845**
Custody at first appearance subset	465	**106**	**71**	**288**

The null hypothesis cannot be rejected: $Chi^2 = 3.2$ on 2 df, $p = 0.8$. This gives support to the proposition that these *serious offenders* do indeed occur randomly across the offender categories, at least for the *custody at first appearance* subset. However, some 20 per cent of male offenders in the 1958 cohort receive one or more custodial sentences at some point in their criminal career. If we define these individuals as *serious offenders* then the *custody at first appearance* subset includes less than a quarter of them.

Custody Rates

For the discussions which follow, we need to define three types of custody rate, the overall custody rate, the custody rate at particular appearance numbers and the individual custody rate. The overall custody rate is defined as the proportion of convictions resulting in a custodial sentence. We consider all court appearances of male offenders in the 1958 cohort and find that the overall custody rate is 14.2 per cent. But the custody rate is not the same at all appearance numbers. At first appearances only 4.6 per cent of offenders receive a custodial sentence. The custody rate then increases with each subsequent appearance number to 20 per cent at the fourth and 40 per cent at the eleventh appearances. Custody rates at appearance numbers above the eleventh show considerable variation but with an average of 40 per cent and no discernible trend.

There are several possible explanations for the relationship between custody rate and appearance number. The most likely explanation is a progressive lowering of the seriousness threshold for custodial sentences, and certainly previous convictions are an aggravating factor in sentencing decisions. A second possible explanation is an escalation of offence seriousness as the criminal career progresses. To explore the second possibility we need to look at individual custody rates, ie the proportion of an individual's convictions that result in a custodial sentence. We will return to this issue in the next section where we consider *serious offenders* in more detail.

Serious Offenders

The *serious offenders* subset (offenders with one or more custodial sentences up to age 35) does not exhibit the same statistical structure as the cohort sample overall (see the recidivism plot in Figure 4.1). The initial slope, the solid line on the graph, represents a recidivism probability for *serious offenders* of 0.865 which is significantly higher than the 0.80 (dotted line on the graph) estimated for the high-risk category of the whole sample. For the data, points on the graph, the slope appears to get steeper with higher appearance numbers suggesting reducing recidivism probability as the career progresses. However, the incremental recidivism probability[2] of the *serious offenders'* subset is consistently higher than that of the high-risk category of the whole male offender sample.

From the analysis of the *custody at first appearance* subset there appeared to be a higher proportion of low-risk offenders than in

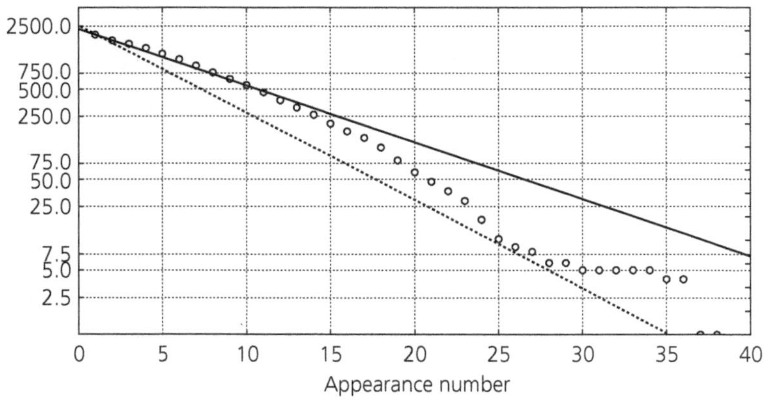

Figure 4.1 Recidivism of *serious offenders*

Source: 1958 cohort Offenders Index.

[2] The incremental recidivism probability is that value of p for which the number of offenders with n convictions is given by $N * p^n$.

the whole sample, but these low-risk, *custody at first appearance*, *serious offenders* represent less than 11.5 per cent of all *serious offenders* and the effect of their lower recidivism is masked by the much greater number of high-risk category offenders in the *serious offenders* subset.

The above *custody at first appearance* analysis also suggests that *serious offenders* might be just like offenders in general. However, if we examine the individual custody rate, that is the proportion of an individual's convictions resulting in custody, for offenders in the whole *serious offenders* subset, we find that the mean custody rate does not increase significantly with career conviction count. In fact, the highest individual custody rates occur for *serious offenders* with only one or two convictions (see Figure 4.2). The average individual custody rate initially falls to a low of 26 per cent, for *serious offenders* with six convictions (up to age 35), and then increases gradually to an average of 45 per cent for *serious offenders* with 24 convictions. The average individual custody rate for *serious offenders* with three or more convictions is 30 per cent, so some 70 per cent of their offences fall below the custodial threshold, despite the threshold reducing as the career progresses. For these persistent *serious offenders*, the median custody rate is 27 per cent, with an inter-quartile range from 18.5 per cent to 38.5 per cent.

Figure 4.2 Average individual custody rate plotted against career conviction count

Source: 1958 cohort (Male Serious Offenders), Offenders Index.

To summarize, using custody as an indicator of offence seriousness leads us to classify some 20 per cent of male offenders as *serious offenders*. These individuals are versatile in the seriousness of their offending, and on average only 30 per cent of their convictions result in custody. Among these *serious offenders* the high-risk of recidivism category are over-represented, despite them being under-represented in the *custody at first appearance* subset. The over-representation of high-risk offenders among *serious offenders* is, in part, due to the increased probability of a custodial sentence for offenders with several previous convictions. As a corollary, offenders in the low-risk category who receive custody are very likely to have committed very serious offences and hence attract long sentences, which provides a possible explanation for the lower recidivism rates observed for offenders released from sentences of over six years compared with those released from sentences of under six years.

We have seen from the *custody at first appearance* analysis that serious first offenders appear to be a random sample from the risk/rate categories identified in the whole cohort, inasmuch as they exhibit similar recidivism probability and reconviction time distributions. But a custodial sentence at a first conviction is a relatively rare occurrence, with only 4.6 per cent of male offenders overall and 23 per cent of *serious offenders* sent to prison at their first court appearance. The majority of *serious offenders* exhibit very different characteristics with higher recidivism probabilities and a disproportionate number of custodial convictions.

Less Serious Offenders

The subset of *less serious offenders*, with no custodial convictions up to age 35, exhibits the same statistical structure as the whole sample but, again, with very different parameter values. The proportions in the risk categories are 58 per cent and 42 per cent for high and low-risk categories respectively, apparently the reverse of the whole sample values. As explained in Chapter 2 the unequivocal allocation of offenders to specific risk/rate categories is problematic and the removal of *serious offenders* from the sample blurs the distinction between risk categories so that low-risk offenders with more convictions and high-risk offenders with fewer appear to be more similar. The probabilities of reconviction for the high and low-risk *less serious offenders* are 0.58 and 0.10 respectively, which are very much less than the corresponding values for the whole sample of 0.8 and 0.25. As we saw with the male and female subsets in Chapter 2, parameter estimates are dependent on the conditioning of the sample and are in fact characteristics of the sample population rather than of the individuals within it. The removal of *serious offenders* leaves behind sub-categories of offenders who not only commit less serious offences but who, as a group, also have lower recidivism probabilities.

Serious Offences

We can now turn our attention to serious offending and examine the subset of the *serious offenders'* convictions which resulted in custodial sentences and look at custodial recidivism and inter-imprisonment times. We begin by following the procedure described in Chapter 2 to obtain the custodial values for the 'λ's, 'p's and the allocation of offenders to the risk/rate categories (see Table 4.3 for the results obtained from the 1953 cohort).

We can see from Table 4.3 that the high-risk/low-rate category has apparently disappeared, leaving just two categories. We now propose a model with 'high' and 'low' categories only, where the high and low categories are substantially equivalent to the high-risk/high-rate and low-risk/low-rate categories of Chapter 2 respectively. We will also introduce a simpler approach to the modelling of assumption 5 of Chapter 3. In order, to account for the apparent rise in crime during adolescence, we will assume that one or more

Table 4.3 Allocation of serious male offenders to the risk/rate categories for the 1953 cohort

	Offenders		Total
	High-risk of re-incarceration $p_h = 0.681$	Low-risk of re-incarceration $p_l = 0.136$	Offenders
High-rate of incarceration $\lambda_h = 0.451$	58%	–	58%
Low-rate of incarceration $\lambda_l = 0.129$	–	42%	42%
Total	58%	42%	

early custodial opportunities[3] are dealt with either informally or by other CJS disposals.

Simplified Modelling of Convictions for Serious Offences

We show in the Appendix that if the offending rate is constant over age and the time to the next offence is distributed as a negative exponential then, from any point in time, the time to the second offence (committed after that point in time) is distributed as a gamma distribution with shape parameter 2, and to the **n**th offence as a gamma distribution[4] with shape parameter **n**.

Equation 4.1 gives the general form of the gamma distribution.

$$y(t) = A * \lambda * \frac{(\lambda * t)^{n-1}}{\Gamma(n)} * e^{-\lambda * t} \tag{4.1}$$

Where:

$y(t)$ is the number offending in unit time at time t from the chosen point in time,

A is the total number of future offenders at the chosen point in time,

λ is the rate parameter,

n is the gamma distribution shape parameter,

$\Gamma(n)$ is, for integer n, equivalent to factorial $(n - 1)$.

In order to model age at first custody we can make the assumption that one or more of the initial custodial opportunities result in non-custodial disposals. So the observed age at first custodial conviction curve is in fact the age to the second, third, or fourth custodial opportunity. This would result in a weighted sum of gamma distributions with shape parameters (c_i) where ($c_i - 1$) is the number of custodial opportunities ignored prior to the first custodial conviction for the **i**th section of offenders and the weight w_i is the proportion of offenders in that section. For computational convenience

[3] A custodial opportunity is a cleared-up offence which could have resulted in a custodial sentence had the offender been older or had had a number of previous convictions.

[4] This formulation of time to a subsequent conviction number can also be derived directly from the solution of differential equations assuming a constant rate of conviction (see the Appendix).

we will simply divide our offenders into two sections. For one we will ignore only the first custodial opportunity and for the second we will ignore one additional custodial opportunity. In this instance if we assume that the two sections are of equal size then we can say that we have ignored 1.5 custodial opportunities to arrive at our first actual custody.

Our motivation for these simplifications is to provide a basis for forecasting the prison population up to ten years ahead, which we will describe more fully in Chapter 7. The mathematical model implementing our theory had to be easily programmed to permit the direct computation of the age profiles for each imprisonment or conviction number. We also need a parameterization of the model based on all the data available which provides a satisfactory fit over the period up to 1993 and beyond. We begin by following the procedure described in Chapter 2 to obtain the custodial values for λ and p for the high and low categories aggregated over all the cohorts. The results are given in Table 4.4.

In fitting the rate of custodial conviction (λ), we must consider the time offenders have been in prison and subtract this from the inter-incarceration times. As it turns out we get a very similar value for λ if the time spent in custody is ignored. This is because the majority of 'times served' are relatively short and often a proportion of this time is served on remand prior to the conviction date. Also, the slopes of the graphs constructed in Chapter 2, which give us the conviction rate, are not greatly changed by adding on this extra time, which merely moves the entire graph to the right by an amount equivalent to the average time served under sentence.

The next step was to try to fit the age–imprisonment curve for various values of the proportion who are criminal (q). The fitting was done against each separate imprisonment, first, second, third, etc. Because the 'high' category has a higher recidivism probability it will dominate the high custody number graphs. This allows the high category parameters to be set before moving to the low category.[5] As well as q it is also possible to estimate the first age at which

[5] The reader might wonder why a more algorithmic approach was not used, for example some form of maximum likelihood approach. The authors are proponents of the 'likelihood school' of statistics as described by Edwards (1972). However, it is important to remember that likelihood (and in particular maximum likelihood) estimation can only act as guide to the expert judgement of the analyst. The standard example is that of a coin taken from the pocket, thrown in the air and landing heads. The most likely hypothesis regarding the coin is that it has

Table 4.4 The aggregated parameters obtained for offenders convicted of offences for which they were imprisoned before 1993

Table 4.4a: Male	'High' category	'Low' category
Imprisonment rate $\boldsymbol{\lambda}$ (years)$^{-1}$	0.50 +/– 0.05	0.20 +/– 0.05
Re-incarceration probability $\boldsymbol{p}$	0.67 +/– 0.03	0.18 +/– 0.02
Proportion of criminal population $\boldsymbol{q}$	0.55 +/– 0.03	0.45 +/– 0.03
Criminality $\boldsymbol{c}$	0.073 +/– 0.004	
Temporal adjustment $\boldsymbol{\delta}$ years	–0.6	
Number of custodial opportunities ignored	1	
Age of first imprisonment (years)	15	
Table 4.4b: Female	**'High' category**	**'Low' category**
Imprisonment rate $\boldsymbol{\lambda}$ (years)$^{-1}$	0.35 +/– 0.05	0.09 +/– 0.01
Re-incarceration probability $\boldsymbol{p}$	0.67 +/– 0.05	0.15 +/– 0.02
Proportion of criminal population $\boldsymbol{q}$	0.3 +/– 0.1	0.7 +/– 0.1
Criminality $\boldsymbol{c}$	0.0040 +/– 0.0001	
Temporal adjustment $\boldsymbol{\delta}$ years	–0.6	
Number of custodial opportunities ignored	1	
Age of first imprisonment (years)	15	

someone is likely to be imprisoned and the number of custodial opportunities ignored before actual imprisonment occurs. The best fitting parameter values, for males and females separately and aggregated over all cohorts, are shown in Table 4.4a and 4.4b.

two heads. On the basis of his theory of the world the analyst may consider it more probable that the coin has a tail on the other side. In addition a likelihood analysis can only be carried out where one has a good idea of the error structure and inherent variability of the data. True, here one will have near-Gaussian counting errors, but there will also be unknown effects due to criminal justice system changes in the period and an approximation of unknown accuracy in the treatment of early offences. Also the model being used in this instance is a further approximation of a large scale theory. Even if one were to attempt to put together a likelihood function for this situation, expert judgement on the basis of how well the graph was seen to fit by eye would have to guide the analysis. In this case it seems more honest simply to admit that the fits were 'judged by expert opinion'.

The table includes a 'temporal adjustment' parameter δ which we will consider in some detail later.

Figures 4.3a and 4.3b show the results of the simplified model compared to the actual age-custody data from the 1958 cohort from the Offenders Index. The lines on the graphs show the predictions of the model for the annual numbers imprisoned or otherwise detained at a given age. The first four imprisonments are shown, on one graph, Figure 4.3a, and the fourth to the seventh imprisonments are shown on separate graphs in Figure 4.3b. The annual data for the 1958 cohort from the Offenders Index is shown as points on the graphs. There are no data points over the age of 34 as members of the 1958 cohort were under 35 at the time the sample was extracted from the Offenders Index.

As we can see the results are quite good for such a simple model. Although the three category model derived in Chapters 2 and 3 does fit the data better, the computational advantages of this (gamma distribution based) model outweigh the marginal reduction in fit. This simple two category model provides an explicit formula for the age/custody curve at each custody number, greatly facilitating practical applications of the theory. Clearly this model is not describing everything that is going on, and there are no doubt many second order effects which are important. It should also be remembered that custody rates did in fact change over the period.

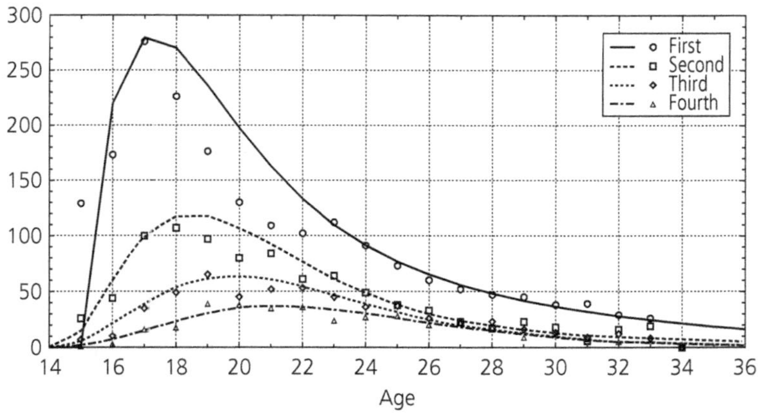

Figure 4.3a The predictions of the two group age-custody model compared with data from the Offenders Index (custodies 1 to 4)

Note: 1958 cohort offenders who were incarcerated before 1992.

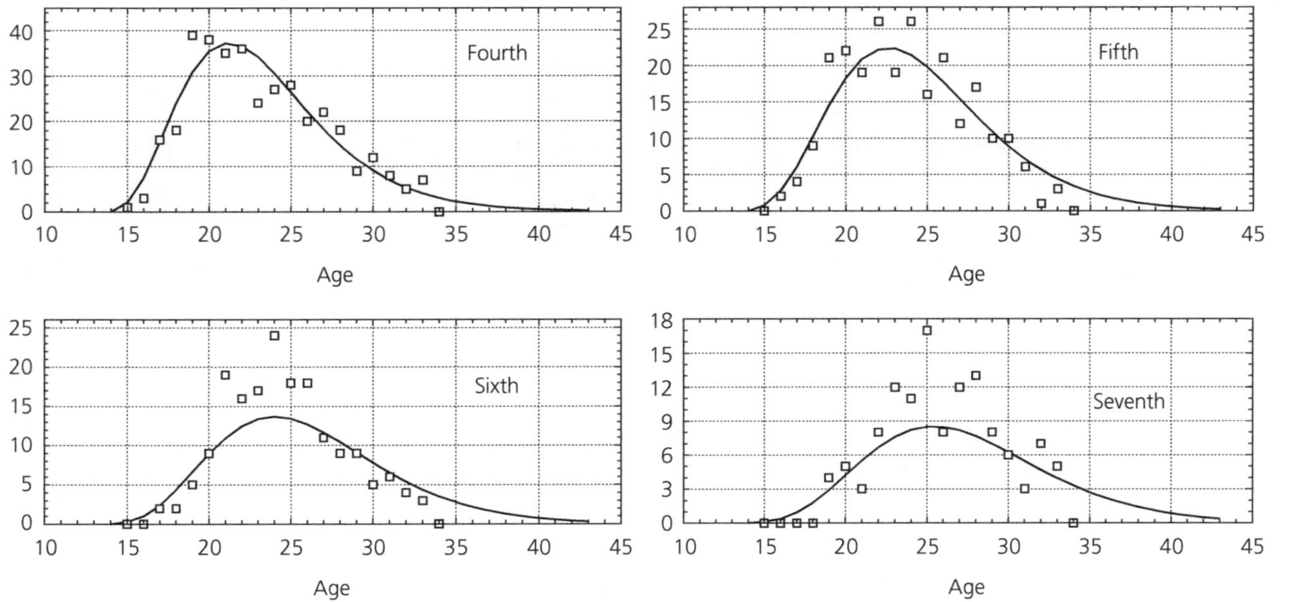

Figure 4.3b The predictions of the two group age-custody model compared with data from the Offenders Index (custodies 4 to 7)

Simplified Modelling of all Convictions

The two category model can also be applied to all standard list convictions, not only those leading to imprisonment. The results are shown in Figure 4.4 and Table 4.5. Figure 4.4 shows the modelled age curves for the first four conviction numbers (lines on the graph) and the corresponding numbers of offenders at each age/conviction number from the 1958 cohort (points on the graph). Again the fit is reasonable, but as ever there are other things going on. We have seen in Chapter 3 that a three category model can produce a better fit to the age–crime curves, both for individual conviction numbers and overall. The two category fit for early ages is quite poor. However this model is very simple and we would not expect an 'ignore the first two conviction opportunities or so' model to accurately reflect the complex processes involved in dealing with young offenders.

As we saw in Chapter 2 there is evidence of a category of offenders with a high recidivism probability and a low rate of offending. These offenders will in general have long careers and still be offending when other high (recidivism) risk offenders have given up. Their influence has been to reduce the value of λ for the high category in the two category model. The high category is in fact an amalgamation of both high-rate and low-rate offenders, in the ratio 70:30, which reduces the high-rate parameter from well over 0.85 (see the estimates in Table 2.2) to 0.63 (see Table 4.5a). This reduction in

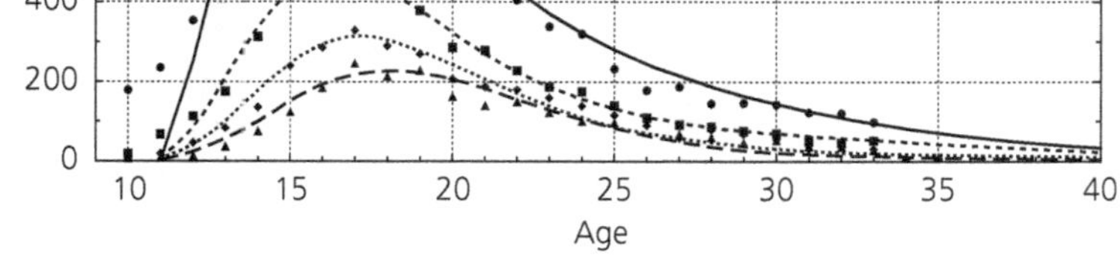

Figure 4.4 The predictions of the two group standard list conviction model compared with data from the Offenders Index

Source: 1958 cohort, Offenders Index.

Table 4.5 The parameters obtained for the two category model for offenders convicted of standard list offences before 1993

Table 4.5a: Male	'High' category	'Low' category
Conviction rate **λ** (convictions per year)	0.63 +/– 0.08	0.22 +/– 0.02
Reconviction probability ***p***	0.82 +/– 0.03	0.29 +/– 0.02
Proportion of criminal category ***q***	0.40 +/– 0.05	0.60 +/– 0.05
Criminality ***c***	0.33 +/– 0.02	
Temporal adjustment **δ** years	–0.6	
Number of conviction opportunities ignored ***g***	2.4*	1.4*
Age of first conviction (years)	11	
Table 4.5b: Female	**'High' category**	**'Low' category**
Conviction rate **λ** (convictions per year)	0.58 +/– 0.08	0.27 +/– 0.05
Reconviction probability ***p***	0.78 +/– 0.04	0.21 +/– 0.02
Proportion of criminal category ***q***	0.10 +/– 0.05	0.90 +/– 0.05
Criminality ***c***	0.087 +/– 0.003	
Temporal adjustment	–0.6	
Number of conviction opportunities ignored ***g***	2.8*	1.8*
Age of first conviction (years)	11	

* Where ***N.n*** means a fraction (1–0.***n***) have ***N*** informal convictions and 0.***n*** have ***N*** + 1.

λ necessitates the introduction of the temporal adjustment (δ) of –0.6 years into the mathematical representation of the two category model. The temporal adjustment is needed to bring the peaks of the age–conviction (custody) curves in line with the observed data for each conviction (custody) number. To achieve this, the gamma distribution model is modified as follows:

$$y(t) = A * \lambda * \frac{(\lambda * (t - \delta * (n-1)))^{n+first-2}}{\Gamma(n)} * e^{-\lambda*(t-\delta*(n-1))} \tag{4.2}$$

Where:

y(t) is the number offending in unit time at time t from the earliest conviction/custody age,

A is the total number of offenders in the category,
λ is the rate parameter,
n is the actual conviction/custody number,
first is the number of the conviction/custodial opportunity resulting in actual conviction/custody,
$\Gamma(n)$ is, for integer n, equivalent to factorial $(n - 1)$,
δ is the temporal adjustment.

This approximation of the theory into two offender categories provides us with a very simple mathematical model which adequately fits the data for both custodial and all convictions before 1993. In particular the similarity between the predicted and actual curves for those incarcerated suggests that the two category model is an excellent description of the age profile of those receiving custodial sentences in this period.

An important point to notice is that, the proportion of 'high' category offenders is greater for male custodial convictions (0.55) compared with all male convictions (0.4). Similarly, although there are many fewer offenders who are imprisoned in their lifetimes (as measured by the criminality parameter) the imprisonment rate λ is only very slightly less than the conviction rate (0.5 per year as opposed to 0.6 for the high category and almost identical for the low category). This result reinforces the conclusion that serious offending is not simply a random sample of standard list offending, as suggested by the analysis of the *custody at first conviction* subset, because overall *serious offenders* disproportionately commit the more serious offences. The 'high' category dominates among *serious offenders*. We can calculate for example that more than three quarters of the receptions into prison can be attributed to members of the 'high' population.

We need to be a little careful here. A member of the high offending category will appear before the courts a number of times (on average five). The higher imprisonment rate of the high category may simply be because they are recidivists. This means that although there will be many more of the high category in prison, the low category will be disproportionately represented amongst those who have committed very serious offences, and therefore have very long sentences.

Versatility or Specialization in Offending

As illustrated in Figure 4.2, *serious offenders* do not in general specialize wholly in serious offences. With very few exceptions, only *serious offenders* with just one or two convictions in their criminal careers have individual custody rates much greater than 40 per cent. *Serious offenders* may however exhibit some specialization by offence type. To investigate the level of specialization we can look at the transition matrices from one offence type to another. Table 4.6 is a transition matrix for *serious offenders* given a custodial sentence for the column offence whose previous custodial sentence was for the row offence. The cell entries are the counts of offenders making each transition and the percentages are of the row total.

If all offenders were complete specialists then only the leading diagonal (violence to violence, rape to rape etc) highlighted in bold, would have non-zero cell values. The off-diagonal entries therefore suggest a degree of versatility in offending. Examination of the leading diagonal shows that only the burglary to burglary transition exceeds 50 per cent; thus for all other offences the next custodial sentence is more likely to be for a different offence type. Complete versatility on the other hand would result in cell entries being in direct proportion to the product of row and column totals, the familiar null-hypothesis estimator for contingency tables. The complete versatility hypothesis can be tested using the (one tailed) ***Chi***^{2} test, and this hypothesis was rejected (***Chi***^{2} = 735 with 64 ***df***., critical value at $p = 0.001$ is 104). Thus *serious offenders* are neither completely specialist nor completely versatile. The degree of specialization or versatility can be measured using the Forward Specialization Coefficient proposed by Farrington (1986; see also Farrington, Snyder, and Finnegan 1988). The FSC can be calculated directly from Table 4.6 using Equation 4.3:

$$FSC = \frac{(O - E)}{(R - E)} \tag{4.3}$$

Where:

O is the observed (diagonal table entry)

$$E = \frac{R * C}{N}$$

R is the row total.

C is the column total excluding the 'first custody' row, and

N is the sum of the observations.

Table 4.6 Transition matrix for custodial sentences of 1958 cohort male offenders

Previous Custody	Violence	Rape	Sex	Burglary	Robbery	Theft	Fraud	Drugs	Other	Total
Violence	**64** **25.30%**	2 0.79%	1 0.40%	67 26.48%	11 4.35%	65 25.69%	11 4.35%	8 3.16%	23 9.09%	253
Rape	1 16.67%	**0** **0.00%**	0 0.00%	2 33.33%	0 0.00%	3 50.00%	0 0.00%	0 0.00%	0 0.00%	6
Sex	1 5.00%	2 10.00%	**5** **25.00%**	5 25.00%	1 5.00%	4 20.00%	1 5.00%	0 0.00%	1 5.00%	20
Burglary	83 7.50%	4 0.36%	8 0.72%	**575** **51.99%**	64 5.79%	264 23.87%	47 4.25%	18 1.63%	42 3.80%	1106
Robbery	15 13.89%	0 0.00%	2 1.85%	46 42.59%	**10** **9.26%**	27 25.00%	1 0.93%	1 0.93%	6 5.56%	108
Theft	84 9.66%	4 0.46%	8 0.92%	258 29.66%	35 4.02%	**365** **41.95%**	48 5.52%	17 1.95%	51 5.86%	870
Fraud	18 15.38%	0 0.00%	1 0.85%	36 30.77%	1 0.85%	31 26.50%	**18** **15.38%**	2 1.71%	9 7.69%	117
Drugs	3 7.89%	0 0.00%	0 0.00%	10 26.32%	1 2.63%	5 13.16%	1 2.63%	**17** **44.74%**	1 2.63%	38
Other	18 15.13%	0 0.00%	1 0.84%	33 27.73%	3 2.52%	40 33.61%	5 4.20%	2 1.68%	**17** **14.29%**	119
First Custody	309 15.28%	24 1.19%	25 1.24%	612 30.27%	97 4.80%	598 29.57%	140 6.92%	104 5.14%	111 5.49%	2022
All Offence types	596	36	51	1644	223	1402	272	169	261	4659

Table 4.7 shows the FSCs for *serious offenders* in the 1958 cohort. We now need to interpret the FSC. Stander et al (1989) suggested that specialization was in evidence if the FSC was significantly different from zero. In Table 4.7 all the same offence transitions meet this criterion, with the exception of the transition from rape to rape, but in that case the cell entry in Table 4.6 is zero and only six previous custodial sentences were for rape. Alternatively it could be argued that versatile offending is in evidence if the FSC is significantly different from 1. Again all FSCs in Table 4.7 meet that criterion. The FSC therefore needs to be interpreted as a measure of versatility versus specialization. Perfect versatility is indicated by FSC = zero and perfect specialization by FSC = 1. The most specialized *serious offenders* would appear to be involved in the more serious drugs offences but even there the FSC suggests a marked degree of versatility. For all offence types the tendency is towards versatility rather than specialization.

The next question is, do *serious offenders* become more or less specialized as the career progresses? We therefore need to explore whether transition probabilities change as the custody number increases. We followed the procedure outlined in Stander et al (1989). This procedure involves the construction of intermediate matrices for each previous offence type in which the rows represent the custody number from two to five, the columns represent the offence types at the corresponding custody number, and the cell

Table 4.7 Forward Specialization Coefficients for each of the offence types

Offence type	Forward specialization coefficient
Violence to Violence	0.16
Rape to Rape	0.00
Sex to Sex	0.24
Burglary to Burglary	0.21
Robbery to Robbery	0.05
Theft to Theft	0.16
Fraud to Fraud	0.11
Drugs to Drugs	0.43
Other to Other	0.09

entries are the counts of offenders making that transition. The analysis was restricted to the first four transitions to maintain the total transition count at each custody number to more than 200. ***Chi*²** was calculated for each intermediate matrix and summed over the nine matrices. Since ***Chi*²** = 154 on 167 *df*. (the critical value at $p = 0.05$ is 198), the null hypothesis, that the transition probabilities were the same at each custody number, could not be rejected. Similarly the ***Chi*²**s for the four intermediate matrices were all non-significant, replicating Stander et al's findings. It should be noted here that for some of the transitions where the number of offenders involved was low, both expected and actual counts were zero and these cells were not included in the degrees of freedom calculations.

The analysis of offence type transitions above has concentrated on custodial convictions only. We now look at all convictions of both *serious offenders* and offenders with no custodial sentences, the *less serious offenders*. Table 4.8 replicates Table 4.7 with the addition of the FSCs for the conviction transitions of *serious offenders* with at least one custodial sentence; *less serious offenders* with no custodial sentences up to age 35; and the whole 1958 cohort sample.

Table 4.8 Forward Specialization Coefficients for various subsets of the 1958 cohort

Offence type	Serious offenders custodial only	Serious offenders all convictions	Less serious offenders	All offenders
Violence to Violence	0.16	0.16	0.18	0.17
Sex to Sex	0.24	0.21	0.22	0.21
Burglary to Burglary	0.21	0.19	0.14	0.19
Robbery to Robbery	0.05	0.06	0.00	0.05
Theft to Theft	0.16	0.13	0.14	0.14
Fraud to Fraud	0.11	0.09	0.08	0.09
Drugs to Drugs	0.43	0.37	0.40	0.38
Other to Other	0.09	0.14	0.15	0.14

The Rape to Rape transition has been omitted from Table 4.8 as only one offender in the 1958 cohort was convicted of a second rape. Also, rape was a relatively rare offence in the 1958 cohort with only 40 convictions for rape out of a total of 32,803 convictions overall. It can be seen from Table 4.8 that variations in the FSCs, for the same offence transitions, between the various subsets of offenders are very small. Even between the two disjoint subsets, *serious offenders* (all convictions) and *less serious offenders*, the differences are small. *Serious offenders* appear to be marginally more specialized in burglary and robbery and marginally less specialized in all other offence types.

Specialization in the sense used above is about the likelihood of an offender being convicted of the same offence on consecutive court appearances. We now look at the distribution of offence types over all convictions and compare the distribution for *serious offenders* (those with one or more custodial sentences in their careers up to age 35) with the distribution of offence types for *less serious offenders* (those without any custodial convictions up to age 35).

Figures 4.5a and 4.5b show the offence type distributions for the two subsets respectively. The percentages shown on the histograms are the proportions that each offence type is of the total convictions sustained by *serious* and *less serious offenders*. Table 4.9 presents the proportions of convictions for each offence type committed by these two offender subsets.

In the 1958 cohort there are a total of 12,417 offenders (male and female), 2,164 (17.4 per cent) of whom fall into the *serious*

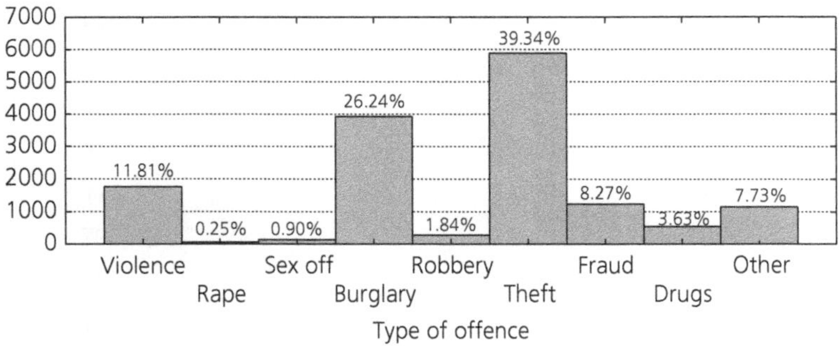

Figure 4.5a Offences of *serious offenders*

Note: Offenders with one or more custodial sentences up to age 35.

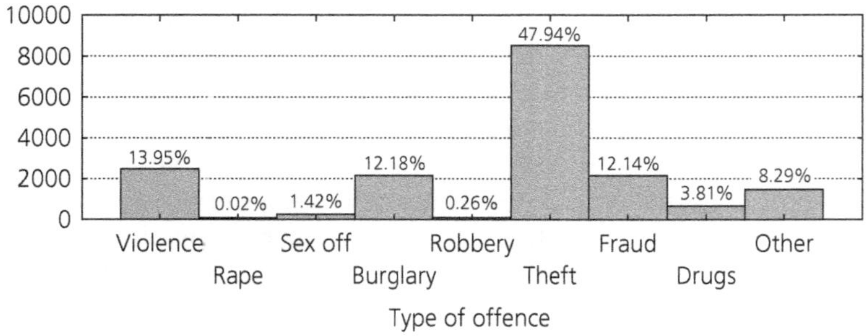

Figure 4.5b Offences of *less serious offenders*

Source: 1958 Cohort Offenders Index.
Note: Offenders with no custodial sentences up to age 35.

offender subset. Collectively *serious offenders* were responsible for 45.7 per cent of convictions and disproportionately responsible for convictions in all offence types. It is perhaps not surprising that these offenders are over-represented in offence types with a high probability of custodial sentences (rape, robbery, and burglary) but their over-representation in all offence types suggests that in general they are more prolific and more versatile as well as committing

Table 4.9 Numbers and proportions of convictions for each offence type attributable to the *Serious* and *Less Serious Offender* subsets

Type of offence	Serious offender subset		Less serious offender subset		Total convictions
Violence	1765	41.60%	2478	58.40%	4243
Rape	37	92.50%	3	7.50%	40
Sex	134	34.63%	253	65.37%	387
Burglary	3922	64.45%	2163	35.55%	6085
Robbery	275	85.67%	46	14.33%	321
Theft	5881	40.85%	8516	59.15%	14397
Fraud	1236	36.44%	2156	63.56%	3392
Drugs	543	44.54%	676	55.46%	1219
Other	1156	43.97%	1473	56.03%	2629
All Offences	14949	45.70%	17764	54.30%	32713

the more serious offences. Among *serious offenders*, 26.3 per cent of them had more than ten convictions in their careers up to age 35 and the highest career conviction count was 38. For the 10,236 *less serious offenders*, less than 0.5 per cent sustained more than ten convictions up to age 35 and the highest career conviction count was only 15.

Finally we explore versatility of offending in relation to career conviction counts. For each count we calculated the average number of different offence types (maximum 9) committed during the career. Figure 4.6 shows how the average type count increases as the number of convictions increases for both the *serious* and *less serious offenders*, circles and plusses on the graph respectively. The solid line on the graph is a logarithmic fit to the combined data suggesting that the variety of offence types is proportional to the log of the number of offences committed.

In interpreting this graph it must be remembered that offender numbers diminish as the career conviction count increases. Only one *less serious offender* reached a career conviction count of 15, but 210 *serious offenders* had 15 or more convictions. Figure 4.7 shows the distribution of offence type counts for the *serious* and *less serious offender* subsets. The *y* axis is the proportion of the subset with the given offence type count. One-fifth of *serious offenders* have just one offence type, but over two-thirds of this 20 per cent, 14.5 per cent of *serious offenders*, have only one conviction. The

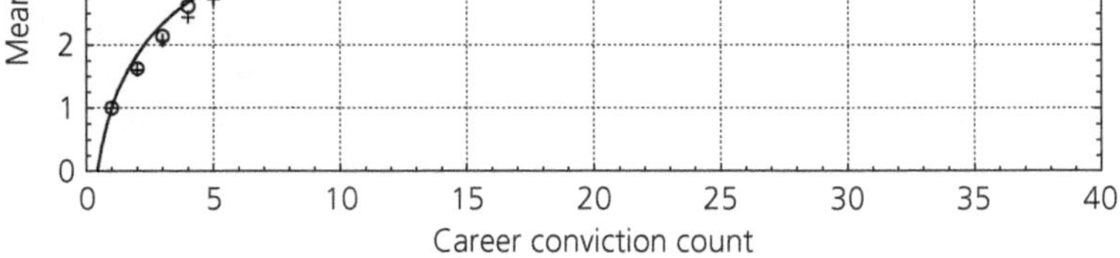

Figure 4.6 Plot of the average number of different offence types against career conviction count

Source: 1958 cohort, Offenders Index.

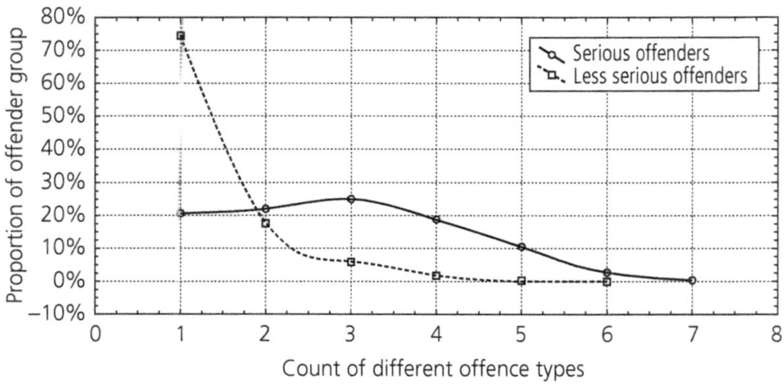

Figure 4.7 Proportions of serious and less serious offender groups against the count of offence types

Source: 1958 cohort, Offenders Index.

proportion then increases slightly with offence type count to 25 per cent at three offence types, and then falls back to 19 per cent at four, 10 per cent at five and less than 3 per cent with six or more and only seven offenders convicted of seven different offence types. The decline in the proportion reflects the diminishing numbers of offenders with higher career conviction counts. *Less serious offenders* show a different pattern; 75 per cent have just one offence type but 65 per cent have only one conviction. The proportion of *less serious offenders* at each type count diminishes rapidly as the type count increases reflecting the lower recidivism probability of this subset and the smaller number of offenders with more than six convictions.

Despite the very real differences in the distribution of offence type counts between the two categories, the relationship between type count and career conviction count is very similar for *serious* and *less serious offenders*, circles and plusses on the graph in Figure 4.6 respectively. Offenders without custodial sentences up to age 35 may appear more specialized but only because their career conviction counts are much lower.

Trivial Offenders

The analysis presented so far has concentrated on those (standard list) offences recorded in the Offenders Index. There are many less serious offences tried exclusively in the magistrates' courts which are not recorded on the Offenders Index. These offences include various forms of antisocial behaviour, drunkenness, disturbing the peace, minor assaults, motoring offences, breach of regulations governing trade and other activities, etc. All breaches of the criminal law, rather than the civil law, are technically crimes and non-standard list summary convictions constitute the majority of criminal convictions recorded in England and Wales. Because these offences were not recorded on the OI there is little information available regarding the offenders and in particular there is no criminal history information available.

Data on convictions for non-standard list offences were however available from the 'Court Appearance' computer system, run by the Research, Development and Statistics Directorate of the Home Office. This system collected information from all courts in England and Wales. The records for standard list convictions were copied to the Offenders Index and retained but records on the Court Appearance system were not retained longer than was necessary for the compilation of Criminal Statistics publications. We were able to extract magistrates' court data from the 1996 court appearance data set. Although all convictions (court appearances) are included, the age information for a little under half of the offenders convicted and sentenced during that year was not recorded by the courts. About one third of the convictions were for standard list offences, many of which would have been committed for trial in the Crown Court and would include the serious offences analysed above. The remaining summary offences are investigated below. Male offenders are again considerably more numerous than females and we have restricted our analysis to males.

The missing age data on well over half of the non-standard list conviction records causes problems for the analysis. However it was possible, by making some reasonable assumptions, to investigate the characteristics of the offenders committing less serious offences. Missing age is recorded with a date of birth as 01/01/1971 in the 1996 raw data. To correct for this we have, as a first step, replaced the recorded count of convictions at age 25, circa 360,000, with 20,500, the average conviction count for ages 24 and 26. Figure 4.8 shows the age profiles obtained from the raw data with that adjustment.

It can be seen from Figure 4.8 that the standard list convictions exhibit the familiar age–conviction curve first encountered in

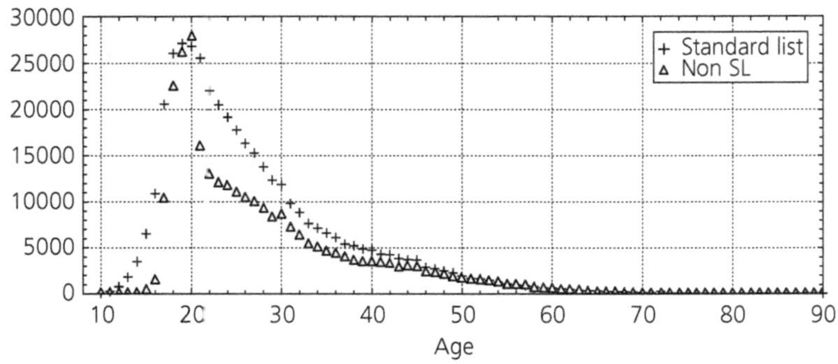

Figure 4.8 Age profiles for offenders appearing in the magistrates' court in 1996

Source: 1996 Home Office court appearance data.
Note: Raw data corrected at age 25.

Chapter 3, which is not surprising as the OI has been derived from the same basic data source. The non-standard list convictions however do not at first sight conform to the profile. They peak at age 20, the rise in convictions is steeper and delayed to the late teenage years, and it then drops to nearly half the peak at age 21. Also, although non-standard list convictions account for two-thirds of the annual total, due to the missing age data the profile shows fewer non-standard list convictions at almost every age, compared to standard list convictions. The steeper rise in the late teenage years is because many summary offences, regulatory offences in particular, are not available to juveniles, or to other offences being routinely dealt with outside the court system when committed by juveniles. The apparent rapid decline at age 21 is entirely due to the missing age data.

Correcting for missing data for summary offences is problematic as we have no firm information on why age is recorded for some convictions and not for others. In the courts, for many offences, it is quite important to identify juveniles and young adults but much less important to record the age of adults. The main exceptions to this are the less serious motoring offences and we will return to these later. Examination of the standard list convictions from the OI suggests that missing age data occurs randomly over offence types and does not appear to distort the age–conviction curve at ages other than 25. For simplicity we have assumed that, for the standard list offences, non-recording of age after age 20 is

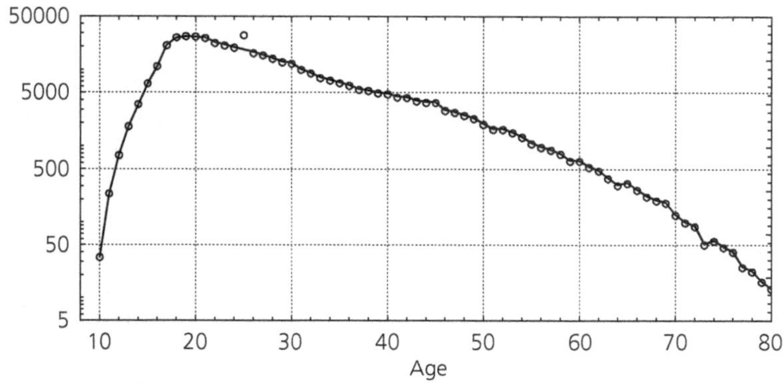

Figure 4.9 Standard list age–conviction curve (with and without missing data adjustment)

Source: 1996 Home Office court appearance data.
Note: For the solid line the outlier data points represent the total number of standard list convictions in 1996 at the age shown in one-year increments of age. The outlier at age 25 has been replaced by the average of age 24 and 26 and the surplus distributed pro-rata over all ages ≥ 21.

random, and we have therefore spread the excess count from age 25, pro rata, over the 21+ data points. Figure 4.9 shows the results of this adjustment; the circles on the graph are the raw data points and the line is the corrected profile, using a logarithmic *y* axis. The corrected profile is not very different from the original data ignoring the age 25 outlier.

For the non-standard list (non-SL) convictions the corrections needed to be more complicated. Applying the above correction to the non-SL age–conviction curve created a large step increase at age 21 which we believe is unlikely to represent the true situation. Separating motoring offences from the non-SL data shows that the number and proportion of summary motoring offences increase dramatically at age 17, representing nearly two-thirds of all non-SL offences thereafter. For many of these post-17 motoring offences, age would not be of any particular concern to the magistrates and is thus more likely not to be recorded. Non-motoring offences on the other hand are more likely to follow the age recording practices outlined above where age is more important before age 21 than after. We have assumed that the peak age for non-SL offences remains at age 20 and that at age 21 the conviction count is a nominal 6 per cent less than at age 20. All age counts above 21 were then increased in the same proportion, thus eliminating the step decrease at age 21. The resulting total number of corrected convictions was then subtracted from the known total non-SL conviction count and the difference added pro-rata over conviction counts for all ages above 16. The corrected profile was then age-weighted to reflect a constant male birth rate of 330,000 over the entire age range.

The result of this procedure is shown in Figure 4.10. On the graph the lower plot is the raw non-SL data, with the outlier (missing age data) at age 25. The upper plot is the corrected age–conviction profile and the straight line is an exponential fit to the corrected profile between ages 20 and 50. The slope of the corrected profile, over the 20 to 50 age range is very similar to the slope derived from the standard list subset (Figure 4.9), suggesting that after age 18 similar processes are at work for both standard list and non-standard list convictions.

Prior to age 18, the profiles are very different. As outlined above many offences are not available to juveniles. However, those that are might be expected to give a similar age profile to the standard list offences already discussed, especially if repeated frequently. What we actually see is very few, non-SL convictions, less than 3 per cent of the peak rate (convictions per one year age band) at and before age 16, jumping to 60 per cent at age 17. For standard list convictions, at age 16 the rate is 45 per cent of the peak and numerically an order of magnitude greater than the non-SL rate.

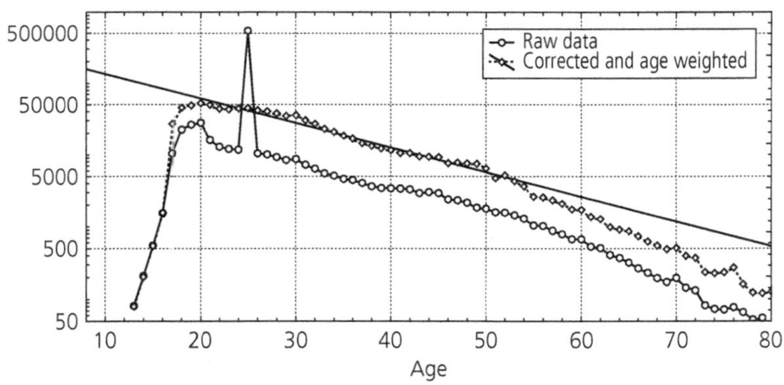

Figure 4.10 Male non standard list age–conviction curve

Note: The graph shows raw data and raw data corrected for missing age data and normalised to a 330,000 annual birth rate. The outlier at age 25 in the raw data has been redistribute as described in the text to produce the corrected curve.

In the main the non-SL offenders would seem to have a different age–conviction curve from their standard list offender counterparts. This is not to say that there is no overlap between the two; several of the non-SL offences are just less serious versions of indictable offences and, as we have seen, offenders are versatile both in offence type and seriousness. Having said that, the non-SL convictions are far more numerous, for adults, than the standard list convictions and it is unlikely that the same people are wholly responsible for both.

We therefore suggest that there is a group of trivial offenders, living on the margins of legality, who commit the bulk of regulatory offences, unconcerned by the requirements for licences, hygiene, or health and safety regulations, or parking and speeding restrictions, and they may also be involved in minor acts of public disorder and antisocial behaviour. Some of these offences in the extreme could well be included in the standard list. These trivial offenders may also be inclined to evade taxation or defraud the benefit system which again would bring them into the realm of standard list offences and hence contribute significantly to our group of high-risk/low-rate offenders of Chapters 2 and 3 or more generally to the *less serious offenders* analysed above. Trivial offenders could therefore be characterized as antisocial individuals with a general disregard for others and the law, but who usually stop short of more serious offending.

Grove (2003, pp 95–102), in fitting the simplified model to the male non-SL conviction data, suggested that some 10 per cent of the male population were involved in petty crime with very high recidivism probabilities and conviction frequency ($p = 0.955$ and $\lambda = 0.85$). Approximately one in six of these convictions would be for a less serious standard list offence creating a (trivial) sub-category of the high category offenders in the simplified model of Offenders Index data. Although this simplified high, low, and trivial, model improved the SL fit and was successful in predicting the impact of changes in the re-classification of some summary offences as standard list, the model did not take account of many non-SL convictions with missing age information. In effect Grove did not redistribute all of the 'missing age' motoring convictions as was done above; in addition he assumed that the majority of non-SL/non-motoring offences were committed by offenders who occasionally committed SL offences.

The lack of detailed information on the criminal careers of non-SL offenders makes the allocation of these convictions to specific offender categories difficult. Below, we take an alternative approach and consider a range of assumptions about the composition of a trivial offender category. The shape of the age–crime curve for non-SL convictions (Figure 4.10) suggests that the behaviour of juveniles in this group is largely overlooked or dealt with in other ways. We therefore assume that non-SL criminal careers start at 17, coinciding with leaving full time education and legally driving motor vehicles. There is also no justification for assuming different capture/conviction probabilities for first and subsequent convictions.

Solving Equation 3.7, without the separate first conviction component, for a single trivial category and differentiating the result gives the following expression for the age profile for age ≥ 17:

$$y(t-17) = A*(1-p)*\lambda*e^{-(1-p)*\lambda*(t-17)} \qquad (4.4)$$

Where:

$y(t-17)$ is the total convictions per year at age t,
A is the total number of convictions, over all ages,
p is the recidivism probability,
λ is the conviction rate parameter (convictions per year).

If p is zero then $y(t)$ represents first offences and A is the trivial offender category size. Thus for non-zero p the ratio of total convictions to trivial offender category size is $1/(1-p)$.

We have normalized the non-SL conviction profile to a total male cohort of 330,000 and the normalized total number of convictions is 907,000. It is very unlikely that all males in the population are eventually convicted, so, as a reasonable assumption and even allowing for motoring offences, we have assumed that some 40 per cent of males remain conviction-free throughout their lifetime. This implies that some 60 per cent males in a population cohort will have at least one non-SL conviction giving us an estimate for p of 0.78 for petty offences. This figure provides us with a lower bound for the trivial offender recidivism probability.

We also have an estimate for $(1-p)*\lambda = 0.097$, from the exponential fit in Figure 4.10. The lower bound for λ is thus 0.44 convictions per year. If we exclude all standard list offenders, and assume they are not separately convicted of non-SL offences, we are left with about 20 per cent of males in the trivial offender category. This gives us upper bound estimates, for the trivial offender category, of 0.93 for recidivism probability and 1.4 convictions per year for λ. Including the high-risk/low-rate offender category, identified in Chapter 2, in the trivial category reduces the recidivism estimate p to 0.92 and the λ estimate to 1.15 convictions per year. These last estimates for p and λ are probably our best guess but clearly changing the assumptions about the composition of the trivial category changes the estimates.

Conclusion

In this chapter we have examined in some detail the aggregate characteristics of offenders committing the most serious offences, those leading to custody, and compared them with *other offenders*, who have no custodial sentences up to age 35. Offenders with *custody at their first appearance* appear to be a small but random sample of offenders as a whole. A large proportion of these offenders are at low-risk of recidivism but will have committed very serious offences. Offenders receiving custodial sentences later in their careers are predominantly drawn from the high-risk of recidivism category, are the most persistent, and are disproportionately convicted of the most serious offences.

We have seen that, by considering only custodial convictions, the high-risk/low-rate category of offenders identified in Chapter 2 did not appear to be represented in the serious offender subset. This observation led to a simplification of the mathematical representation of our theory. An approximate two-group gamma distribution-based model was found to fit the age–custody curve for each custody number. Extending this model to the age–conviction curves of all offenders it was found to approximately fit the data at each conviction count.

Various aspects of specialization versus versatility have also been explored. Offenders in general were found to be neither wholly specialized nor completely versatile. For the *serious offenders'* custodial transitions, only burglary to burglary exceeded 50 per cent, and all other custodial sentences were more likely to be preceded by some other custodial offence. Similarly for all convictions the most likely transition from any offence type is to a different type. Using Farrington's (1986) Forward Specialization Coefficient, we found that there were only small differences in the degree of specialization between *serious* and *other offenders*. The highest degree of specialization was in drugs offences followed by sex offences and burglary, ranked in that order. The FSCs were marginally higher for custodial transitions but that possibly reflects the fact that those offences were the more serious in the offender's repertoire.

We explored versatility more directly by counting the number of different offence types in offenders' careers. We found that on average the variety of offending was proportional to the logarithm of the career conviction count. On average offenders with 12 or more convictions will have been convicted for half of the available types of offences. The tendency for all offenders is towards versatility; over 80 per cent of offenders with more than one conviction have been convicted of more than one offence type. At the other extreme no offenders in the 1958 cohort have been convicted of every offence type and only seven offenders have convictions for seven of the nine offence types. *Serious offenders* appear more versatile but that is mainly because they have higher career conviction counts.

Turning our attention to the other extreme of seriousness, we examined convictions for non-standard list summary offences. These offences include various forms of antisocial behaviour, drunkenness, disturbing the peace, minor assaults, motoring offences, breach of regulations governing trade and other activities, etc. We discovered that, after correcting for large amounts of missing age data and weighting for age, the age–conviction curve for adults showed similar characteristics to the standard list offenders analysed in previous chapters. Juveniles, however, were significantly under-represented in the non-SL convictions. This under-representation was accounted for in part by many non-SL offences not being available to juveniles and those that are being dealt with informally. We made the assumption that non-SL criminal careers started at age 17 and by applying our theory we were able to estimate upper and lower bounds on the recidivism probability p and conviction rate λ for a proposed category of trivial offenders. Although we believe that there is good evidence for the existence of the trivial offender category, its precise composition is uncertain. This uncertainty can only be resolved by collecting better data on trivial offenders, including better recording of age and criminal history.

5

Is Age the Primary Influence on Offending?

Orientation

In Chapter 2, we proposed a theory based on the idea that convictions occurred at random (according to a Poisson process). We proposed that there were three categories of offenders: high-risk/high-rate, high-risk/low-rate, and low-risk/low-rate. Both the risk of reconviction and the rate of offending are assumed to be constant over age. In Chapter 4 we investigated serious, less serious, and trivial offenders. We showed how our simplified two category model adequately deals with particularly serious offences and approximately fits all serious offences. We also investigated the specialization and versatility of offenders and showed that the tendency is towards versatility rather than specialisation. We then extended our theory by the introduction of a category of offenders who commit mostly trivial offences and showed how a one category model could be used to explain the age profile of non-standard list convictions and make estimates of the recidivism probability p and conviction-rate parameter λ for trivial offences. These parameter values depended on the assumed size of the trivial offender category which may or may not include the high-risk/low-rate category of standard list offenders.

Introduction

The principal evidence in favour of our theory, and the models derived from it, is that we can reproduce the age–crime curve (the graph of the number of offenders convicted at any given age), both overall and for each conviction number first, second, third, and so on. This is despite the fact that our theory and models assume no causal relationship between the age of offenders and their criminal behaviour. The fall in the number of convictions at older ages is explained, at least until offenders become too infirm to offend, by older offenders, on average, having been convicted more often, being more likely to have 'retired' from offending, with probability $(1 - p^n)$. The rise in the number of convictions during the early teenage years is explained by the progressive change from informal sanctions for antisocial/criminal behaviour, through police warnings and cautions to the 'last resort' use of formal prosecution and conviction in the magistrates' or Crown courts.

More conventional theories (discussed in Chapter 1) either assume that individual age–crime curves are similar to the aggregate age–crime curve or that both onset and desistance are age-dependent. Certainly the former types of theory and many of the latter types also assume that the rate of offending λ varies both between individuals and over time, λ increasing to a peak in the teenage years and then decreasing as offenders get older. Our theory is inconsistent with these assumptions and in this chapter we set out to test whether the cohort data can be explained by these types of variable-λ and/or age-dependent theories.

Generally, in our models, we have considered that the antisocial behaviour of young active offenders, over the period when convictions are increasing with age, has stayed constant. It is however possible that some offenders may desist from crime as a result of informal sanctions, reprimands, formal warnings, or cautions. As ever we must be careful to say that our statements refer to offending which could lead to conviction. There may well be age-dependent effects in the nature and rate of offending which do not show up in convictions. For example the nature of the crimes committed by

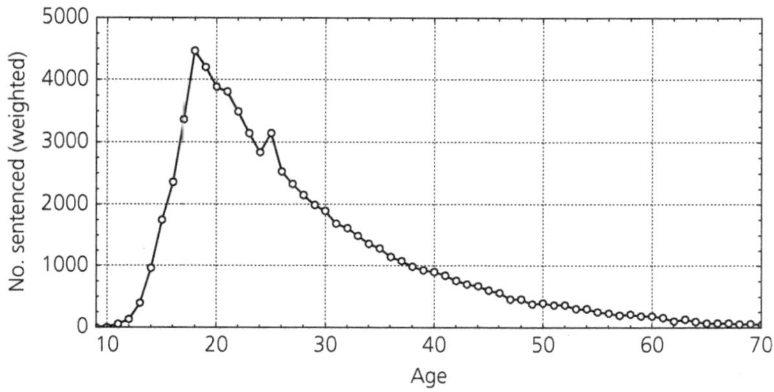

Figure 5.1a Age–crime curve 1997 sentencing sample

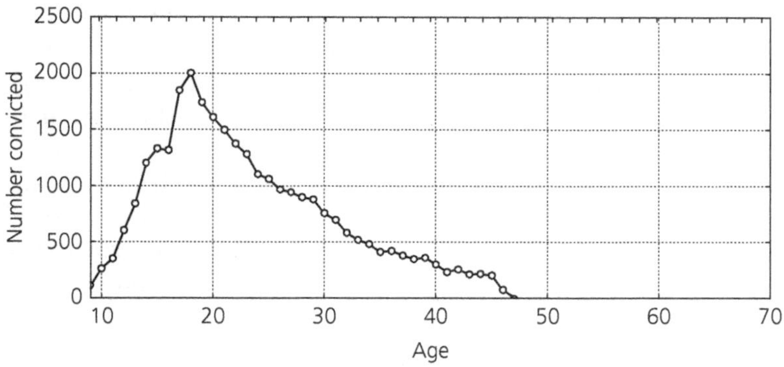

Figure 5.1b Age–crime curve 1953 cohort

offenders may well change as they get older or progress further into a criminal career (LeBlanc and Frechette 1989; Piquero et al 2003; Tarling 1993). Despite what we believe to be compelling evidence for our theory, a critic might wonder if it is possible to fit the Offenders Index data with a more intuitive theory suggesting that offending behaviour, as measured by convictions, is causally dependent on age. We will now consider this possibility.

Possible Types of Age Dependence

A typical age–crime curve[1] is shown in Figure 5.1a, in this instance for the sample of offenders convicted in 1997. The sample was drawn from the Offenders Index of all those convicted and sentenced during the first week of alternate months from February through to December 1997. The data plotted in Figure 5.1a has also been standardized (age-weighted) to a fixed number of individuals of each age in the community. This is very similar to the age–crime curve for the 1953 cohort shown in Figure 5.1b.

[1] There are some features of the age–crime curves in Figure 5.1 which need further explanation. In Figure 5.1a there is a small secondary peak which is caused by the recording of unknown age as 25. In Figure 5.1b there is a step rise in crime during the teenage years at age 16 caused by the introduction of formal cautioning by the Metropolitan Police in 1968. Many offences at age 16 in 1969 led to unrecorded cautions rather than convictions, whereas offences at age 17 in 1970 (17 was the minimum age for the adult court) led to conviction. There is also an apparent earlier onset age in the 1953 cohort than in the 1997 sentencing sample, a point that we shall return to later.

One possible explanation for this similarity is that offenders are homogeneous in nature and that the aggregate curve directly indicates the probability of offending of each individual at each age (Gottfredson and Hirschi 1990). We will call this, and similar theories, 'variable λ' theories, since they imply that the individual frequency of offending varies with age. In this kind of theory it is age itself, acting as an average measure of psychological and social development (eg self-control) which determines the probability and rate of offending. The age–crime curve for an individual is assumed to be similar to the aggregate curve.

A second kind of explanation suggests that the rate of offending λ over a given period is in fact constant from the 'age of onset', when offending starts, to the 'age of desistance' when offending ceases (Blumstein et al 1986). Each individual has a fixed career duration. By choosing suitable probability distributions of the ages of onset and desistance, when averaged over all offenders each with their individual onset and desistance ages, it should be possible to reproduce the aggregate age–crime curve. For example, Shinnar and Shinnar (1975), in their calculations of the incapacitative effects of custody, explicitly assumed that λ was constant over age and that career length was exponentially distributed. Figure 5.2 shows a hypothesized criminal career for one individual. Each individual in the population of offenders would have their own similar career pattern but with a different λ, onset age and desistance age. Thus, the aggregate age–crime curve is very different from each individual age–crime curve. We will call these 'fixed career length' theories.

Obviously variable λ and fixed career length theories fall at extreme ends of a whole range of theories, with varying probabilities of offending for a given individual at a particular age on the one

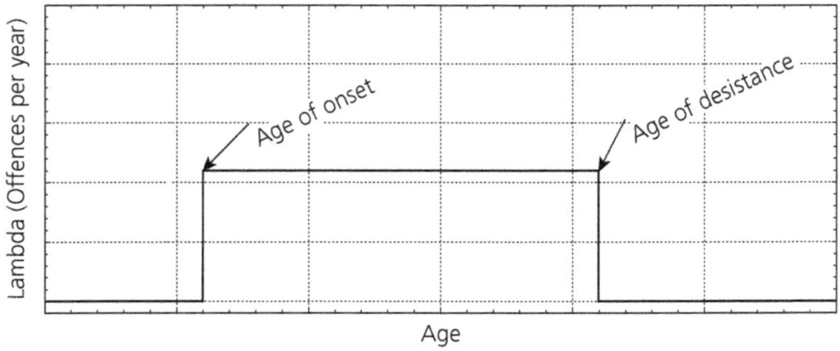

Figure 5.2 A hypothesized individual criminal career

hand and varying onset and desistance distributions for the beginning and end of offending on the other. This may be further complicated by the existence of hybrid theories consisting of multiple developmental trajectories with differing parameters (Sampson and Laub 2005). However, if we can show that no theory or model with the features of either a variable λ theory or fixed career length theory can fit the Offenders Index data, then we have ruled out all but the most contrived theories in which age is the main determinant of offending behaviour.

Testing the Theories

We begin by considering variable λ theories. Here there exist one or more categories with varying rates of conviction at different ages. Each category in this sense has a particular relationship between age and the probability of conviction. To study this we can look at offenders who in their lifetime gather a large number of convictions, say more than five. Looking at the inter-offence times between successive convictions will show how their offending rate (measured in convictions) changes with age. In our models we have explained the behaviour of these prolific offenders by suggesting that they tend to be dominated by two high-risk categories, one with a fixed recidivism probability and a high offending rate and a second group with the same recidivism probability (for standard list offences) and a considerably lower rate of offending.

A pure 'variable λ' theory explains this as a group of crime-prone individuals each with their own propensity to offend which varies with age according to the age–crime curve. Gottfredson and Hirschi (1990) maintain the invariance of the age–crime curve and attribute the decline in adult crime with age to maturation processes and increasing self control slowing down the offending rate. The main point is that, if variable λ theories are true, we should have a group of offenders over the age of 18 who, as they are getting older, would have a reducing rate of offending and, as a consequence, increasing inter-conviction times.

The conviction rate λ (which we have defined as the conviction rate between onset and desistance) is usually measured in quantitative research as the number of convictions or arrests in some time period divided by the number of offenders. This measure is problematic in a number of ways: firstly, if the time period is short, say one year, then what is the correct divisor? Is it the total number of offenders in the group, or the number who are actually arrested or convicted in the time period? In the first case, desisters would be included in the denominator while in the second case, active offenders who happened not to be arrested or convicted in the time period would be excluded. It is also generally assumed that, for individuals, crime counts follow a Poisson distribution with mean λ, which implies that inter-conviction times are exponentially distributed with mean $1/\lambda$.

In Chapter 2 we saw that there is a graphical way of displaying the rate of conviction which overcomes the above measurement problems. We plot (with a logarithmic scale on the *y* axis) the numbers surviving a specified time between consecutive convictions. If this plot is a straight line, the slope of the line gives a measure of the rate of offending. Indeed, it is the mean offending rate of the associated exponential distribution. As an example, a group of offenders about to be convicted for the seventh time will, on average, be at least a year older than those being convicted for the sixth time. If we therefore plot the inter-conviction survival time distribution for different offence serial numbers (for offenders aged over 18 on conviction) the change in the slope of the distributions will indicate any changes in the rate of offending with age.

What would we expect to see given a variable λ theory? As offenders with higher conviction numbers are on average older, they should have progressively lower rates of offending. The slopes should therefore decrease as we go to higher conviction numbers. This is indicated in Figure 5.3. The graph shows the postulated survival time distributions of inter-offence times from the fifth to sixth, sixth to seventh conviction (etc), assuming a variable λ theory. The graph is as usual on a logarithmic *y* axis scale. The graph is based on a cohort size of 2,000 with a mean inter-conviction time of 1.1 years between the fifth and sixth convictions, increasing by 15 per cent for each subsequent conviction number.

What actually happens, in the Offenders Index 1953 cohort, for offenders over the age of 18 at increasing stages of the criminal career, is shown in Figure 5.4. The lines plotted in Figure 5.4 are not 'best fit' curves but are the actual survival time data from one conviction to the next for the specified conviction serial numbers. The uppermost curve is the combined inter-conviction survival times from first to second, second to third, third to fourth, fourth to fifth, and fifth to sixth appearances. The lower curves are for the inter-conviction survival times for the pairs of conviction serial numbers

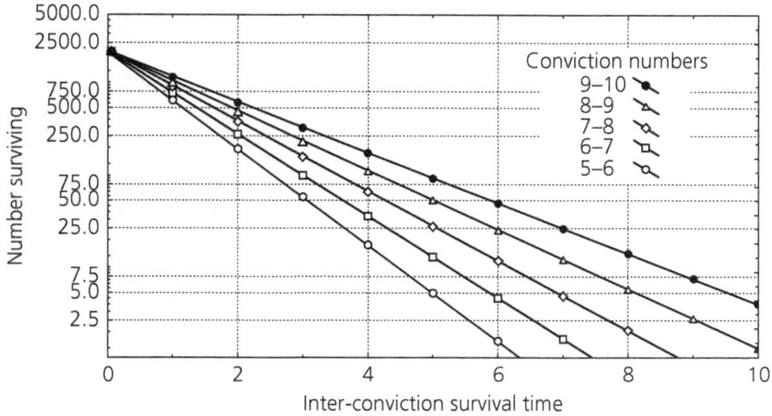

Figure 5.3 Hypothetical survival time plots for increasing conviction number

(AppNo) specified in the legend, with the steeper curve combining all inter-conviction survival times to conviction serial numbers greater than the twelfth.

For conviction numbers (AppNo) between the sixth and the twelfth the survival time curves are essentially parallel, indicating constant survival time distributions differing only in the size of the subsets. The survival curve for convictions up to and including the sixth again appears to be parallel. For convictions over the twelfth

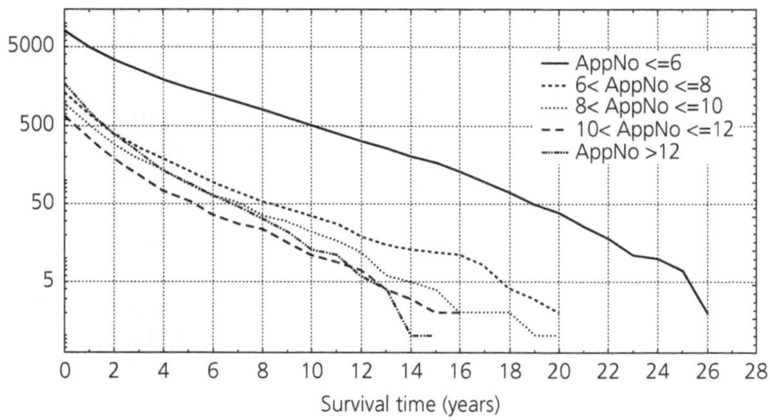

Figure 5.4 Survival time curves for the 1953 cohort (Age at conviction >18)

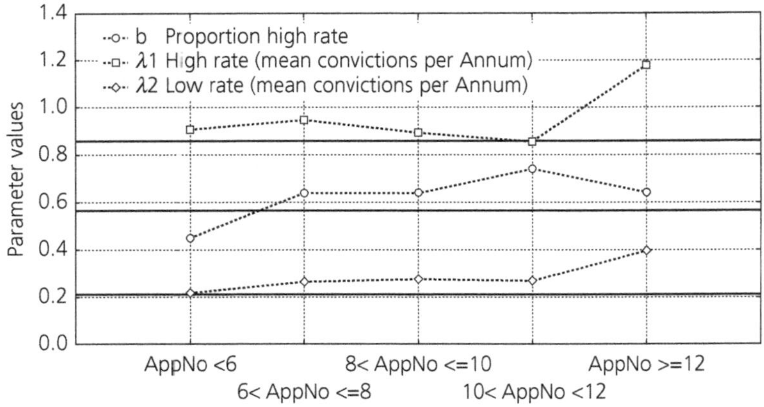

Figure 5.5 Best fit parameter values for the data in Figure 5.4

the curve is steeper than the other curves. This suggests that for higher conviction numbers, and therefore older offenders, the inter-offence times apparently get shorter and offending speeds up. However, under our theory we would expect this apparent speeding up because of the cut-off point of the cohort data at age 46. Fitting the double exponential survival functions derived in Chapter 2 confirms that the parameters are essentially constant as the conviction serial numbers increase.

Figure 5.5 plots the parameter values for the 'best fit' double exponential survival functions to the curves in Figure 5.4. As our theory predicts, the mean number of convictions per year for the high and low-rate parts of the curves, parameters ***λ1*** and ***λ2*** respectively,[2] remain essentially constant as the conviction serial numbers increase. The anticipated increase in the rate for serial numbers above 12, due to censoring, is also evident. There is no evidence that the slopes get shallower, ie that offending is slowing down.

For a variable ***λ*** theory to adequately explain the age–crime curves the rate parameters would need to be reduced by about 15–20 per cent between each offence. The solid horizontal lines in Figure 5.5 are the parameter values for the complete 1953 cohort.

[2] The parameters λ_1 and λ_2 are equivalent to the **λ**s used in other quantitative studies but are estimated directly from the slopes of the inter-conviction survival time curves and not by counting convictions in given time periods.

The proportion (high-rate) parameter '*b*' for conviction serial numbers under seven is significantly less than the complete cohort value, indicating the preponderance of low-risk/low-rate offenders in this group. For conviction serial numbers over six, *b* is higher than the complete cohort value.

The above analysis demonstrates that at any stage in the criminal career the distribution of time to next conviction is invariant and not dependent on prior criminal history. As a further illustration, if we look at individuals who in their lifetime accrue eight or more convictions, our theory would predict that early convictions, those with serial numbers less than eight, would have rate parameters consistent with both those for serial numbers greater than eight and those of the cohort as a whole.

Table 5.1 compares the 'best fit' parameter values for inter-conviction survival times for offenders with at least eight convictions in their criminal career, separately for later convictions, with serial numbers greater than seven and for earlier convictions with serial numbers less than eight. From Table 5.1 we can see that the proportion of high-rate offenders is higher for later convictions, in line with our theory's prediction that low-rate offenders will be less likely to reach the higher conviction numbers. Although both rate parameters are lower for the later convictions, suggesting a slight slowing down in offending, the difference is very small and cannot account for the observed age–crime curve. We can thus rule out variable λ theories for all those offenders who commit standard list offences.

This leaves us with fixed career duration theories, in which the offenders offend at a constant rate but their onset and desistance ages are given by some distributions. Shinnar and Shinnar (1975) used a negative exponential distribution for residual career length in their incapacitation calculations. We observe in the Appendix

Table 5.1 Comparison of survival time distribution parameters for early and late convictions for offenders with 8 or more court appearances

Conviction number	Proportion high-rates: b	High-rate parameters: λh	Low-rate parameters: λl
(Late) >7	0.70	0.95	0.30
(Early) <8	0.63	0.98	0.38

that the average residual career length of both the high and low categories, who commit offences serious enough to be sent to prison, is around 5.3 years (the high category being a little shorter, the low category a little longer). The Offenders Index data that we have considered so far could therefore be approximately modelled by a fixed career length theory with two categories of offenders with constant (but different) rates of conviction and a (negative exponential) distribution of career length with a mean of 5.3 years.

This model could theoretically be tested in an experiment in which we have two groups of serious offenders convicted over the same period. We take one group out of circulation for a period of say about seven months; the other group is immediately put back into society so that they can offend again. The recidivism of the two groups is then compared over a fixed period at liberty (say two years) having corrected for the seriousness of offences originally committed by the two groups. Because the group who could not offend for seven months will be on average seven months older, a proportion $(1 - e^{-7/(5.3*12)}) = 10.4$ per cent would have reached the end of their offending careers and we should therefore see a reduction in the proportion reconvicted of 10.4 per cent. But we would only expect about half of the reconvictions to occur in the two year follow-up period, resulting in a 5 per cent reduction in the two-year reconviction rate for custody compared with non-custodial disposals. This experiment is similar to experiments comparing the effects of custodial and non-custodial sentences (see eg Killias et al 2010).

We now look at one such study based on the Offenders Index. This is described by Kershaw (1999). The two-year reconviction rates of offenders discharged from prison over the period 1987 until 1996 were compared with those receiving community penalties. After correcting for seriousness of offence and so called 'pseudo-reconvictions',[3] no discernable difference (–0.7 per cent, 1995, and –1.3 per cent, first quarter of 1996) can be seen in the reconviction rates; certainly less than the –5 per cent predicted for the average of seven months spent in prison by those receiving custodial sentences. The correction for pseudo-reconvictions has raised issues about the validity of drawing conclusions from Kershaw's study about the additional individual deterrent effect of a prison sentence. However, with no correction, the two year

[3] A 'pseudo-reconviction' is where an offender is subsequently (re-)convicted for an offence committed prior to the date of the current sentence.

reconviction rate for community penalties is the same as that for imprisonment, which provides no support at all for a fixed career duration theory.

Ideally we would like to look at total career recidivism following custodial and non-custodial sentences, but recidivism rates following specific disposals may not be reliably calculable from a cohort sample. This is because the nature of disposals may change over the time span of the cohort, particularly for non-custodial sentences. It could also be argued that, as the same offenders reappear many times in the sample of conviction occasions, the results are in some way biased. However, despite these reservations we now assume that the effectiveness of custody and community penalties did not change over the observation period. We can also control for seriousness and type of offender by looking at the subset of offenders who have at least one custodial sentence and more than four convictions.

In the 1953 cohort, 1,141 offenders fall into this subset, accruing a total of 7,016 convictions; 2,561 of these resulted in custody and 2,172 of these were followed by a further conviction. The overall reconviction rate for custodial sentences was therefore 84.8 per cent. In the same subset of offenders, of the 4,455 convictions not resulting in custody 3,703 were followed by further convictions and the overall reconviction rate for non-custodial sentences was 83.1 per cent. Both of these reconviction rates are consistent with the high-risk reconviction probability of 0.84 estimated for the whole 1953+ cohort (see Table 2.1). Again we see no evidence of the reduced recidivism following custody that is predicted by a fixed career length theory.

It could be argued that both cohort analysis (see above) and short follow-up times are unreliable in detecting the expected reduction in recidivism due to career termination whilst in custody. We therefore need to use a longer follow-up time cross-sectional analysis to directly estimate recidivism for different disposals on a more consistent basis. The follow-up period usually used in reconviction studies is two years; this period is long enough to allow a substantial proportion to be reconvicted but short enough not to appear to be out-of-date in policy terms. However, we have shown from our earlier analysis that reconviction times, for a significant proportion of cohort members, are very much greater than two years.

We can replicate Kershaw's (1999) analysis using the 1997 sentencing sample, drawn from the Offenders Index, with a much

Table 5.2 Proportion of offenders reconvicted during a 4 year 3 week follow-up period for the 1997 sentencing sample

	Not reconvicted		Reconvicted		Total
Fine	13143	56.6%	10077	43.4%	23220
Supervision	5534	37.5%	9224	62.5%	14758
Custody	3629	35.6%	6559	64.4%	10188
Other	4882	48.5%	5189	51.5%	10071
Total	27188	46.7%	31049	53.3%	58237

longer follow-up period. Table 5.2 shows the numbers and proportions reconvicted during a follow-up period (to 31 December 2001) of those convicted of standard list offences during the first week of alternate months from February through to December 1997 (six weeks in all). Where individuals were convicted in more than one of the sample weeks the earliest conviction has been taken as the target conviction for the analysis. No corrections have been made for pseudo-reconvictions or time served in custody, either on remand before conviction or under sentence during the follow-up period. The follow-up period varies between four years 11 months for the earliest convictions to four years and three weeks for the latest convictions, but for the purpose of the analysis only, reconviction times less than four years three weeks have been counted as reconvictions.

It can be seen from Table 5.2 that those with custodial sentences had the highest reconviction rate at 64.4 per cent. Sentences involving supervision in the community had a similar rate at 62.5 per cent but fines and other disposals had significantly lower rates at 43.4 per cent and 51.5 per cent respectively. However, it seems likely that different disposals are given to different kinds of offender, and it is important to control for these differences. As a first step we can assume that the magistrates and judges take account of at least some of the characteristics of the offenders and aspects of their criminal careers in making their sentencing decisions. Supervision and custody are often regarded as alternatives for the lower end of more serious offending and should therefore be directly comparable. However, the difference in recidivism probabilities between them (which is significant at $p = 0.01$; $Chi^2 = 9.15$ on $1df$) is in the wrong direction to support a fixed career length theory.

If we exclude first convictions from the comparison the difference in recidivism probabilities between custody and supervision diminishes to less than 1.2 per cent (which is not significant at $p = 0.05$, $Chi^2 = 2.94$ on1*df*). Excluding more of the early convictions further diminishes the difference in reconviction rates between supervision and custody, but the rates themselves increase with each successive conviction omitted from the comparison. With conviction numbers greater than six the proportions reconvicted after supervision or custody are 82.3 per cent and 82.9 per cent respectively ($Chi^2 = 0.51$ on 1*df*, not significant). If adjustments were to be made for pseudo-reconvictions and/or time spent in custody during the follow-up period, these would have the effect of widening the gap by reducing recidivism for supervision and increasing it for custody. As with Kershaw's analysis, this later sample with a longer follow-up period provides no evidence of age related desistance or lower reconviction rates following custody and no support for fixed career duration theories.

As a by-product of his calculation of the incapacitative effect of a prison sentence, Tarling (1993, p 145) showed that the assumption that recidivism probabilities of offenders in the Offenders Index are generated by a fixed career length theory, implies that the average residual career length would be about two to three years. We have seen that a direct analysis of the Offenders Index shows that the average is nearer five years for high-risk/high-rate offenders and 10 to 15 years for high-risk/low-rate offenders. Again there is no support for fixed career length theories in the Offenders Index data. The lack of any unequivocal evidence for such a reduction in recidivism (McGuire 1995) suggests that we can rule out fixed career length theories.

In general, then, we can rule out any theory (variable λ, fixed career length or any mixture) in which offending behaviour is dominated by the effects of age, at least for those offenders who commit standard list offences, the high and the low-offending rate categories. This is not to say that offending does not depend on age at all, only that: offenders in these categories do not desist from crime only or mainly because they are getting older.

Conclusion

It is clear from the many studies of age and crime that there is an aggregate relationship between age and criminal offending.

Our theory, derived in Chapters 2 and 3, explains this relationship as the result of a process of capture, conviction, and sentencing of individuals. Homogeneous categories of individuals have constant probabilities of offending in given time periods and have constant probabilities of recidivism after each conviction. The only part of our theory which is age-dependent is the apparent initial rise in crime during the early teenage years, when society's response to criminal behaviour changes with age. The largely informal response at the age of 10 becomes progressively more severe with an increasing proportion of offenders subjected to full criminal proceedings as they approach and enter adulthood.

Our criminal career theory fits the Offenders Index data without assuming that adult offending (convictions) depends on age. The decline in crime with age in the adult population is entirely explainable by the constant (within each group) proportion of offenders desisting after each conviction. The apparent reduction in the frequency of offending of older offenders is due to the increasing proportion of low-rate offenders in the active population as age increases. There is no support in the Offenders Index data for any change in the (within Category) rate of offending with age.

In testing the fixed career duration type of theory, in which each individual has his or her own fixed career length which when aggregated over all individuals produces the age–crime curve, no reduction in recidivism was observed after custodial sentences. This result is consistent with our proposition that desistance occurs at the time of conviction and that on release prisoners, who have not desisted, simply rejoin the active offender population. This also implies that there is no major reduction in crime caused by keeping people in prison, given the current average time served. The only way to create a reduction in crime by incapacitation is to constantly increase the prison population and/or keep offenders in prison for much longer periods. We will return to this topic in our discussion of the significance of our theory for criminal justice policy in Chapter 8 and in the Appendix.

One important point should be made here. Age-based theories tend to assume, like Shinnar and Shinnar (1975) and Gottfredson and Hirschi (1990), that offenders grow out of crime and that the effects of the criminal justice system on offending are minimal, except through incapacitation. In our theory custody in itself 'does not work' (either by individual deterrence or incapacitation, except for those who are removed for very long periods from society).

There is no support for age-based desistance in our analysis as we have shown that the expected residual career length for a recidivist is exactly the same when released from prison as it is when leaving court with a non-custodial sentence.

This chapter has explored alternative age-based theories and has shown that theories that assume explicit age dependence cannot fit the data. However, our theory does suggest that the operation of the Criminal Justice System, in repeatedly convicting offenders, is the most important factor in reducing the number of active offenders and is essential in the control of crime.

6

Characteristics of Individuals

Orientation

Our theory, proposed to explain aggregate age–crime curves, assumes that there are three categories of offenders: high-risk/high-rate, high-risk/low-rate, and low-risk/low-rate. Each category has a constant rate of offending and a constant probability of reoffending. In Chapter 5 we showed that a theory assuming that offending was strongly determined by age, and that individual rates of offending increased to a peak in the teenage years and then decreased, could be ruled out. In this chapter, we investigate the psychological characteristics of offenders and whether these characteristics can be used to allocate individuals to the risk/rate categories.

Introduction

We have constructed very successful predictive models on the basis of our theory. However, the evidence for the underlying theory, the existence of a small number of categories with simple offending behaviours, is circumstantial. The theory is the simplest possible that explains the main features of the aggregate statistical data. Even making successful predictions of the number of convictions at any given age (the age–crime curve) for *each* offence number (first, second, third, etc) does not necessarily confirm the existence of distinct categories. As we have seen it is difficult to find more intuitive theories that can fit the known criminal career information. But, until we can demonstrate that the categories really do differ in their psychology, due to genetic, social, or other environmental factors, the suspicion might remain that all we are seeing is some statistical coincidence or artefact of the data.

Unfortunately, neither of the databases that we have relied upon so far, the Offenders Index (OI) and the Court Appearances database contain psychological information. The direct analysis of such factors is thus impossible. On the other hand large databases of psychological information seldom contain criminal career information of sufficient detail to enable comparisons with the offender categorization we propose. We were therefore very grateful that the Home Office Offender Assessment System (OASys) database was made available to us for analysis. Initially approximately 2000 offender records collected in the pilot phase of OASys were provided for analysis. Since then the use of OASys has become routine for the probation and prison services and a second sample of linked OASys and PNC records were made available to us for further analysis. The two analyses used different methodologies and are reported on separately below.

In Chapter 2 we identified our high- and low-risk categories, not from the characteristics of individuals, but from the statistical properties of the offender population with respect to the distribution of conviction numbers. In this chapter we show that OASys assessments of individuals can be used to dichotomize the offender population into two groups one of which displays the recidivism characteristics of the high-risk category and the other, dual-risk characteristics in the proportions predicted by the OASys score distributions. This result suggests that psychological assessments can be used to allocate individual offenders to the risk categories more effectively than criminal history information on its own.

The Rationale and Development of OASys

In common with most jurisdictions the Home Office has a statistically based tool for estimating the aggregate probability of reconviction for a group of offenders with a particular set of characteristics (eg previous convictions, gender, and age). The Home Office tool is called OGRS (Offender Group Reconviction Score). The first version of the system is described by its developers in Copas et al (1998), and since then it has been further refined and developed by the Home Office. It was found that the best predictors of future offending were based purely on criminal history information. This is of course entirely consistent with expectations based on our theory where the categories have a very regular offending behaviour as seen in official statistics. However it is a rather static predictor.

One might ask, however, what about the underlying psychological factors which are believed to cause offending? These have been extensively reviewed (see eg Farrington 2007, 2010; Jolliffe and Farrington 2010). However, although offending behaviour is driven by psychological characteristics, it is much easier to measure past offending than to directly measure the underlying offender characteristics. Previous offending may be the best surrogate measure of the psychological characteristics which influence future offending.

Since the mid-1990s, large-scale programmes seeking to reduce the criminality of offenders have been introduced, both within prisons and in the community. These programmes have led to the development of a tool to predict future offending on the basis of so-called 'dynamic' factors. The difference between a 'dynamic' factor, such as taking drugs, unemployment, peer group influences, etc, compared with the 'static' factors of age, gender, and previous conviction history, is that the 'dynamic' factors might be changed by offender programmes and other social policy. In addition, by measuring the change in the 'dynamic' factors it should be possible to measure the effectiveness of a programme while an offender is being treated, rather than having to wait to see if they are reconvicted. (For reviews of risk assessment, see eg Andrade, 2009; Otto and Douglas, 2010.)

The National Probation Service and the Prison Service of England and Wales (now the National Offender Management Service) have co-operatively developed the Offender Assessment System (OASys), to use as their tool to calculate a 'dynamic' factor reconviction score. OASys is actually rather more than this, being a system for risk assessment and management as well as a way of producing and reviewing a sentence/supervision plan. The OASys pilot study was a first step towards a national computerized database of ongoing assessments for most offenders entrusted to the care of the probation and prison services. Following the successful pilot, phased implementation of the system was set in train. This should be a very useful resource for future criminal career research.

OASys consists of an extensive questionnaire to be completed by prison/probation staff, in the course of offender interviews and from the offender's documented criminal record. The questions which are of particular interest to our research are contained in sections 7, 11, and 12 of the questionnaire (see Table 6.1). Like most of the questions throughout the questionnaire the answers are scored 0, 1, or 2, where 0 is benign or positive, and 2 is problematic. Section 7, entitled Lifestyle and Associates, consists of

Table 6.1 OASys Questionnaire sections 7, 11, and 12

7. Lifestyle and Associates	
7.1	Community integration (Attachments to individual(s) or community groups. Participation in organized activities not linked to offending, including in prison, eg sports clubs, faith communities, etc) (Absence of any links = 2) Score 0, 1, 2
7.2	Regular activities encourage offending (Do the leisure activities most commonly engaged in create opportunities to offend, or contribute to the need to offend eg gambling in prison?) Score 0, 1, 2
7.3	Easily influenced by criminal associates (Are most offences committed with others? When in the community does s/he spend a large amount of their time with other offenders?) Score 0, 1, 2
7.4	Manipulative / predatory lifestyle (Does s/he exploit others or abuse friendships, relationships, positions of trust? Does s/he use others, live off others without reciprocation, bully others?) Score 0, 1, 2
7.5	Recklessness and risk-taking behaviour (Lifestyle includes excessive thrill-seeking and risk taking activities. Demonstrates intolerance for boring, unchallenging or unchanging situations: Needs excessive excitement or stimulation) Score 0, 1, 2
11. Thinking and behaviour	
11.1	Level of interpersonal skills (Are the offender's social/interpersonal skills adequate ie to their background and normal circumstances?) Score 0, 1, 2
11.2	Impulsivity (Does offender prefer to act rather than plan, take decisions which are later regretted, become bored easily, require stimulation?) Score 0, 1, 2
11.3	Aggressive/controlling behaviour (Does offender show aggression to others, or use violence or threats in order to resolve conflicts with others, eg domestic violence?) 0 = no aggressive behaviour. Score 0, 1, 2
11.4	Temper control (Does offender lose his/her temper easily and often. Does s/he have a low tolerance, is s/he poor at conflict resolution, unable to control emotions) 0 = no problems controlling their temper. Score 0, 1, 2

11.5	Ability to recognize problems (Does the offender have insight into areas of their life which are problematic?) Score 0, 1, 2
11.6	Problem solving skills (Is the offender's approach to solving problems illogical? Does s/he employ inappropriate strategies? Does s/he recognize contribution of others? Is s/he unable to think flexibly?) Score 0, 1, 2
11.7	Awareness of consequences (Does the offender recognize that most courses of action have a mixture of positive and negative outcomes: Is s/he able to balance these?) 0 = is aware of consequences. Score 0, 1, 2
11.8	Achieves goals (Does the offender fail to set goals in all areas of their life? Are they unrealistic and unsupported by planning? Does s/he lack motivation to achieve goals? No examples of reaching goals) 0 = Achieves goals. Score 0, 1, 2
11.9	Understands other people's views (Is the offender unable to interpret social situations correctly or form acceptable relationships with peers and those in authority? Does s/he fail to demonstrate feelings for others or remorse for victims?) 0 = is able to understand others. Score 0, 1, 2
11.10	Concrete/ abstract thinking (Does offender hold rigid dogmatic views or have difficulty in thinking in general terms rather than about specific incidents. Is s/he unable to consider problems in the abstract, infer general principles and adapt to circumstances) Score 0, 1, 2
12. Attitudes	
12.1	Pro-criminal attitudes (Does s/he express attitudes supportive of criminal behaviour in general? Does s/he believe everyone offends given the opportunity?) Score 0, 1, 2
12.2	Discriminatory attitudes/ behaviour (Evidence from offending or lifestyle of attitudes or behaviour which may be considered as racist/sexist or degrading to any group in society.) 0 = no discriminatory attitudes or behaviours: Score 0, 1, 2
12.3	Attitude towards staff (Has s/he accepted and co-operated with authority?) Score 0, 1, 2
12.4	Attitude towards supervision/licence (Past experience of supervision if applicable. Does s/he view supervision favourably or unfavourably? Is s/he likely to co-operate with supervision?) 0 = no problems with being supervised. Score 0, 1, 2

(cont.)

Table 6.1 *(cont.)*

12.5	Attitude to community / society (Does the offender acknowledge the rights of others, accept the necessary limits on personal freedom. Does s/he express a wish / willingness to be part of the community) 0 = acknowledges the rights of others. Score 0, 1, 2
12.6	Does the offender understand their motivation for offending (How well does the offender recognize which of their own attitudes, beliefs, emotions and needs are linked to their offending? How much insight do they have into their own behaviour?) Score 0, 1, 2

five questions which address issues of interaction with others. Section 11, entitled Thinking and Behaviour, consists of ten questions covering self-control, empathy and awareness. Section 12, entitled Attitudes, covers just that. In offender assessments the total scores from each of these sections are combined with the scores of the other sections (technically, by using a non-linear transformation followed by a linear weighting) to arrive at a summary measure related to the overall probability of reconviction.

Analysis of the Pilot OASys Data

To test the Offender Assessment System 'in action', a pilot study was undertaken of around 2,000 offenders convicted in late 1999 and early 2000 who were either placed in the care of the probation service or received a custodial sentence. The OASys assessments were carried out by carefully trained assessors, assuring a relatively high quality of assessment. Limited criminal career information was obtained for each of the 2,000 offenders from the Police National Computer.

The OASys pilot database contained paper records for around 1,600 male offenders. These records provided limited psychological information. Data from section 11 of the assessment questionnaire was made available to us together with basic information, from the Police National Computer (PNC), on the offender's criminal careers. The section 11 questions loosely fall into two categories. Questions 11.1 to 11.4 address factors such as impulsivity, which might, if unchecked, lead to offending behaviour, while 11.5 to 11.10 look at factors influencing offenders' ability to control their behaviour, such as their 'awareness of consequences'. Improving offenders' ability to control their behaviour by the use of so called 'cognitive behavioural' programmes is the approach that has the greatest backing, from empirical evidence, for reducing recidivism (see eg Bernfeld, Farrington and Leschied 2001; Lipsey and Landenberger, 2006; McGuire 1995). Initially, however, we will consider only the total section 11 score.

In this analysis we confined ourselves to male offenders, as there are too few females for meaningful analysis. The offenders assessed in the pilot study had received relatively severe sentences, prison, or probation, presumably for relatively serious offences. We therefore expect them to be members of the offender categories identified in Chapters 2 and 3.

The fact that criminal career information in the database comes from the PNC, rather than the Offenders Index, raises three issues. The first is simply that the PNC records offences to a lower level of seriousness than the Offenders Index. We therefore expect the recidivism of the high- and low-risk categories to be higher in the PNC data compared to recidivism calculated from the OI. The second issue is that the PNC is an operational rather than statistical database. The focus of users of the PNC will be such as to minimize operational rather than statistical problems. Comparisons that have been carried out between the OI and the PNC (Francis and Crosland 2002) suggest that they both have missing data but with rather different patterns. Finally, we must remember that the PNC data is not complete before 1995 (see Chapter 2).

The first step in this analysis was to establish that the criminal career data for the male offenders included in the OASys pilot sample conforms to the recidivism patterns identified in Chapter 2. The small sample size and cross-sectional nature of the pilot data did not permit the joint estimation of the parameters (a, p_h, and p_l) as was done with the much larger cohort samples. However, following the procedures outlined in Chapter 2 and illustrated in Figure 2.3, we can estimate the high- and low-risk parameter values. We first estimated the high-risk probability, from the slope of the logarithmic plot of the conviction number frequency data for conviction numbers from 6 to 23. The parameter value obtained was then substituted in Equation 2.2 (see the inset graph of Figure 6.1). The residuals from the high-risk recidivism line were then calculated for the counts of conviction numbers one to eight, enabling the estimation of the

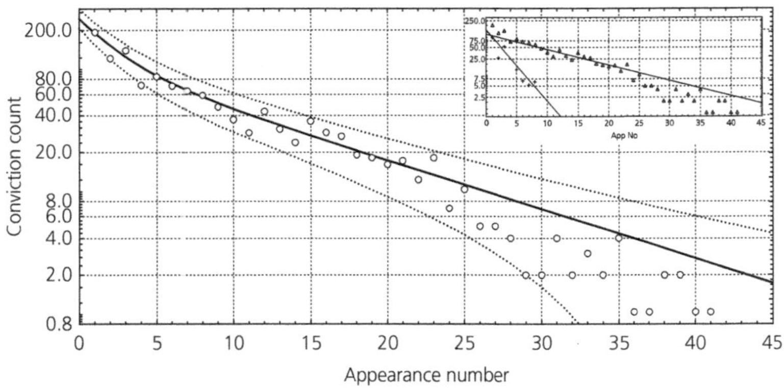

Figure 6.1 The dual risk recidivism model fitted to the conviction count data from the OASys pilot, male offenders

low-risk probability. The high- and low-risk parameters were then substituted into the dual-risk recidivism model (Equation 2.4).

The main graph in Figure 6.1 shows the OASys pilot data (points on the graph), the dual-risk recidivism model (central solid line), and the $\pm 2\sigma$ bounds (95 per cent confidence interval, dotted lines on the graph) assuming a Poisson distribution of counts at each conviction number. It must be pointed out at this stage that we could not have reliably identified the dual risk recidivism model directly from the OASys/PNC data had we not known what to look for. But, despite that, the model does adequately describe the data as virtually all the data points fall within the expected bounds.

The recidivism parameters calculated for the dual risk recidivism model from the OASys/PNC pilot data are: $a = 0.52, p_h = 0.91, p_l = 0.65$. The probabilities are higher than the cohort and sentencing sample values of Chapter 2, derived from the Offenders Index, but closer to the values derived in Chapter 4 when considering *serious offenders*. The proportion of offenders in the high-risk category is also very much higher than in the 1953 and 1958 cohorts. As explained previously the parameters are characteristics of the sample of offenders rather than of the individuals within the sample and are therefore conditioned by the selection criteria for the sample. In this instance all the offenders in the sample will have been convicted for relatively serious offences and few if any of the low-seriousness offenders (who make up the majority of the low-recidivism risk category of the cohorts) are likely to be included.

Also we expect PNC data to produce higher recidivism probabilities for all categories and as we shall see later in this chapter the estimates are broadly consistent with those from a much larger sample of OASys/PNC data.

The Distribution of Section 11 Scores

As mentioned above, each of the questions in section 11 is coded 0, 1 or 2, where 0 represents 'normal' for the general population and 2 indicates serious problems. The expectation is that high scores are indicative of high criminal propensity and should be correlated with other measures of criminality. Table 6.2 shows the frequency distribution of total section 11 scores. The total score with the highest frequency occurs at zero with 124 offenders assessed as having no problems with any of the constructs covered in section 11 of the questionnaire. The next most frequent score occurs at a total score of 7, with 114 offenders. Only nine offenders are assessed as having serious problems with all of the constructs.

The distribution of scores can be described as bimodal, ie with two humps, with a general trend of reducing numbers of offenders as the scores increase. Criminality, as measured by number of previous convictions, on the other hand shows a reducing trend with only one maximum at zero (one conviction) (see Figure 6.1). The relationship between the two measures is clearly more complicated than a simple correlation.

The bimodal nature of the section 11 score is suggestive of a mixture of two separate homogeneous distributions which hopefully would be correlated with the risk categories identified above

Table 6.2 Frequency distribution of total section 11 scores

Total section 11 score	0	1	2	3	4	5	6
Count of offenders	124	79	92	95	85	100	100
Total section 11 score	7	8	9	10	11	12	13
Count of offenders	114	96	108	94	95	76	63
Total section 11 score	14	15	16	17	18	19	20
Count of offenders	51	38	39	19	23	13	9

Note: Based on 1,513 male offenders from the OASys pilot data.

(see Figure 6.1). If this is the case what would we expect to see? Offenders in the low- (recidivism) risk category should have lower scores on all constructs with few of these offenders having total scores above say 5. We must also bear in mind that the measuring system for each construct is very coarse. A borderline, 0 or 1, score on all 10 constructs could result in a total score of anything between 0 and 10. However, even with such coding uncertainties, we would expect the frequency of higher scores to diminish very rapidly perhaps distributed as a negative exponential with a mean around 2 or 3.

The high-recidivism risk category, on the other hand, should dominate the higher section 11 scores. We would not expect many, if any, of the high-risk category to have section 11 total scores of 0 and, if the constructs are not too highly correlated, neither would we expect many to have the maximum score. If our high-risk offenders are indeed a homogeneous group with respect to the section 11 total score, we might expect the scores to be distributed normally with the mean at some central value between say 7 and 11. It could of course be the case that our high-risk category is not homogeneous with respect to the section 11 total score and that the score is strongly correlated with the number of previous convictions. In this latter case we would expect the mean score to increase as the number of previous convictions increased. We will test these propositions against the section 11 data from the OASys pilot.

Because we cannot unequivocally allocate offenders to the high- or low-risk categories simply on the basis of their criminal history we need to use the implications of our theory to try and identify the categories. By looking at the distribution of scores for various subsets of offenders we can confirm or refute the expectations outlined above. The first step is to systematically examine subsets of offenders selected on the basis of conviction number ranges. Figure 6.2 shows the frequency distribution of the section 11 total score for offenders with only one conviction.

The fitted curve is a negative exponential with a mean of 5.7, which is higher than we anticipated for our low-risk category. But, from our dual risk model fit of Figure 6.1, we know that over 50 per cent of offenders with just one conviction are in fact in the high-risk category, perhaps accounting for the small secondary peak at 11. Our dual risk model, for the pilot sample males, also suggests that there are unlikely to be any low-risk offenders with seven or more convictions. Figure 6.3 shows the frequency distribution of

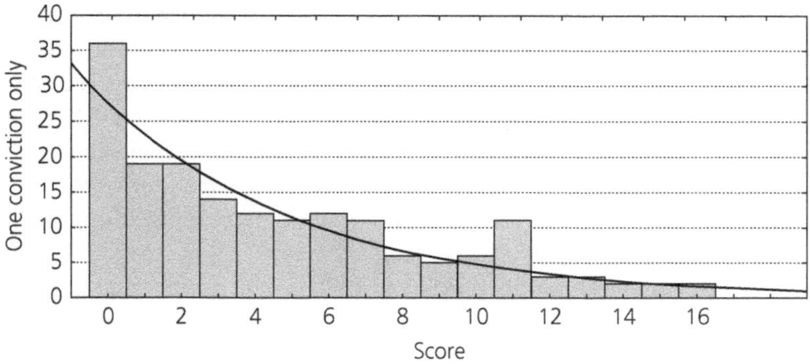

Figure 6.2 Histogram of section 11 total score for offenders with only one conviction, overlaid with an exponential distribution curve

section 11 scores for the subset of offenders with more than ten convictions.

The data in Figure 6.3 has a mean score of 9.9 and a standard deviation 4.6. The data is not significantly different from a normal distribution with the same mean and standard deviation, in line with our expectation. Repeating this analysis for offenders with 15 or more convictions gave a mean of 10.1 and the same standard deviation. Again the data was normally distributed. The distribution of total score for the subset of offenders with more than 14

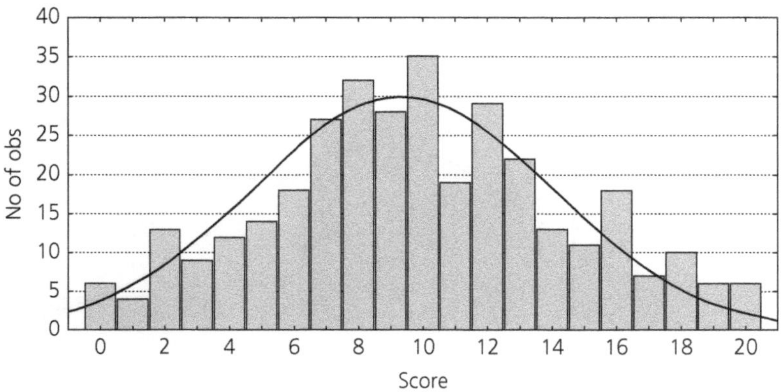

Figure 6.3 Histogram of section 11 total score for offenders with eleven or more convictions, overlaid with the expected normal distribution curve

convictions is clearly not different from the total score distribution for offenders with more than ten convictions. Increasing the subset to include all offenders with more than seven convictions reduces the mean to 9.2 and increases the standard deviation to 4.8. The means of the three nested distributions are consistent with a single normal distribution for high recidivism risk offenders, but the increasing trend, in mean total score with increasing conviction count, is of concern.

A subset consisting of offenders with between seven and ten convictions, inclusive, gave a normal distribution of the total score with a standard deviation of 4.8 but with a mean of only 8.0. This lower mean score for the '7 to 10' subset is significantly different (at $p = 0.01$, two-tailed) from the '7 plus' mean score. However, by overlaying the '7 to 10' histogram, of total score data, with the appropriately scaled normal distribution derived from the '11 plus' data (Figure 6.4), we see that the majority of data points lie within the $\pm 2\sigma$ expected variation (assuming a Poisson distribution about the expected counts). The subsets in this comparison have no data in common.

The difference in means could be interpreted as evidence of heterogeneity amongst the high-recidivism risk offenders, revealing perhaps an additional category: the high-risk/low-rate offenders of Chapter 2 or the *less serious offenders* of Chapter 4. The reduced mean total score could be an artefact of the coarseness of the OASys scoring system. Also, although the constructs measured

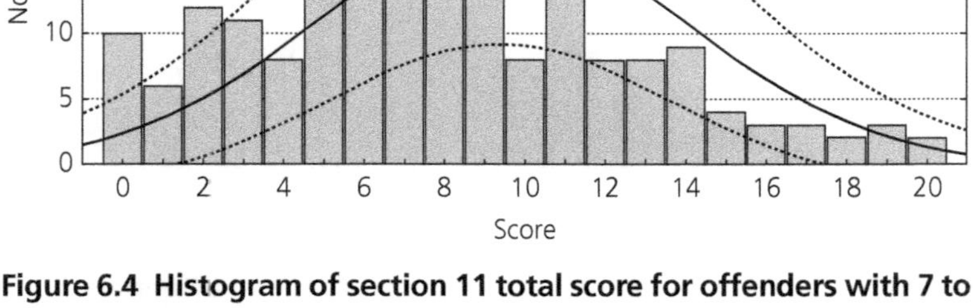

Figure 6.4 Histogram of section 11 total score for offenders with 7 to 10 convictions

Note: The overlaid curve is the scaled normal distribution from Figure 6.3 with $\pm 2\sigma$ bounds.

in section 11 are independent of criminal history, the assessments may not be. For example it could be that, where there is uncertainty, assessors tend to give lower scores for offenders with fewer convictions, and higher scores for those with more convictions.

From the above it is apparent that the total score is not directly correlated with criminal history, certainly for offenders with more than 10 convictions, but we may have evidence supporting a different psychological profile for a third group of offenders. The evidence is not definitive as there is considerable overlap in the distributions and it is not clear how much of the variance in the scores is due to assessment errors caused by the coarse measurement scales and how much is due to real differences between categories of offenders.

The subset of offenders with fewer than seven convictions will contain individuals from both high- and low-reconviction risk categories. From the dual risk model parameter estimates (Figure 6.1) we expect that 484, of the 1161 offenders in the '0 to 6' subset, would be high-risk. We would also expect that the total section 11 scores for these 484 high-risk offenders would be distributed normally with the mean and standard deviation as estimated from the '7 plus' subset. By subtracting the expected (normally distributed) 'high-risk' section 11 score distribution from the distribution of total section 11 scores in this '0 to 6' subset we can get an estimate of the distribution of scores for low-reconviction risk offenders (the low-risk residuals). Figure 6.5 shows a histogram of these

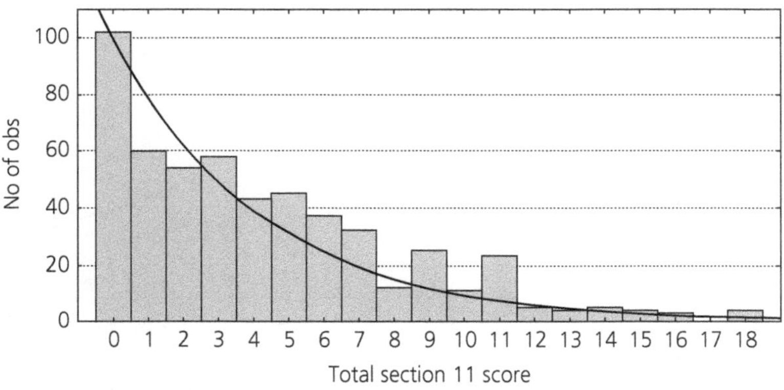

Figure 6.5 Histogram of low-risk residuals of section 11 total score for offenders with fewer than 7 convictions

Note: The overlaid curve is the fitted negative exponential distribution with mean 4.23.

residuals with a fitted exponential distribution overlaid on the graph. The mean of the exponential is 4.23 which is lower than the estimate of the mean of 5.7 derived from offenders with only one conviction (see Figure 6.2 above), but consistent with our expectation that low-risk offenders should have lower scores.

In the above analysis we have explored the relationship between the OASys section 11 total score and criminal history as manifested by the number of convictions sustained by the offenders in the OASys pilot study. It has been shown that the distribution of total section 11 scores is consistent with the expectations from our theory and in particular with the dual risk recidivism model derived in Chapter 2. With the aid of the model we have been able to partition section 11 total score frequency data into two subsets corresponding to our high- and low-recidivism risk categories. For the high-risk category total scores were normally distributed with a mean around 10 and for the low-risk category scores were distributed as a negative exponential with a mode of 0 and a mean of around 4.

At this point critics might argue that all we have done is to manipulate the section 11 total score data to fit our theory. If that were the case we would not necessarily expect to be able to identify our recidivism categories simply from the section 11 total scores. Figure 6.6 shows the distribution of numbers of convictions for offenders with a section 11 total score of six or more. The overlaid curve is the high-risk element of the dual risk recidivism model

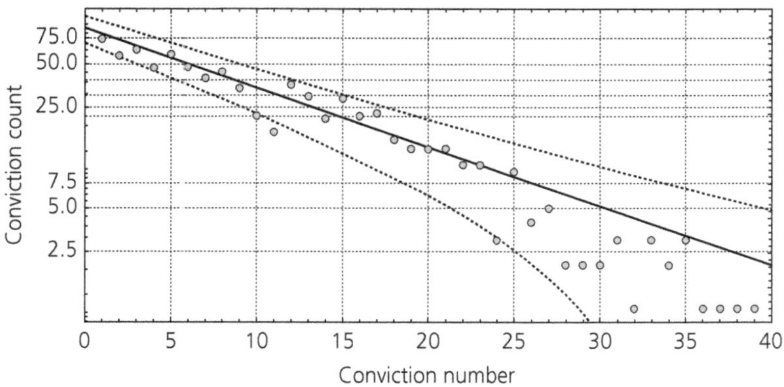

Figure 6.6 Recidivism plot for offenders with section 11 total scores of 6 or more

Note: The solid line is the theoretical recidivism plot with $p = 0.91$, the dotted lines are the $\pm 2\sigma$ bounds.

(Figure 6.2), scaled to 80 per cent, with the ±2σ bounds (95 per cent confidence interval), and the high-risk recidivism probability p_h = 0.91. The scaling down is necessary because we expect some 20 per cent of high-risk offenders to have total scores of less than six (left hand tail of the normal distribution; see Figure 6.3). The overlaid curve is a very good fit to the data, although not quite the best fit which would lie just below and parallel to the central line.

Figure 6.7 shows the distribution of numbers of convictions for offenders with a section 11 total score of less than six. The overlaid curve in Figure 6.7 is the best fit dual risk recidivism model with the high-risk parameter set to 0.91. The low-risk parameter estimated in this fitting process was 0.654, almost identical to the 0.65 calculated above and the estimated proportion of high-risk offenders is tolerably close to the 20 per cent not included in Figure 6.6.

The above analysis of the section 11 total score has demonstrated that the theory developed in Chapters 2 and 3 has some basis in a relatively independent measure of individual psychological characteristics. (This finding is similar to that of Blumstein et al (1985) which was discussed more fully in Chapter 1 pp 9–11.) In particular the offender categorization suggested by the dual risk recidivism model can in large measure be identified from the OASys section 11 total score. There is inevitably some overlap between the high and low section 11 total score groups but some 80 per cent of our theoretical high-risk category are identified simply from the

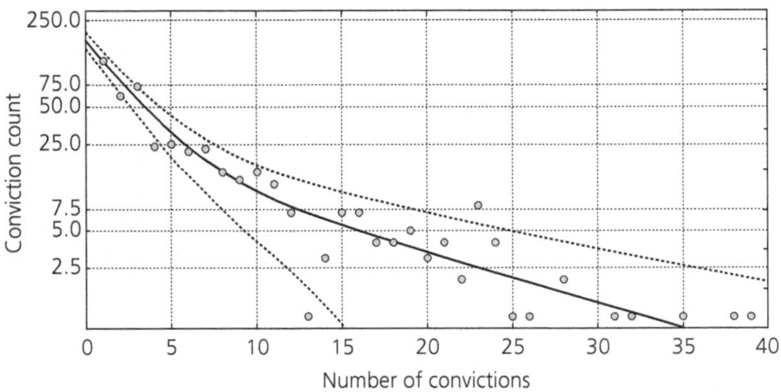

Figure 6.7 Recidivism plot for offenders with section 11 total scores less than 6

Note: The solid line is the theoretical dual risk recidivism plot with ***a*** = 0.29, p_h = 0.91 and p_l = 0.65; the dotted lines are the ±2σ bounds.

section 11 score. Low conviction count offenders with higher scores appear in precisely the numbers predicted by our model. Offenders with low scores account for all of the low-risk offenders predicted by our model and also the correct number of offenders with higher conviction counts predicted by the score distribution for high-risk offenders.

Is there Structure in the Section 11 Information in OASys?

So far we have looked only at the total of the section 11 scores for each offender. We noted earlier that the questions naively fall into two distinct categories. Questions 1 to 4 (see Table 6.1) measure characteristics which might lead to criminal behaviour and questions 5 to 10 measure the lack of ability to check this behaviour. This classification can be investigated using a technique called non-metric multi-dimensional scaling (NMDS) (Davies and Coxon 1982). Here we will briefly review the technique and what it tells us.

Non-metric multi-dimensional scaling takes pair-wise information about the dissimilarities of a collection of objects and creates a picture in a multi-dimensional (most usefully, two- or three-dimensional) space which in some sense 'best' represents the dissimilarities between the objects. Thus ideally, if the point representing object A is further away in the picture from the point representing object C than it is from the point representing object B, then A is more dissimilar to C than B. That is, the closer the points representing the objects in the picture are, the more similar they are. NMDS makes the fewest possible number of assumptions about the data, and does as little as possible to make its pictures more than a very intuitive representation of the dissimilarities. (A good NMDS package will allow the user to look at the effects of changing even these minimal assumptions.) It can be shown both theoretically and from practical studies that the pair-wise dissimilarity information can recover most of the structure in a dataset, whereas the stronger assumptions of more usual statistical techniques merely force the data into the structure of the technique's assumptions.

We can carry out an NMDS analysis of the OASys data by taking each section 11 question as an NMDS 'object'. The dissimilarities between pairs of questions are defined on the basis of the correlations within the entire OASys pilot dataset (male and female) of the scores on those questions; the lower the correlation, the more dissimilar are the questions. One of the features of NMDS is that it does not matter precisely how the correlations are converted to dissimilarities, as long as this is done in a consistent manner, as this in itself conveys no information about the data. It turns out that two dimensions are adequate to represent the main structure in the OASys section 11 pilot data. Figure 6.8 shows the results. The top plot is for the section 11 question scores only; the central plot includes the section 11 total score as an additional NMDS 'object'; and the bottom plot is for the section 11 scores with the measured, post-assessment, 18-month reconviction results (R18FEB02) as an additional NMDS 'object'.

In interpreting the plots in Figure 6.8, the following features need some explanation. The scales on the plots are unimportant and have been omitted, as it is the relative positions of the plotted points which convey the information. The ellipses on the plots indicate the grouping of the points representing questions 5 to 10

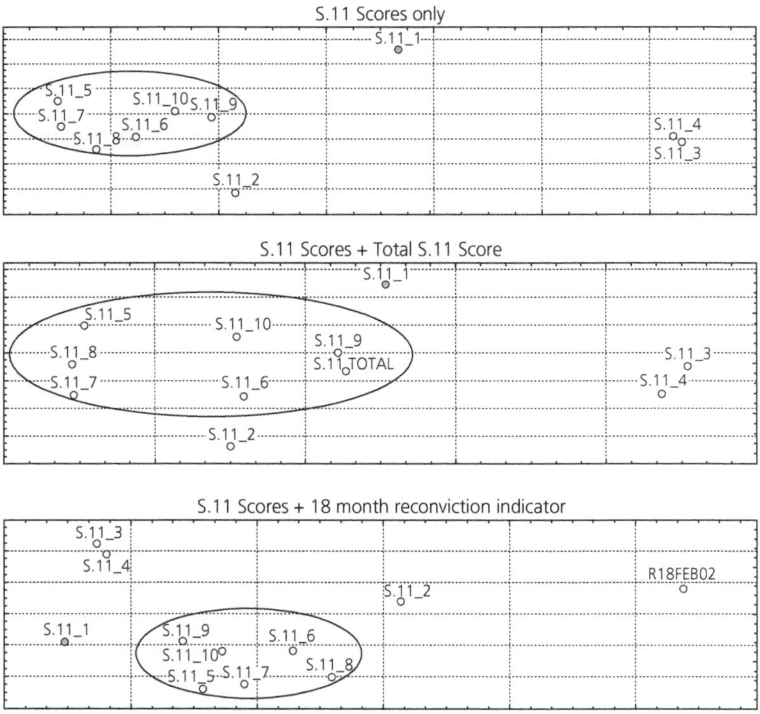

Figure 6.8 Two dimensional non-metric multi-dimensional scaling (NMDS) plot for the questions in section 11 of OASys

of section 11, suggesting that these questions measure related constructs. Similarly questions 3 and 4 seem closely related to each other but separate from the other measures. The addition of extra NMDS objects changes the relative positions of all the objects but, as can be seen from the plots, the grouping of questions 5 to 10 persists and questions 1 to 4 remain separate from the main group. Adding the total score tends to reduce the dissimilarity of the individual scores and the total score is itself positioned within the 5 to 10 grouping. However, perhaps most interestingly, adding the 18 month reconviction indicator seems to emphasize the '5 to 10' grouping but suggests that reconviction, within the 18 months after the OASys assessment, is not strongly related to any of the section 11 scores.

In summary, questions 5–10 do seem to measure essentially the same thing whereas questions 1–4 measure something different from questions 5–10. Also questions 2 and 3 are distinct from questions 1 and 2, which are also distinct from each other. From now on we will describe questions 1–4 as the heterogeneous section 11 questions, and 5–10 as the homogeneous ones.

Homogeneous and Heterogeneous Section 11 Questions

Repeating the above analysis for the total scores of the heterogeneous group of section 11 questions gives the results displayed in

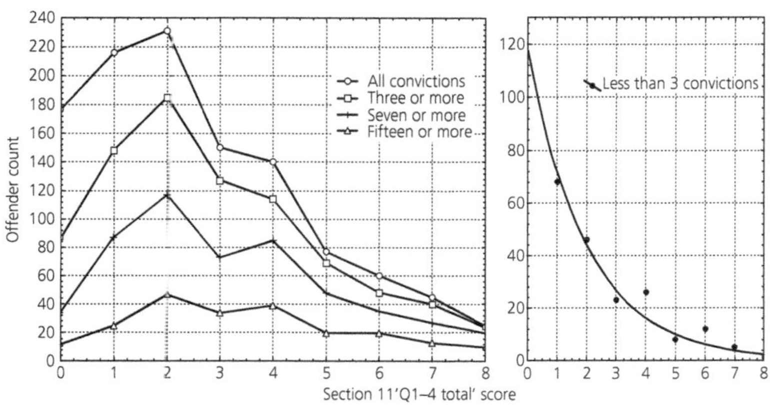

Figure 6.9 Plots of offender count against total section 11 score for questions 1–4 for various subsets of offenders with different conviction counts

Figure 6.9. The left hand graph is made up of subsets of offenders. The bottom most, line, is the 'Q1–4 score' distribution for offenders with more than 14 convictions. The next line is the distribution of scores for offenders with more than 10 convictions and the area between the lines represents the score distribution for offenders with Q1–4 scores from 11 to 14. The third from bottom line is the score distribution for offenders with seven or more convictions and the top most line is the score distribution for all offenders. The right hand graph shows the plot for offenders with less than three convictions; the overlaid line is a negative exponential curve like the one we encountered above in Figures 6.2 and 6.5.

In this analysis of the heterogeneous questions, Q1–4, we see evidence of the low-risk group in the right hand graph, which shows the score distribution for offenders with less than three convictions. In the left hand graph we see a similar distribution shape for all the offender subsets. This is consistent with the view that they measure personality attributes that are less amenable to change (see eg Roberts and DelVecchio 2000). It is also interesting to note that the distribution is skewed towards the lower scores which is consistent with the view that the constructs are relatively independent. The peak frequency at 2 and a mean score of only 2.6 suggest that the majority of offenders in the pilot scored badly on only one or two of the questions, with only 2.25 per cent attaining the maximum score.

In a similar analysis of the homogeneous questions, Q5–10, we see a different picture. The results of that analysis are shown in Figure 6.10. The 'all convictions' score distribution is bimodal

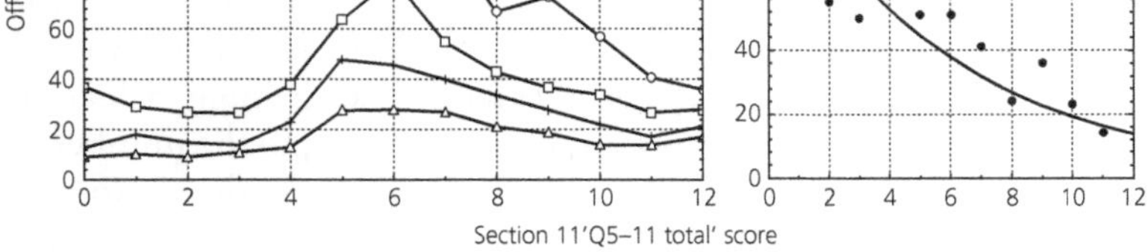

Figure 6.10 Plots of offender count against total section 11 score for questions 5–10 for various subsets of offenders with different conviction counts

suggesting a mixture of two offender types. The right hand graph, showing the distribution of scores for offenders with a Q5–10 score less than 7, again providing evidence of the low-risk category offenders. However, for offenders with higher numbers of convictions (7+), there appears to be a level area in the distribution for scores less than 4, followed by a steep rise to the peak at around 6 and a shallower decline to the maximum score of 12.

Questions 5–10 of section 11 measure cognitive-behavioural skills and it is believed that these can be improved by appropriate programmes, leading in turn to reduced recidivism. The scope for overall crime reduction is however quite small, in part because only the high-risk offenders score highly on these questions and there are relatively few of them, but also because even the most successful of these programmes are unlikely to reduce this element of the score to zero.

Conclusions from the OASys Pilot Data Analysis

Using conviction number information from the Police National Computer, we have shown in Figure 6.1 that the OASys pilot data displays the dual risk category structure that we previously identified in the Offenders Index data in Chapter 2. Our analysis of section 11 of the OASys questionnaire, total score, also indicates that there are two groups of offenders: one group with Normally distributed (mean ≈ 10, $\sigma = 4.8$) total section 11 score and one group with lower scores (exponentially distributed, mean = 4.23). By dichotomizing the data, on the basis of section 11 total score, we have also shown that offenders with high (≥ 6) OASys section 11 total score account for 80 per cent of the high-risk category offenders identified in Figure 6.1. As illustrated in Figure 6.6 these high-scoring offenders also exhibit the same recidivism probability (0.91). The offenders with low-OASys section 11 total scores (< 6) are predominantly (70 per cent) made up of offenders with the recidivism properties (see Figure 6.7) of the low-risk category identified in Figure 6.1. The number of offenders in the high-risk component of Figure 6.7 corresponds, almost exactly, to the number in the left hand tail (total section 11 score < 6) of the fitted Normal distribution of high-risk offender scores (see Figure 6.3). We have also shown that there may be evidence for the existence of a group of moderate scoring offenders not identified by the dichotomy but perhaps accounting for some of the high-risk element in the offender group with score < 6. We thus have strong evidence that our high- and low-risk categories actually exist as distinct sub-populations, with different psychological characteristics. The low-risk category offenders displaying relatively normal psychology and the high-risk category offenders displaying problems in areas of self-control, empathy and awareness.

It is important to stress here that our risk categories are inferences from the statistical structure of the offender population resulting in some difficulty allocating many individual offenders unequivocally to one or other of the risk categories especially for offenders with low conviction counts. The total section 11 score dichotomy on the other hand allocates *individuals* to the high- and low-risk categories on the basis of characteristics independent of criminal history and with much greater certainty if conviction count is used as an additional discriminant.

By means of an NMDS analysis, we split the section 11 questions into two sets, one set measuring underlying predispositions to criminal activity and the other measuring cognitive behavioural skills which might control criminal activity. The two score distribution groups are evident in both sets of questions. The higher scoring (normally distributed) group has a high-recidivism probability and the lower scoring (exponentially distributed) group has a lower recidivism probability. The distribution of scores measuring cognitive behavioural skills suggests a link between the lack of these skills and a high-recidivism probability. There is some evidence that these skills can be improved by treatment programmes leading to small reductions in recidivism.

We can also create a picture of a typical high-recidivism risk offender as someone who has several of the characteristics of being impulsive, aggressive, or having difficulty controlling his or her temper. In general they will also have difficulty in controlling the behaviour generated by these features of their personality because of their poor problem-solving skills and failure to consider the consequences of their actions.

A puzzle remains, however. The low-risk offenders generally score less than 6 and typically 0 to 2 on the OASys section 11 total score, indicating that their underlying impulsivity, aggression, and cognitive behavioural skills differ little from the general population, at least as compared with the high-risk category offenders. In Chapter 4 we saw some suggestion that very serious offences are disproportionately committed by the low-risk category offenders, possibly explaining the lower reconviction probabilities for those serving very long prison sentences. This suggests that, while high-risk offenders are impulsive and have difficulty controlling themselves, low-risk offenders might be more calculating.

Analysis of Operational OASys Data

Following the successful pilot study, OASys was rolled out to the prison and probation services in England and Wales. From March 2000 a computerized database was established and an anonymized copy of the assessments up to March 2005, containing over 400,000 OASys assessments on 154,000 offenders, was made available to the authors. In addition a subset of PNC records for offenders convicted during April 2004 were also made available for analysis. Again the records were anonymized but could be linked to the OASys data.

The data of interest in the OASys dataset were the scores for individual questions in sections 7, 11, and 12 (see Table 6.1), and also the criminal history data in the form of the number of convictions sustained up to the latest assessment. Many of the offenders (53 per cent) in the OASys dataset have multiple assessments, potentially by several different assessors. However, despite the possibility of inconsistency in the scoring, 62 per cent of the multiple assessments were wholly consistent across the 21 questions in sections 7, 11, and 12. Also, for individual questions, from 85 per cent to 96 per cent of the scores did not change between assessments. In view of the coarse nature of the scoring, this level of consistency is reassuring. In cases where the score did change the average was used in the following analysis.

As with the pilot sample above, the first step in the analysis was to establish that the criminal career data, this time for both male and female offenders, included in the operational OASys data conforms to the recidivism patterns identified in Chapter 2. The results of the maximum likelihood fit of the model are given in Table 6.3 and Figure 6.11. The fit accounted for over 99.7 per cent of the variance in the data for both male and female subsets.

As with the pilot data, offenders in the OASys operational data base will in general have either committed more serious offences or simply more offences than offenders in general and the explanation of the higher parameter values for these subsets is the same as outlined above for the pilot. Males and females have similar recidivism

Table 6.3 Dual-risk recidivism model parameter estimates for offenders in the operational OASys database

	a	p_h	p_l	Cohort equivalent number of offenders N
Male	0.65	0.90	0.48	17429
Female	0.33	0.89	0.51	4440
Pilot male	0.52	0.91	0.65	192

Note: a = proportion high-risk, p_h = high reconviction probability, p_l = low reconviction probability. The cohort equivalent number of offenders is the number of first convictions in the data.

probabilities but, like the cohorts and OI sentencing samples, the proportion of high-risk is very much smaller for females than for males. Most importantly however, the structure of the data is consistent with the analysis of Chapter 2.

The next step in the analysis is to explore the sections 7, 11, and 12 data for internal statistical structure. In analysing the pilot data, we saw that section 11 question scores exhibited structures which were related to the recidivism characteristics of the offenders in the pilot. We now extend that analysis by including sections 7 and 12, 'lifestyle and associates' and 'attitudes' respectively. The analysis tool used in what follows is Principal Component Analysis (PCA). We start as before, in the NMDS analysis, with a correlation matrix, this time for the 21 individual questions in the three sections. Principal components are the combinations of questions which best describe a feature of the data (ie an underlying construct) independently of

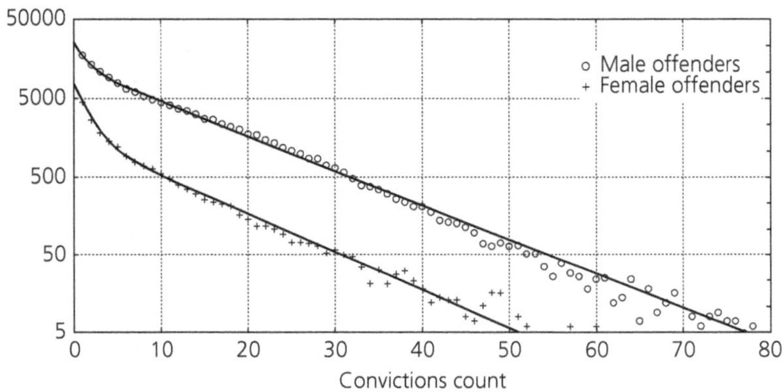

Figure 6.11 Dual risk recidivism model fit to OASys operational data

the other components. By way of simple explanation: If we draw a line on a map we can describe it using a start position on the map grid followed by distances north and east to get to the end point, and moving the line will change all of the coordinates. The map grid initially has the *y* axis north south and the *x* axis east west. However if we rotate the grid so that the *x* axis lies along the line we only need one component (x) to describe the length of the line, and moving the line in the y direction does not change my description of the length. The new x direction is then the principal component of the line. This idea can be applied to the 21 measures contained in sections 7, 11, and 12 of the OASys questionnaire.

To find the principal components of a set of data we first need to compute the eigenvectors and eigenvalues of the correlation matrix of the data. Eigenvectors all have length one and are independent of (orthogonal to) all others. Each eigenvector has an associated eigenvalue which is the relative contribution that the eigenvector makes in the overall description of the data set. Large eigenvalues indicate which eigenvectors are important. These eigenvectors are the principal components of the data set and, if used to create single measures, show the greatest variation between individuals. Conventionally, eigenvalues greater than one are taken to indicate principal components. Figure 6.12 is a scree plot of the eigenvalues which shows that the first four (largest) are all greater than one but that the first factor is significantly larger and its corresponding eigenvector accounts for almost 35 per cent of the variation in the data.

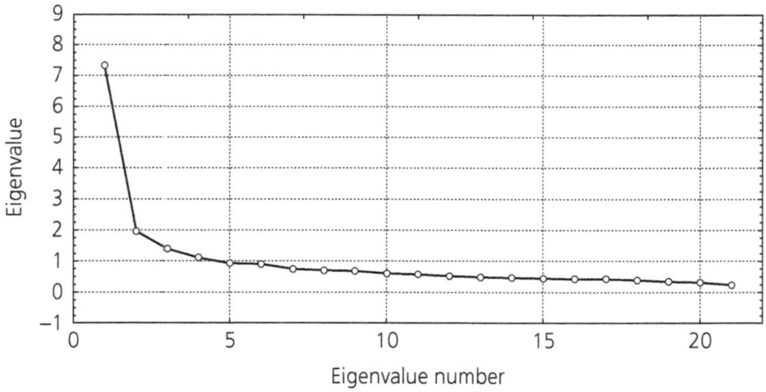

Figure 6.12 Scree plot of eigenvalues of the sections 7, 11, and 12 correlation matrix

Our task now is to explore whether we can identify our criminal categories from the principal components. As we did above, for the total section 11 score in the analysis of the pilot data, we need to choose a dichotomy point for the Factor 1 score. Our aim is to identify two groups of offenders, one with a high Factor 1 score and the other with a low Factor 1 score, and to test whether these groups correspond to our risk categories. Using what is essentially a trial and error procedure a dichotomy point of 0.9 was chosen with the results shown in Figure 6.13. The circles on the graph represent the number of offenders with a Factor 1 score less than 0.9 and conviction counts as indicated on the x axis. The plusses on the graph represent offenders with a Factor 1 score greater than or equal to 0.9. The solid curves are the best fit recidivism models to the two subsets of the dichotomized data. The upper curve (Factor 1 score <0.9) is characteristic of a single group of 108,821 offenders with recidivism probability $p = 0.905$ (high-risk category) and the lower curve is characteristic of two groups, one of 13,675 offenders with $p = 0.870$ (high-risk category) and one of 16,185 offenders with $p = 0.496$ (low-risk category).

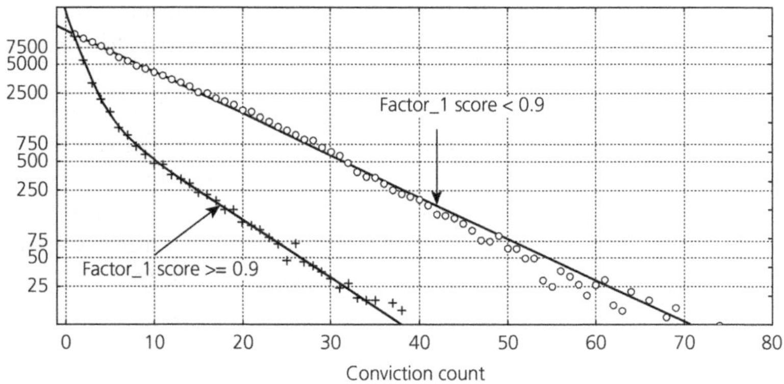

Figure 6.13 Recidivism plot for OASys operational dataset (all offenders) with dichotomy point of Factor 1 score 0.9

The recidivism probability estimates from the operational OASys data and the dichotomized subsets are given in Table 6.4. At this point we must remind the reader that the OASys data is cross-sectional but the model is based on longitudinal cohort data. In the OASys data each offender appears only once whereas in the cohort data an individual may appear several times, once for each

Table 6.4 Dual risk recidivism model parameters for the OASys operational data, all offenders and the dichotomized subsets

OASys subsets	a	p_h	p_l	Cohort equivalent number of offenders	Number of offenders	
					High	Low
All Offenders	0.58	0.902	0.477	20215	119639	16234
section 11 total ≥ 6	1.00	0.910	-	7011	77900	-
section 11 total < 6	0.26	0.89	0.522	13204	31209	20441
Factor 1 < 0.9	1.00	0.905	-	10338	108821	-
Factor 1 ≥ 0.9	0.18	0.870	0.496	9877	13675	16185

Note: a = proportion high-risk, p_h = high reconviction probability, p_l = low reconviction probability.

conviction during the career. The two types of data-set are equivalent if the process is stable over time and both demographics and criminality proportions are relatively constant. In Chapter 2 we showed that these were reasonable assumptions for the Offenders Index data and we now assume that they hold for the current analysis.

For cross-sections the cohort equivalent number of offenders is given by the number of first convictions in the data. In Table 6.4 the first row, 'All offenders', gives the dual risk recidivism model parameters, the actual number of first convictions in the OASys operational data set, and the modelled number of high- and low-risk offenders. The modelled total is 135,873 which is within 2 per cent of the 138,615 offenders in the OASys data set. The rows below repeat these estimates for the subsets created by both the 'Section 11 Total Score' dichotomy and the 'PCA Factor 1' dichotomy.

Including more of the principal component factors in the discriminant function provided no improvement in the separation of offenders into high- and low-risk categories. However, from our theory, we know that the low-risk offenders are very unlikely to have conviction counts greater than six. With this additional criminal history information an extra 5,000 offenders with a Factor 1 score ≥0.9 could be identified as high-risk.

Reducing the number of section 7, 11, and 12 raw scores included in the principal component analysis progressively reduces the discriminating power of the principal component. However, several subsets of raw scores produced similar results: in particular section 11 scores only, section 7 and section 12 scores together, and the combinations of section 11 scores identified in Figure 6.8 all identified the two risk categories in the dual risk recidivism model. It is clear that all of the constructs measured are related to criminality and that they all make an independent contribution. None of the scores was found to be redundant, but at the same time much of the information relating to criminality is contained in most of the scores to the extent that disjoint subsets of scores provided similar discriminating power. The best discrimination was found when all the section 7, 11, and 12 scores were included in the principal component analysis.

Analysis of April 2004 PNC Conviction Data

The operational OASys data analysed above only contained conviction number information and no inter-conviction times. Only the risk element of our theory could be explored in relation to psychological and behavioural constructs. Also no information is available in that dataset on convicted offenders who have not been assessed using OASys. To remedy this deficiency an anonymized extract of PNC records for all offenders convicted of standard list offences during April 2004 was made available to the authors for analysis. The extract was drawn late in 2005 providing reconviction times up to sixteen months and also criminal history information that enabled inter-conviction times to be calculated. Sufficient information was provided to enable linkage with the OASys data analysed above.

In total 16,164 individuals were convicted of at least one offence during April 2004. Of these 14,340 were adult offenders, over 18 years of age at their conviction, who were thus eligible for assessment using OASys. However only 4,833 offenders, those sent to prison or put under the supervision of the probation service, were actually assessed and their records linked to the OASys data. The information available from the PNC extract included the offender's date of birth, gender and the dates of all the individual's convictions. An offender's target conviction (court appearance) was taken as their earliest conviction in April 2004. From this the appearance number, time from the previous conviction and time to the next conviction were calculated. The previous conviction times were used to estimate the distribution of inter-conviction times for the various subsets of the April 2004 data.

Repeating the analysis of Chapter 2 on the various subsets of the April 2004 data produces the risk and rate model parameters given in Table 6.5. The risk parameters derived from the OASys operational data are included in Table 6.5 for comparison. From Table 6.5 we can see that the high-risk probability is very consistent across subsets. Its value at about 0.9 is higher than that estimated from the cohorts but consistent with our expectation from cross-sectional data from the PNC. The 1997 Sentencing sample from the OI gave a value of 0.88, and we also expect PNC data to yield higher estimates.

The low-risk reconviction probability estimate for the whole April 2004 sample is again a little higher than the Chapter 2 estimates but not inconsistent with them given the different data source. The estimates of the λs are broadly consistent between subsets but are generally higher than the cohort estimates from Chapter 2. The difference could either be the result of speeding up the reconviction process in recent years, which has certainly been a policy priority, or simply due to the change in the data source. The increase in proportion of high-risk offenders amongst adults compared with all offenders can be explained by the omission of juveniles which resulted in a significant reduction in the numbers of first and second convictions and smaller reductions in higher conviction counts. The proportion of high-rate adult offenders is consistent with the whole sample value. Our theory suggests that average inter-conviction times, within categories, are consistent throughout the criminal career and not dependent on age.

Assessed adult offenders present quite different characteristics. They all appear to be high-risk, and also appear to reoffend at

Table 6.5 Model parameter estimates from April 2004 PNC extract and OASys data

Subset	a	p_h	p_l	B	λ_h	λ_l	Subset size
2004 all	.40	0.904	0.357	0.65	1.23	0.65	16,164
2004 adults	.49	0.906	0.299	0.63	1.17	0.63	14,340
2004 assessed	1	0.906	-	0.68	1.57	0.24	4,833
OASys	.58	0.902	0.477	-	-	-	141,219

Notes: a = proportion high-risk; p_h = high-risk reconviction probability, p_l = low-risk reconviction probability; b = proportion high-rate, λ_h = high reconviction rate; λ_l = low reconviction rate.

higher rates with an increased proportion in the high-rate group. We suggest that, in large part, these apparent inconsistencies are due to selection effects for the assessed offender subset. All will have been convicted of relatively serious offences resulting in either custodial or supervisory sentences. Many will also be prolific offenders and may have received this particular sentence because their previous convictions were considered as aggravating factors in the sentencing decision. In addition there are no juveniles in the assessed offender subset, with a consequential reduction of early convictions in the data. Figure 6.14 shows the frequency distribution of conviction count (recidivism plot) for assessed offenders from the April 2004 sample, together with the plus and minus two sigma bounds, assuming a Poisson distribution about the expected count at each conviction number. It can be seen that for conviction numbers less than 8 the data falls on or below the lower bound, supporting our contention of selection effects.

Although our analysis of OASys operational data suggests that there should be a significant proportion of low-risk offenders among the April 2004 assessed offenders, there is, apparently, no evidence of them in Figure 6.14. However, by applying the Factor 1 dichotomy to the April 2004 assessed offender subset we obtain a recidivism plot very similar to Figure 6.13. In Table 6.4 we estimated the numbers of offenders in each of the risk categories in the Factor 1 dichotomized OASys data. Repeating those calculations for the assessed offenders in the April 2004 PNC data gives the

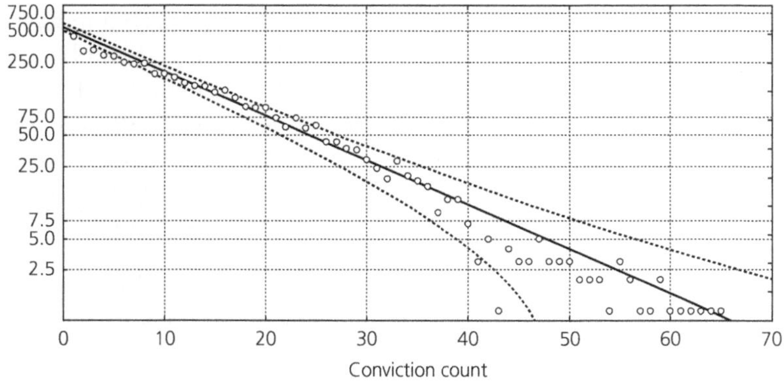

Figure 6.14 Recidivism plot for assessed offenders in the April 2004 PNC data extract

Table 6.6 Estimated numbers of offenders in the risk categories for the Factor 1 dichotomized data for the assessed April 2004 and the OASys datasets

Data set	Factor 1 < 0.9	Factor 1 > = 0.9	
	High-risk	High-risk	Low-risk
OASys operational data	109234	13638	16076
	78.6%	9.8%	11.6%
April 2004 assessed subset	3122	525	170
	81.8%	13.7%	4.5%

results tabulated in Table 6.6, with the OASys results repeated for comparison.

At first inspection, the proportions in each of the categories seems inconsistent between the two sets of data. However the OASys data includes individual offenders convicted during a five-year period, whereas in the April 2004 data the period is only one month. High-risk individuals will be over-represented in short sampling periods because the probability of their conviction in the period is high compared with low-risk offenders. As the sampling period is increased the high-risk offenders may have several convictions but will only be counted once and low-risk offenders have an increasing probability of being included. It is therefore not surprising that the proportions in the risk categories are different.

Using the time from the previous conviction, the λs were estimated for the April 2004 assessed offenders and these values were used in the calculations which are described below. The theory and models developed in Chapter 2 allow us to estimate the expected number of offenders who will be reconvicted in a given period, in the set of April 2004 assessed offenders. To do the calculation we need estimates of the reconviction probabilities (p_h and p_l) for the high- and low-risk categories. For these we use the estimates derived from the OASys operational data analysis as this is the largest data set available. For estimates of the proportions (***a*** and ***1–a***) we use the Factor 1 (0.9) dichotomy data and for (***b*** and ***1–b***) and the λs (λ_h and λ_l) for the high- and low-rate categories, we use the values derived from the April 2004 assessed offender subset. For each of the risk/rate categories the proportion (r) reconvicted within time t is given by:

$$r = p * (1 - e^{-\lambda * t}) \quad (6.1)$$

In the April 2004 data we have reconviction information for up to 16 months after the target conviction but have censored that data at 15 months (1.25 years). If we had assumed that our initial analysis of the April 2004 assessed offender data was correct, (Figure 6.14), then our estimate of 15-month reconvictions would have been 3,023, some 12.75 per cent above the actual number reconvicted of 2,681.

However, if we apply the Factor 1 (0.90) dichotomy to the assessed offender data and, using Equation 6.1, calculate the number of reconvictions for each of the theoretical categories so defined, then we obtain the results given in Table 6.7. These predictions are a good prospective test of both the basic model and the link between our risk/rate categories and the psychological characteristics of offenders. Our overall prediction is now within 1 per cent of the actual value and for the subset of offenders with Factor 1 scores less than 0.9 the number reconvicted is within 1.25 per cent of the predicted value. Assuming that reconvictions occur as a Poisson process, these figures are well within one standard deviation (1.9 per cent) of the estimate.

The success of these predictions adds considerable support to our theory, particularly as we have relied on the OASys assessments to identify our low-risk offenders, who were otherwise hidden

Table 6.7 Fifteen-month reconviction prediction results

Dichotomy	***a*** or (***1–a***)	***p***	Total offenders in risk/rate category	λ	***b*** or (***1–b***)	$p*(1-exp(-\lambda*1.25))$	Number reconvicted: Estimate	Number reconvicted: Actual
Factor 1 score < 0.9	1	0.90	2862	1.57	0.71	0.774	2214	2461
		0.90	1169	0.24	0.29	0.237	277	
Factor 1 score ≥ 0.9	0.38	0.87	195	1.57	0.36	0.748	146	220
		0.87	346	0.24	0.64	0.126	44	
	0.62	0.48	221	0.24	1.00	0.126	28	
Estimate			4792				2708	
Actual			4833					2681

amongst a group of what appeared to be exclusively high-risk offenders.

Conclusions

The PCA analysis of the operational OASys data has confirmed the pilot study findings with regard to the link between psychological characteristics (associated with self control, empathy, and awareness) and our high- and low-risk offender categories. Considering the small size of the pilot sample the parameter estimates were remarkably consistent with those derived from the operational data. In the pilot, OASys section 11 total score provided a satisfactory discriminator enabling the majority of high-recidivism risk offenders to be identified. However, the more sophisticated principal component analysis on an expanded set of OASys questions, sections 7, 11, and 12, (including measures of Lifestyle and Associates, and Attitudes) provided a significant improvement in identifying high-risk offenders.

Using the Factor 1 (0.9) dichotomy allocated 22 per cent more of the offenders (in the operational OASys database) to the high-risk group than would have been allocated using the 'Total section 11 score ≥ 6' dichotomy. The improved discrimination however owes more to the PCA technique than to the increased number of questions included in the analysis. Selecting disjoint subsets of the OASys questions for use in the PCA only marginally reduced the discrimination. Sections 7 and 12 combined performed as well as section 11 on its own. None of the OASys questions were identified as redundant in the analysis, but it would seem that the information contained in the principal component, Factor 1, is spread across most of the questions and can, in large part, be extracted from subsets of them.

Using our theory and the Factor 1 dichotomy, applied to a subset of a sample of offenders convicted in April 2004, we produced prospective predictions of reconvictions during a 15-month period from the target conviction. The overall number of actual reconvictions was within 1 per cent of the predicted number. This result provides convincing support for both the basic theory and the link between psychological characteristics and our high- and low-risk offender categories.

7

Applications for Managing the Criminal Justice System

Orientation

In Chapter 2, we proposed the theory that there are three categories of offenders: high-risk/high-rate, high-risk/low-rate, and low-risk/low-rate. In Chapter 6, we showed that these categories differed in their psychological characteristics. In this chapter, we use the theory to make forecasts of the prison population and of the number of offenders in the DNA database.

Introduction

In 1996 the Operational Research Unit of the Home Office, in which two of us (John MacLeod and Peter Grove) then worked, was asked to develop a new long-term methodology to forecast the prison population in England and Wales. The requirement was to be able to predict the average population (disaggregated by age, gender, and type of offence) in any year up to five years in advance. The purpose of these long-term forecasts was to inform the Prison Agency's programme of estate management (eg how many new prisons to build, how many to refurbish, how many to close). The methods of projection existing at the time were essentially based on regression and time series models. Although effective for short-term forecasts or in stable conditions these models cannot cope with radical change.

In 1993, following 25 years of relative stability, there was a sudden and dramatic increase (10 to 15 per cent), year on year, in the use of custodial sentences by the courts. It is difficult to see how a time series or regression approach could be helpful in such circumstances. As a result it was decided to build a model which could be used to test the consequences of various policy scenarios (eg reduce the use of custody by 10 per cent for non-violent crime, 'three strikes and you're out', etc). The model was intended to be easily used by policy makers to test the results of various policy options.

Some years prior to the 1996 request, a casual conversation led to a preliminary exploration of newly generated cohort data extracted from the Offenders Index. That exploration sparked the ideas which led to an embryonic theory of age and crime. The prison population forecasting project provided the impetus to develop and expand the theory which is now described in this book. The theory, and mathematical models implementing it, provided one element of the prison population forecasting system.

The other element is a flow model which keeps track of prisoner numbers over time and is also capable of reflecting actual and potential changes in demographics and penal policy. The theory provides the required understanding of the behaviour of offenders when confronted with the criminal justice system. We will see that together the 'flow model' and the theory of offending/conviction make accurate predictions of the prison population. The forecasting model described here was in regular use for over a decade[1] and with some development can be expected to provide useful forecasts well into the future.

The Flow Model

One of the reasons for using a flow model is the inherent stability of the prison population when considered over a period of a few years. This is partly due to the contributions to the population of those with long sentences. We have good information about the current prison population and in particular about long sentence prisoners. These make a large contribution to the total (generally, one 'two-year' sentence has the same contribution as two 'one-year' sentences), and thus make up an important, slowly changing, and in principle easily predicted, part of the future prison population. The other contribution to stability is the high rate of recidivism. The recidivism probability for custodial sentences, ie the proportion of offenders who return to prison after release, approaches 70 per cent for those who have been in prison at least twice (see Table 4.3). As we know a good deal about those offenders currently

[1] See Councell and Simes (2002) and Ministry of Justice (2008) for examples.

in prison, we should be able to predict, on the basis of past data, when these 70 per cent are going to return. This leaves those offenders who will arrive in prison on their first custodial sentence as the major uncertainty.

We can make a very rough estimate of the importance of first time custody cases using the model shown in Figure 7.1. We assume that the prison population is in equilibrium (ie releases balance receptions), which was approximately the case (within 10 per cent) from 1970 until 1993. Then, using the model, we can estimate the number arriving in prison for the first time as follows. In the model: the prison population is N; the average rate of release χ is the weighted sum of the reciprocals of sentence lengths s_i for each offence type $i = 1,2\ldots$; and recidivism (or more accurately the probability of re-imprisonment) is p. Thus we can calculate the number leaving prison as $N*\chi = \Sigma N_i/s_i$, and the number returning each year as $p*N*\chi$.

As the system is in equilibrium, the number returning to prison ($p*N*\chi$) plus the number starting their first custodial sentences (n) must equal the number leaving ($N*\chi$). Therefore the number of first time custodies is given by $n = N*\chi*(1-p)$ (ie the number entering the system is the same as the number of reformed prisoners who will not return to prison). Using order of magnitude data from 1992 Prison Statistics, we have very approximately: $\chi = 0.5$ per

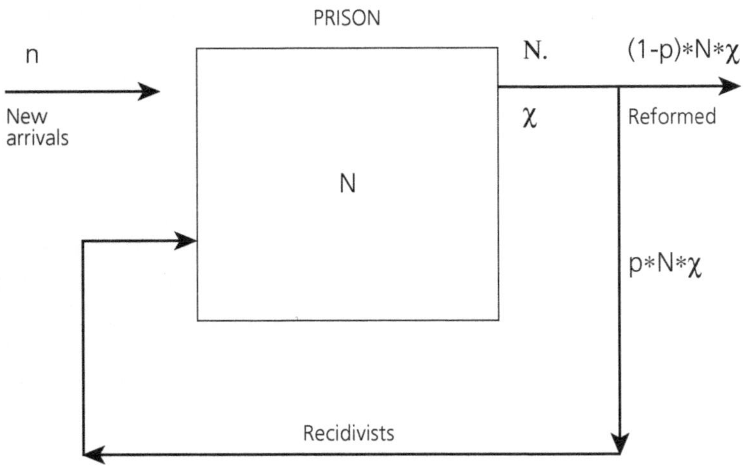

Figure 7.1 The flows into and out of prison

year, $p = 0.7$, giving $n/N = 0.15$ per year. So in any one year the contribution of first custodial offenders is only of the order of 15 per cent of the total intake. However this 15 per cent is the main driver of the flow model and it is important to be able to estimate the number accurately, particularly as it is influenced by factors external to the prison system.

A large proportion of first custodial offenders will have had previous non-custodial convictions so we also need estimates of the rate of reconviction and the age profile of first convictions. The obvious approach is to use historical empirical distributions. Such distributions would be smoothed to provide idealized distributions to be used in the model. An alternative approach is to construct a model of the behaviour of offenders which can reproduce the essential features of the empirical data. In the previous chapters we have described an appropriate theory and developed mathematical models which enable us to calculate the annual number of first offenders and recidivists.

The forecasting methodology described here was built on the two category simplified model of Chapter 4. The two offending categories are separately parameterized for those offences leading to imprisonment before 1993 and again for all standard list offences (the probability of being imprisoned for any significant length of time, more than a few weeks, for a non-standard list offence is very small). In the prison forecasting methodology the high recidivism, rapidly offending category is described as the 'high' population and the low-recidivism, slowly offending category as the 'low' population. The parameter estimates for the simplified two-category model are listed in Tables 4.4 and 4.5 in Chapter 4.

Predicting the Prison Population

With the offending model we have the means to deal with the two 'difficult' parts of modelling the prison population. We can, from the numbers born in each year over the previous 70 years, predict the number and age profile of offenders at first, second, third, etc convictions, up to ten years into the future.[2] Knowing the first-custody rate, at each conviction number, we can calculate the number of offenders (n) entering prison for the first time. Similarly we

[2] Beyond 10 years, progressively, we cannot predict juveniles, young offenders, etc., simply because they are not yet born.

can predict the proportion of those released from prison who will reoffend, be convicted and receive another custodial sentence and the timescale for that reincarceration. The rest is accounting, although somewhat complicated by the disaggregation by offence type, conviction number and gender.

In a little more detail, the model makes the following calculations. Knowing the current prison population size, the future population, for successive quarters, can be calculated by: adding the new intake, consisting of recidivists and those receiving prison sentences for the first time; ascribing the new intake sentence lengths based on current sentencing distributions; and subtracting the number released, which can be calculated from the sentence lengths ascribed to previous intakes. The custody rate information for each offence, together with remission and sentencing policy over the time of the forecast, form a 'Scenario'. Scenarios are generated by a graphical scenario editor and then fed into the model. Although simple in principle the calculation is rather complicated and was encoded in a long C++ program.

Initially only a test version of the computer implementation of the model was available. This did not make use of current prison information. Instead the model was run from 1950 with an initial condition of empty prisons. The prison population was then built up entirely on the basis of the model of offending. If the model is an accurate reflection of reality, the results should be comparable to

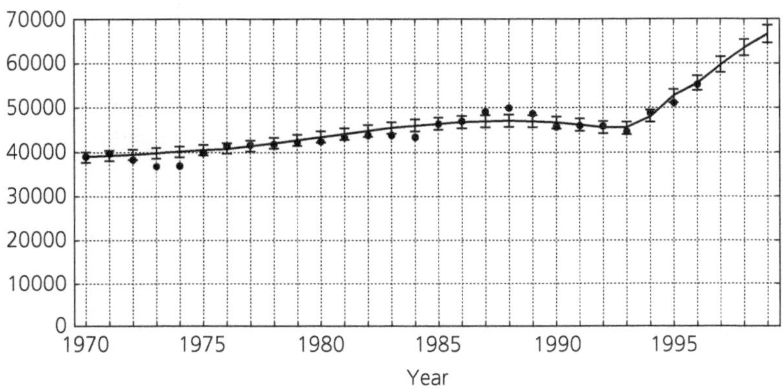

Figure 7.2 Prison population model projection 1970–1999, first scenario

Note: The data points represent the average annual prison population.

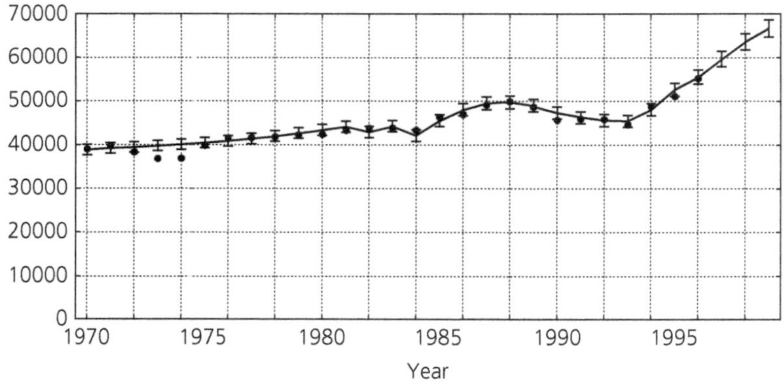

Figure 7.3 Prison population model projection 1970–1999, second scenario

the actual situation from about 1970–75 onwards. The results of three scenarios are presented in Figures 7.2 to 7.4.

Figure 7.2 is a graph of the total prison population based on the first scenario which assumed that, for the whole period prior to 1993, the sentencing policy, and in particular custody rates, were the same as those in 1992; after 1993 the scenario assumed a continuing year on year increasing custody rate to reflect the known situation up to 1996. The 3 per cent error bars on the modelled line (approximately one standard deviation) indicate the possible effect of the stochastic variation in the total number of offenders born in

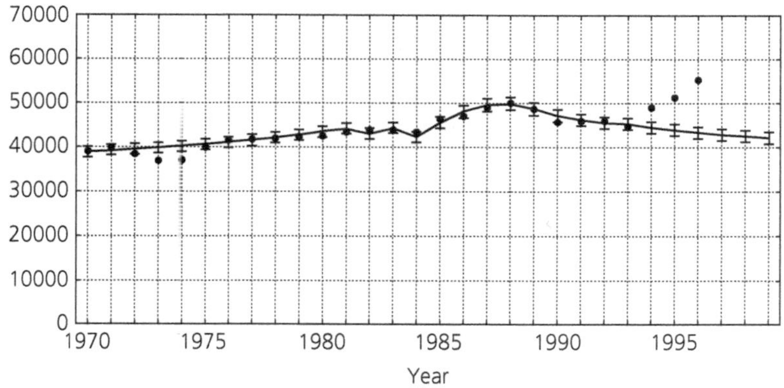

Figure 7.4 Prison population model projection 1970–1999, third scenario

any given year. From Figure 7.2 it can be seen that before 1993 the actual prison population, points on the graph, fell within about three standard deviations of the projection. This is in itself a remarkable fit. Statistically one could not expect a better fit, as the only varying quantity before 1993 is the number of people born in the preceding years. We can also see that over half the variation in the prison population up to 1993 is due to demographics.

Figure 7.3 shows the results of a second scenario in which the actual custody rates for each year from 1975–1993 were used in the model. We see now that all the data points, post 1975, are within the one standard deviation error bars. This fit is 'too good', and this is almost certainly due to the fact that the 'error' calculation is really an upper bound calculation and a more realistic error estimate is about one third this size (ie about 1 per cent). We can conclude that a little less than half of the fluctuation before 1993 (ie that part not due to demographics) was due to changes in custody rates. After 1993 we see that the prison population is well explained by the year on year increase in custody rates. We should emphasize that these projections are not based on any information derived from prisons but only on sentencing information (custody rates and sentence length distributions) obtained from the courts and population estimates derived from census data. The fit is remarkable, indicating that (at least as far as those offences resulting in possible custodial disposals by the courts are concerned) the model of offending is capturing the gross behaviour of the offending population.

For comparison purposes, we modelled a third scenario in which actual custody rates were used for each year in the period 1975–1992 and then held at the 1992 values for the period 1993–1999. This scenario illustrates what might have happened had Home Secretary Michael Howard not made his 'Prison Works' speech.[3] Figure 7.4 shows that, without the increasing use of custody by the courts, post-1993 demographic trends would have caused the prison population to continue the slow decline levelling-off around the turn of the century.

Using our theory and a simple (in principle at least) flow model we have been able to construct a remarkably accurate model of the prison population. The model can be used to predict the effects of changes in sentencing policy by the courts. Of course having an accurate model of what will happen given a particular policy is

[3] Speech to the Conservative Party conference, 6 October 1993.

only half the battle. If we want to know the actual prison population over the next five years it is necessary to predict sentencing policy over the same period. Unfortunately no analytical method exists which can accurately carry out that task, so there was a need to run the model assuming various different scenarios. However, even with this limitation the model has been a useful aid to policy makers in allocating prison resources.

In 1997, a change in policy (focusing more on drugs offences) resulted in all drugs offences being defined as standard list. Although this did not change the behaviour of offenders, who considered many of these offences as rather trivial, it did increase the number of standard list offences, which was the officially recognized measure of relatively serious crime. As a result the proportions of offenders being convicted for particular offence types, within the standard list offences, changed and it was necessary to update the prison model which had to be re-parameterized to reflect the new situation. The change in the total number of standard list convictions was thought to be concentrated on the trivial group of offenders (ie those who would rarely be convicted of offences formerly on the standard list). As the trivial group was not explicitly modelled in the prison model, there was no change in the overall offending parameters. More recent results using the updated model, the actual sentencing practice with and without adjustments to reflect the prison population at the beginning of the projection period, are shown in Figures 7.5 to 7.7.

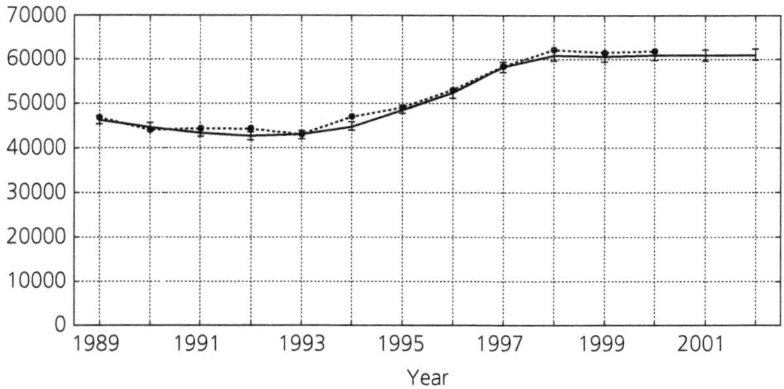

Figure 7.5 Male prison population compared with forecast given actual sentencing policy and practice 1989–2001, no cross-section file

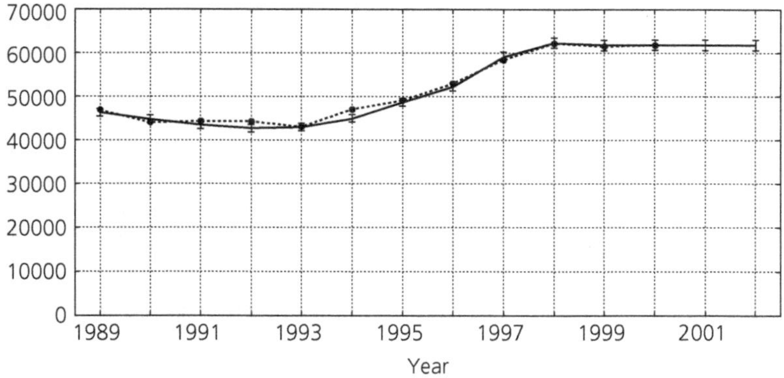

Figure 7.6 Male prison population compared with forecast given actual sentencing policy and practice 1989–2001 with cross-section file set to actual values in 1997

Given the success of the methodology in predicting long-term changes in the prison population, it was decided to produce a similar model for all court disposals. Accuracy similar to that of the prison model was not expected for three reasons. The first is that the averaging over the six months of a typical prison sentence is not applicable to non-custodial sentences. For non-custodial sentences we have to deal with trivial offences and we have found an intrinsic 5 per cent year to year fluctuation in the number of these convictions for males and 10 per cent for females. Finally the data on sentencing policy is considerably less robust for non-custodial sentences.

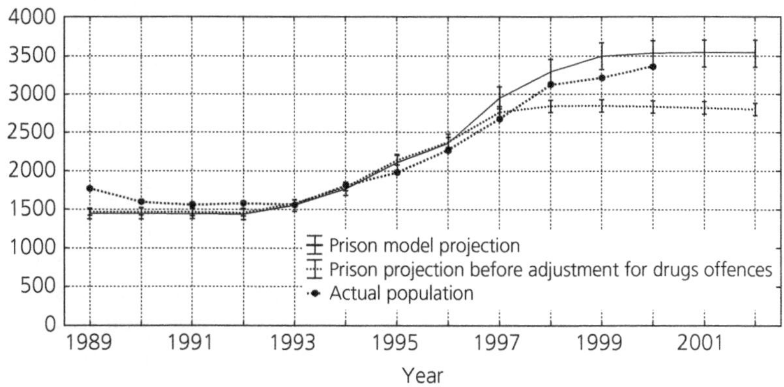

Figure 7.7 Female prison population over period 1989–2001

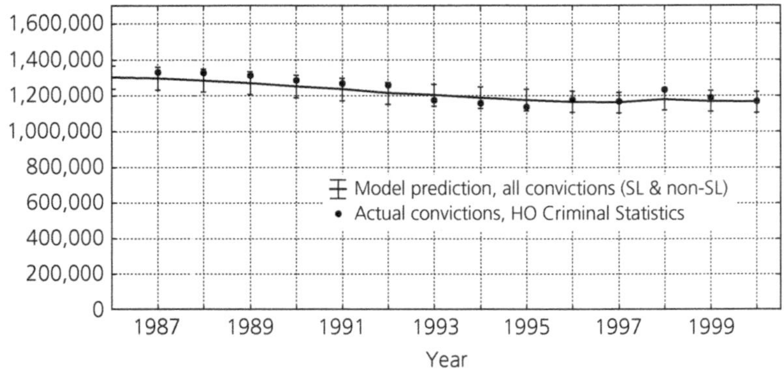

Figure 7.8 A graph of the predicted total male convictions over the period 1987–2000

The methodology is essentially built on the gamma distribution model (Grove 2003) applied to trivial offenders and discussed in Chapter 4. Some changes were required compared with the prison model such as a more sophisticated approach to the temporal parameter (δ). This is modelled by an enhanced rate of offending over the first six months following reconviction, again with the intention of providing an easily implemented approximation to our analysis of Chapters 3 and 4.

A graph of the predictions of the enhanced model (compared to actual number of convictions) for the period 1987–2000 is given in Figure 7.8; offence definitions during this period were fairly constant. The predictions and actual male conviction numbers agree to within the ±5 per cent anticipated error.

Despite the success of the model, we understand that its development, in this form, has been discontinued because of a change of view of the requirements for forecasting in the Ministry of Justice.

The DNA Database

With the possibility of 'matching' DNA taken at crime scenes against that of known offenders, the development of a database of DNA evidence found at crime scenes and of the DNA 'fingerprints' of known offenders was set in train. An important requirement for planning and implementing the database was to know how many new offenders would be entering the database each year and how long it would take to obtain samples from existing offenders who had previously been convicted but had not had their DNA 'fingerprint' recorded. Such information is not available from standard statistics but is precisely the kind the calculation which can be made on the basis of our theory.

DNA evidence is not only recorded on conviction but also on cautioning. As our theory does not explicitly describe cautioning (only its impact on early convictions), we constructed three models based on possible interpretations of the interaction of cautioning and conviction. Each of these models used the full three category models of offending and a fixed annual birth rate of 330,000 males and about 330,000 females. In the year 2000, when the initial forecast was made, there were just under a million records already on the database and this was taken as the starting point.

In the first of the three models, the 'core' model, only first convictions and estimates of reconvictions for active (previously convicted) offenders, were assumed to add to the database. These assumptions represented the slowest possible build-up of DNA profiles on the database and provided a lower bound for our estimates. The second of our three models, the 'total' model, was based on an estimate of the total number of active offenders, excluding all those who would be dealt with informally on their arrest, and calculating when they would be convicted. To this was added the annual number of first cautions. The problem with this model is the lack of understanding of the informal sanctions. It was thought that this model would overestimate the rate of build-up. The final 'intermediate' model was based on taking the cautions element from the 'total' model and the reconvictions element from the core model. This was believed to underestimate the build-up but not as badly as the core model. Figure 7.9 presents the build-up forecasts from the three models. The lower line is the core model estimate, the top line is the total model forecast (the error bars on the line represent the uncertainty due to the variation in the number of cautions year to year), and the central line is the intermediate model forecast.

At the time the forecast was made our expectation was that the size and growth of the database would be between the intermediate and total model forecasts. By mid-2004, the actual database was in line to reach a total size of 2.4 million offender records by the end of that year faster than the intermediate model and a little less than the total model, as expected. A comparison between the actual size of the database and the prediction is given in Figure 7.10. The upper

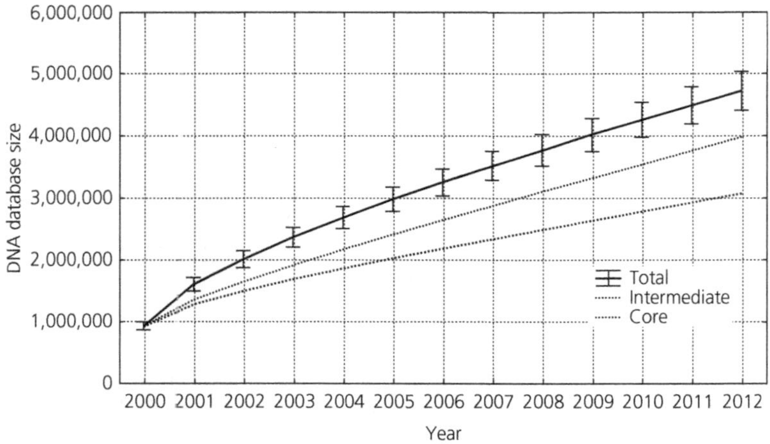

Figure 7.9 The forecast build-up of the DNA database from (June) 2000

and lower lines follow the total and intermediate model projections in Figure 7.9 representing uncertainties due to the variation in cautioning from year to year.

There are two measures of the size of the actual database. The police measure consists of police estimates of the numbers sent to the database excluding certain special routes; and the custodian's measure represents all those offender records believed to have been

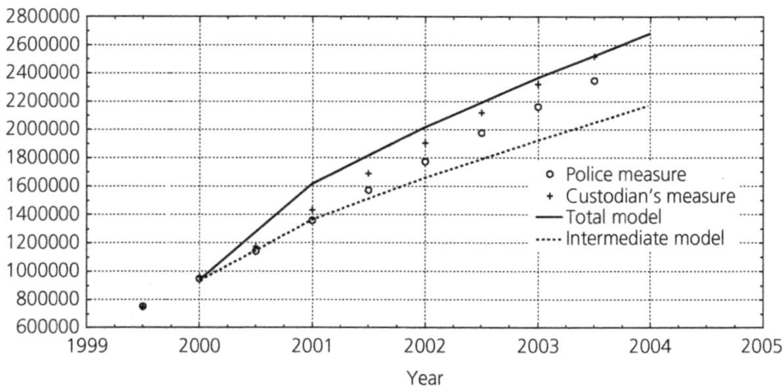

Figure 7.10 Comparison of Police and Custodian's estimates of the size of the DNA database with the models

loaded before weeding for duplicates. The real figure lies somewhere between the two.

June 2000 represented the beginning of a drive to put all known offenders on the database by sampling all those cautioned and convicted. As can be seen the initial rise was slower than expected, probably due to resource constraints in police forces leading to a steady rise rather than the sudden increase that otherwise would have been expected. However, the size of the database in mid-2003 was much as predicted.

Conclusion

In this chapter we have shown that, quite apart from the value of having a theory of criminal careers from a criminological point of view, having a quantitative theory has allowed us to make forecasts of the prison population, court workloads and the growth of the DNA database. The prison population forecasting system, which has been the major subject of this chapter, was used to make annual projections of the long-term prison population for over a decade. These projections were an essential element in the management and planning of the prison building and maintenance programmes for England and Wales. An understanding of possible future scenarios is also a necessary element in many other management issues like the recruitment and training of staff. This particular application of our theory was thus an important factor in the allocation of at least £2,000,000,000 per year.

8

Criminal Policy Implications

Orientation

In this book, we have proposed and tested a simple theory of criminal careers that makes exact quantitative predictions, and we have applied it to several different cross-sectional and longitudinal databases. In Chapter 7, we showed that it could be used to predict the prison population and the number of offenders in the national DNA database. In this chapter, we outline some of the policy implications of the theory, and especially what the theory says about the effect of conviction and imprisonment on criminal careers.

Introduction

The theory has a number of implications for criminal justice policy. Some of these have been touched on earlier but are reviewed systematically here. The main conclusion is that the criminal justice system (CJS) does control crime. The most important single factor leading to significant reductions in crime would be to increase the probability of capture and conviction given an offence. In agreement with this, Farrington and Jolliffe (2005) found that aggregate crime rates in four different countries were negatively correlated with the probability of conviction. However, having convicted an offender, prison should be used only for those offenders who society is prepared to incarcerate for most of their active lives. Treatment programmes for offenders, in the community or in prison, should be targeted at the 'high-risk' category of offenders where the modest individual effects of the programmes will be amplified by repetition.

Overview of the Theory

We begin by reviewing the main features of our theory. We believe that the analysis presented above provides convincing evidence in support of the theory and, if accepted, leads to the following implications:

- Most offences are committed by members of three clearly distinguishable offender categories, whose characteristics are relatively fixed in early childhood and remain so until they desist from crime.
- On reaching the age of criminal responsibility, the proportion of the population in each of the offender categories in any given year has been essentially constant since at least 1963.
- The main reason for offenders desisting from crime is their interaction with the criminal justice system. Offenders do not simply 'grow out' of crime due to either an internal maturation process or by general interaction with their environment. The most important event which causes desistance is *conviction*.
- Apart from those prisoners kept in prison for large fractions of their active lives, there is no overall long-term effect on crime simply due to putting some offenders in prison, unless the prison population is allowed to increase indefinitely.

We cannot, of course, claim that our theory is a true or unique reflection of reality. The categories we define are after all just inferences from the statistical properties of our data. However, what we can say is that our theory is based on simple but plausible assumptions about the offender population and process of conviction and reconviction which replicate those statistical properties. Models based on the theory also predict and explain a wide range other criminal career features and observations.

The Categories

For each gender there are three categories of standard list offenders and a further category of non-standard list trivial offenders. The 'trivial' category of offenders commits a large amount of rather trivial crime (including a large proportion of all motoring offences). They rarely get sentenced to custody but may be very prolific. There may also be substantial overlap between the trivial category and the high-risk/low-rate category of Chapters 2 and 3, as they occasionally commit less serious standard list offences. At the other extreme there is a high-risk/high-rate category of offenders who on average accumulate five or six convictions, for serious offences, and on average are convicted about once a year during their criminal careers.

Some high-risk offenders will accrue large numbers of convictions over many years. Finally there is a low-risk/low-rate category of offenders who typically are convicted only once or twice but for relatively serious offences. For low-risk offenders with more than one conviction, these would be on average four to five years apart.

The high-risk/high-rate and low-risk/low-rate categories have an average criminal career length, from first to last convictions, of about five years whereas the high-risk/low-rate and trivial categories have an average career length of 10 to 11 years. For all categories the range of career lengths (as measured by convictions) is from 0, a single offence/conviction, to the whole active life span but with a rapidly diminishing likelihood of careers longer than the average (see the age–crime curves in Chapters 3 and 4). Most offenders will also have been actively committing crimes prior to their first conviction.

Although the actual numbers (parameters) describing the categories differ, the nature of their behaviour as seen in terms of convictions is qualitatively the same. They are convicted at a constant Poisson rate (committing offences at random) and a constant proportion stop offending after each conviction. Criminality (the proportion of the general population sustaining one or more standard list convictions in their lifetime) was substantially constant for all the birth cohorts, as was the proportions in each of the risk/rate categories. There is much greater uncertainty concerning the trivial offender category. Their offences are technically crimes (regulatory offences, minor public disorder offences, motoring offences, etc) but many in the general population would not consider them as criminals and we have not included them, apart from the subcategory who also commit standard list offences, in our main criminal categories.

The theory and models are 'large scale' in two main respects. The theory does not specifically consider the social or psychological causes of the offending behaviour, although in Chapter 6 we identified significant correlations between our risk categories and psychological assessment scores. Also our group structure is not necessarily complete, in that there are almost certainly special categories and subcategories of offenders. Examples of special categories include those whose offending is induced by mental illness or psychological abnormality (eg paranoid schizophrenics, paedophile sex offenders, serial rapists, and mass murderers) who are all very different from offenders in general but thankfully relatively rare. Another such group probably consists of around half of life-sentence prisoners who have very low probabilities of recidivism. However, in the main, offenders are versatile and commit a wide range of offences over a criminal career. Selecting subsets of offenders leads to some variation in the parameters (proportions in the categories, recidivism probabilities and rates of conviction) although this variation is generally much less than the differences in parameters between the main categories.

With the exception of the mentally ill, our theory assumes that for individuals crime is a lifestyle choice (see also Walters 2006; West and Farrington 1977) and at each offence the individual makes a decision. Without consequences such behaviour is unlikely to change. Being caught is an essential element in desistance, and the greater the certainty of capture the greater the deterrent effect. However, being caught is not, in itself, sufficient. For those destined to join our criminal categories, offenders need to be made aware of the extent to which their behaviour is unacceptable to society at large. In our view it is the criminal justice system process[1] that appears to have the most influence on the life-choice decision to no longer commit crime, or at least to modify behaviour to avoid serious breaches of the law. The penalties imposed on conviction may well serve several other penological objectives, but there is no substantive evidence from our analysis that the particular sentence influences the decision to desist from further offending.

Areas where Policy could Influence Crime

Crime prevention is of course a major vehicle for the reduction of crime, but it is not one that our analysis was concerned with (see Farrington and Welsh 2007; Welsh and Farrington 2009, 2012). Although reducing opportunities for crime could well impact on the parameters of our model it is not clear what that impact might be. We therefore concentrate here on policies which relate to (potential/actual) offenders and the criminal justice system: police, courts and corrections. Our theory suggests that overall crime reduction objectives might be achieved by policies to:

- reduce the likelihood of individuals entering the criminal categories, by means of early intervention programmes for children at risk;

[1] The sequence of events: arrest, charge and court appearances resulting in conviction and sentencing.

- improve the effectiveness of interventions in early criminal careers, for example by informal actions including the handling of antisocial behaviour by society at large as well as the police, and improvements in the effectiveness of the warnings, reprimands and cautions issued by the police;
- increase the efficiency of the criminal justice system. Doubling the probability of conviction given a crime halves the total amount of crime committed by known offenders in the long term;
- make those small reductions in recidivism, mainly in the high recidivism group of offenders, which might be expected from some kinds of offender treatment programmes such as Enhanced Thinking Skills. These will have a disproportionate impact in reducing crime.

Childhood Early Interventions

In the Cambridge Study in Delinquent Development, Farrington (2007; see also Farrington, Coid, and West 2009) identified a number of factors from childhood which could be used to predict later offending and conviction. In a systematic review of evaluations of early intervention programmes, Farrington and Welsh (2007) concluded that many programmes were effective in reducing childhood antisocial behaviour and later delinquency. Beelmann and Raabe (2009), from a review of articles and a meta-analyses of childhood interventions, found that prevention measures addressing high-risk categories produced higher effect sizes than universal strategies.

Common sense, the evidence base, and our theory suggests, that preventing the onset of offending would be a very effective strategy for reducing crime and early intervention would seem to be the most likely option for long-term criminality reduction (see Farrington 2007; Farrington and Welsh 2007). These programmes are not necessarily focused on crime but rather on community cohesion, improving parenting skills, the provision of facilities for families and improving social responsibility and good citizenship. All of these interventions are likely to reduce criminal involvement and have been in the political rhetoric for many years. There have been programmes based on these ideas but, in England and Wales over the time period covered by the Offenders Index (OI) cohorts, not on a scale that would show up in our analysis.

More recently, such programmes have been rolled out on a much larger scale, and in particular Sure Start, a comprehensive community based programme of early intervention and family support. Sure Start was initially aimed at children under school age and their families, particularly in less advantaged areas, and it has shown some encouraging results (Melhuish et al 2008). By 2011 there were more than 3,600 Sure Start Children's Centres in England. Although the effectiveness of the Sure Start local programmes and children's centres is being assessed on many of the anticipated outcomes, the impact on crime and criminality will not become apparent until about 2020–2030 and even then it may be difficult to separate the effects of Sure Start from other interventions and policies.

Early Career Interventions

The next opportunity in the life course would be to deal more effectively with early-onset offending. During the period of the OI cohorts there has been a progressive tendency to divert offenders away from the criminal justice system and a reluctance to prosecute and impose formal sanctions on even quite serious young offenders, particularly for pre- and early teenagers.

In the 1953 cohort some 237 offenders, approximately 2 per cent, were convicted at age 10, but this number reduced in successive birth cohorts to 196, 123, 71, and 39 in the 1958, 1963, 1968, and 1973 cohorts respectively. The pattern is somewhat different if we consider those convicted up to the mid-teens. By age 16 about 20 per cent of offenders in the 1953 cohort had one or more convictions. This proportion reduced only slightly in the 1958 and 1963 cohorts to about 19 per cent of the estimated lifetime offender cohort size. But the proportion of under-16s reduced significantly to 14 per cent for the 1968 cohort and only 7 per cent for the 1973 cohort. Our estimates of criminality (see Table 2.6) remain essentially constant for all the cohorts, with an average of 23 per cent. The 1973 cohort estimate at 20.4 per cent seems low, but because the observation period ended at age 20 the criminality estimate is subject to greater censoring. However, the criminality estimate from the 1997 sentencing sample is also about 20 per cent, and should not be so error prone, suggesting that the 1973 cohort estimate might not be too low.

If correct, this reduction in criminality might be seen as evidence of the success of the police cautioning policies. But if the reduction is due only to those offenders who would have desisted after conviction now desisting after caution, the success is limited to savings in court time and the non-criminalization of young offenders. To effect a reduction in crime would require recidivism after cautioning to be lower than after conviction. However, after controlling for prior differences between cautioned and convicted youth, Farrington and Bennett (1981) and Mott (1983) found little difference in reoffending between them. Criminality estimates in successive cohorts from 1953 to 1968 suggest that, despite the progressively increased use of cautions up to age 16, criminality remained comparable to, or above, the 1953 cohort level. This in turn suggests that convictions were merely delayed with a commensurate increase in pre-conviction crimes (see also Farrington and Maughan 1999). The 1973 cohort and the 1997 sentencing sample, however, do seem to indicate a reduction in criminality. The authors have insufficient information on the effectiveness of cautioning in more recent years to resolve this issue but this is clearly an important area for more rigorous evaluation.

Increasing the Efficiency of Conviction

We define the efficiency of conviction as the ratio of convictions to recorded offences. We assume that offenders, in particular our high-risk offenders, commit many more offences than they are convicted of. For example, Farrington et al (2006) in the Cambridge Study found that there were 39 self-reported crimes for every conviction occasion. Based on a comparison between victim survey and conviction data, Farrington and Jolliffe (2004) concluded that, in England and Wales in 1999, there were only seven convictions per 1,000 burglars, 17 convictions per 1,000 vehicle thieves, six convictions per 1,000 robbers, and 25 convictions per 1,000 assaulters. Our theory suggests that conviction is the trigger for desistance. Therefore if offenders are convicted for more of their offences (increasing λ for convictions but not for offences) and the reconviction probability remains the same, then crime will be reduced.

In the cohort data there is a tendency for higher recidivism probabilities after shorter inter-conviction times. However this does not necessarily imply a causal relationship. In the 1953 cohort, following inter-conviction times of less than six months, the recidivism probability was 0.86, marginally greater than the high-risk value of 0.84. But this apparently higher recidivism probability could well be caused by the pseudo-reconviction problem, in which the pseudo-reconviction is for an offence committed prior to the previous conviction. For inter-conviction times between six months and a year the reconviction probability was 0.84, the same as for the high-risk category. For inter-conviction times greater than a year the probability decreased steadily to about 0.30 at 10 years, reflecting the increasing proportion of low-risk/low-rate offenders among those with longer inter-conviction times.

There is also some evidence that high-rate offenders in particular, tend to slow down between the penultimate and last conviction. This slowing down is unlikely to be an ageing effect as was demonstrated in Chapter 5 (Figures 5.4 and 5.5), where the inter-conviction survival time curves were parallel and parameter values were substantially constant over increasing ranges of appearance numbers and hence increasing age. It would also be counter-intuitive to believe that being caught and convicted more quickly would encourage recidivism rather than desistance. Policies to improve the efficiency of conviction should therefore hasten the end of the criminal career and hence reduce crime.

Offender Treatment Programmes

Goldblatt and Lewis (1998) summarized substantial evidence that various kinds of treatment programmes can reduce recidivism. Such programmes were not widely used in the period from 1963 until 1997, during which time the bulk of data for the research leading to our theories and models was collected. If such programmes are effective in practice they will lead to decreases in the recidivism parameters and would have a significant long-term effect on crime.

Prolific and other Priority Offenders

Criminal Justice: The Way Ahead (Home Office 2001) outlined many policies aimed at reducing crime and improving the operation of the criminal justice system. Among these policies was a commitment to target persistent offenders. The Prolific and other Priority Offender (PPO) programme was implemented in England and Wales on 6 September 2004. In each area PPOs were identified using criteria reflecting local concerns coupled with the offender's criminal history. PPOs were then prioritized by the police, prisons, probation, and other local agencies, with a view to reducing their offending. The three objectives of the programme were to 'Prevent and Deter', 'Catch and Convict', and 'Rehabilitate and Resettle'. The 'catch and convict' element of the PPO programme was intended to improve the efficiency of conviction for these offenders and hence shorten the criminal careers of the PPOs. In the short term, PPOs were also given rehabilitation training and post sentence support to aid resettlement. An important element of the programme was close coordination between all the agencies involved.

Dawson and Cuppleditch (2007) reported on an evaluation of the Prolific and other Priority Offender programme. The evaluation comprised three components: a reconviction analysis, offender interviews, and staff interviews. Although the interview components provided interesting and informative anecdotal evidence of the impact of the programme, our particular interest here is the reconviction analysis and how the theories developed in this book clarify and help to explain the results.

Offenders identified as PPOs were tracked on a computerized system known as JTrack. This system enabled the researchers to extract conviction information on all PPOs identified in the first two months of the programme (the PPO cohort). A monthly count of cohort convictions was made for the three and a half years prior to and one year and nine months after September 2004 (see Figure 8.1).[2]

Figure 8.1 shows an increasing trend in convictions up to the start of the PPO selection period followed by a 30 per cent reduction in the conviction rate in the subsequent three months and a steady decline over the remaining part of the observation period. Dawson and Cuppleditch (2007 p 7) interpreted this as 'a steady rise in their criminal behaviour until they commence the PPO programme at which point there is a sharp decrease followed by a period of steady decline'. The inference was that the PPO programme halted the worsening criminal behaviour, reducing it significantly and setting in train a steady continuing reduction in convictions.

Although not specifically stated in the evaluation report, we suspect that selection as a PPO was triggered by a conviction in,

[2] The data points in Figure 8.1 were taken from the published graph, Figure C in Dawson and Cuppleditch (2007, p 7), and may therefore not be exact as values were estimated to the nearest 50.

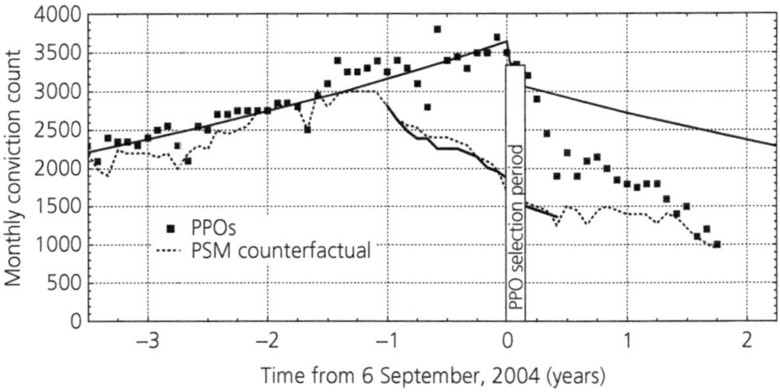

Figure 8.1 Monthly conviction count for PPO cohort and control group, before and after PPO selection

Source: Dawson and Cuppleditch (2007).
Note: The overlaid curves are predictions derived from our theory and models.

or very close to, the selection period. The PPO sample size was 7,400 and the reported monthly conviction rate, in the selection period, was in the region of 3,500. However, for a sample of 7,400 offenders convicted at time $t = 0$, using our rate model with $\lambda = 1.05$ court appearances per annum, we would expect 1,236 offenders to have sustained at least one principal conviction in the previous month. The figure of 3,500 convictions suggests that Dawson and Cuppleditch (2007) counted all convictions rather than just court appearances.

We would also have expected a significant peak in the conviction rate at $t = 0$, in the PPO sample case, spread over two months or so. The high conviction rate is consistent with the PPOs being members of our high-risk/high-rate offender group and we can calculate the distribution of previous convictions prior to 6 September 2004 (conditioned on conviction in the approximately two month selection period): the solid smooth line on the graph shows the expected distribution of conviction rates up to 6 September 2004. Because of the conditioning of the sample and stability in the number of active offenders over time we would expect the build up of monthly convictions to follow the mirror image of the residual career length profile. The solid line up to 6 September shows the expected profile assuming $p = 0.84$ and $\lambda = 1.05$ court appearances per annum.

On conviction in the selection period we would expect 16 per cent of the PPOs to desist and, had there been no intervention, the remainder to continue offending and desisting in line with the residual career length profile[3] as shown by the continuation of the solid line. The apparent rise in criminal behaviour is an artefact of the conditioning[4] of the PPO cohort sample (conviction in the selection period), which is in fact comprised of high-risk/high-rate offenders who are convicted at a constant Poisson rate λ.

In the PPO data the conviction rate reduces more slowly than predicted, over the first three months from September to December, but then continues to fall rapidly for a further two months. We would suggest that the slower than predicted initial decline is the result of the *catch and convict* element in the PPO programme which was intended to speed up the reconviction process with the aim of reducing the active population more quickly. This appears to have happened as after four months the conviction rate (which is proportional to the active population) is well below the prediction, continuing the initial trend. From February/March 2005 through to May/June 2006, the slope of the steady decline is steeper than the model predicts suggesting that, following involvement in the PPO programme, the residual career length is shorter. This can be explained either as an increase in the conviction rate λ as a result of *catch and convict* or as a reduction in the recidivism probability due to *rehabilitate and resettle* or a combination of the two. In any event the PPO programme appears to have been successful and the resulting conviction rate profile has a rational explanation in terms of the theories and models described in this book.

As part of the evaluation, Dawson and Cuppleditch (2007) set up a counterfactual sample of offenders based on Propensity Score Matching (PSM) to act as a control group. Offenders were matched case by case with the PPO cohort sample, on several characteristics including gender, age, and detailed criminal history. Judging from their description, the matching procedures were rigorous. The monthly conviction rates of the PSM sample are plotted as the irregular line in Figure 8.1. However the evaluators were perplexed by the profile obtained. The PSM conviction rate profile was very

[3] See discussions on incapacitation in the Appendix.

[4] Had the sample been a random selection of active high risk/high rate offenders the conviction rate distribution would have been uniform over the observation period, prior to 6 September 2004, at about 600 convictions per month.

similar to the PPO rates from three and a half years to one year before the start of the PPO programme at which point the conviction rate started to decline consistently through to the end of the observation period. These results were described as 'unexpected'.

In our view the problem has arisen due to the conditioning of the counterfactual sample. There is no mention of *date of conviction* in the matching criteria. From the graph we suspect that for the PSM offenders their last convictions prior to the start of the PPO selection period occurred evenly over the previous 12 months and that their inclusion in the sample was not conditional on a conviction during the PPO selection period. If that was the case, our theory would predict that each month, from the start of the PSM selection period, some 16 per cent of those convicted (recidivism = 0.84) would not be convicted again, representing some 6 per cent of the active offenders in the PSM sample. The number of active offenders would therefore be reduced by 6 per cent each month over the period from September 2003 up to, judging from the graph, possibly January 2005. The solid line, overlaying the PSM conviction profile, in Figure 8.1 shows the expected conviction profile over that period based on the above. The profile beyond January 2005 runs approximately parallel to the PPO predicted profile suggesting conformity to the residual career length distribution with λ and recidivism probability as for our high-risk/high-rate group.

The *rehabilitate and resettle* component of the PPO programme contained some elements of offender treatment and our analysis above suggests that recidivism may have been reduced significantly. That programme contained a variety of interventions including drug treatment, close supervision, and assistance with resettlement and it is not clear which element or combination of elements were responsible for the observed results or indeed whether the reduction in recidivism would persist beyond the observation period. Notwithstanding these reservations the indications are encouraging and the reduction in the conviction rate and the apparent shortening of the residual career length suggest a permanent change. A long term, up to 10 years, follow up of the PPO cohort and a more detailed analysis of recidivism and inter-conviction times would be needed to verify the effectiveness of the PPO programme.

Implications and Uses of the Theory

The PPO analysis above has provided a practical example of the way our theory can be used to explain observations which otherwise can be easily misinterpreted. In the PPO programme example the theory provided a plausible counterfactual and was able to explain why the PSM sample produced an unhelpful control, which in the event is entirely consistent if the conditioning of the data is taken into account. In any evaluation research it is very important to have a clear understanding of the processes involved and a well founded expectation against which to measure the outcome. In this section we will outline what we might expect from policy interventions aimed at influencing criminality, recidivism, rate of offending or rate of conviction.

Perhaps the most important implication of our theory is that the criminal justice system *does control crime*. The vast majority of offenders cease offending because of the activities of the CJS. This means that changes to the CJS may lead to reduced or increased levels of crime. However, perhaps the most effective way to reduce crime is to reduce criminality, ie to stop individuals becoming criminal in the first place. For each potential high-risk offender diverted completely from a life of crime by early intervention, an average of between 19 and 31 recorded crimes would be averted. For potential low-risk offenders an average of between 4 and 7 recorded crimes would be averted. These estimates were based on our theory and 'Offences Brought To Justice' statistics (Ministry of Justice 2010).

For high-risk offenders the above estimates are probably very conservative; if unrecorded and unreported crimes are included the averages could be very much greater. Overall approximately 5 per cent of the population fall into our high-risk categories and in Chapter 6 we showed that a significant proportion of the high-risk category could be identified from psychological characteristics. If early interventions were focused on these most vulnerable individuals a disproportionate[5] reduction in crime could be achieved. Low-risk potential offenders would be more difficult to target as they appear to be similar, psychologically, to non-offenders and the bulk of non-standard list trivial offenders. Reducing the size of an offender category would result in a pro rata reduction in the crime committed by offenders in that category.

Policies aimed at reducing recidivism can also have a significant and disproportionate impact on crime. Again this is particularly true for high-risk offenders. In the Appendix we show that overall, at any given time, about 55 per cent of crime is committed by

[5] A well-targeted intervention could be up to 25 times more effective at reducing crime than one randomly allocated in the population at large.

offenders prior to their first conviction. Thus reducing recidivism only impacts on 45 per cent of future crime (see Table A.1). We also show that crime is inversely proportional to the probability of desistance: thus reducing the recidivism probability for the high-risk group by 10 per cent, from 0.84 to 0.76, would result in a 34 per cent reduction in their future offending and, on reaching the steady state, a 14 per cent reduction in overall crime. In making these estimates we are assuming that offender treatment programmes are given to all high-risk offenders and that a 10 per cent recidivism reduction can be maintained. In practice, the results might be more modest.

The results would certainly be modest for low-risk offenders both because only 33 per cent, at most, of their crime would be affected by reducing their recidivism and because programmes aimed at first offenders in this group would be given to individuals of whom 60 per cent had already decided not to offend again. A 10 per cent reduction in the recidivism probability of low-risk offenders, from 0.30 to 0.27, would result in only a 0.5 per cent reduction in overall crime.

Policies aimed at reducing opportunities for crime may well reduce crime overall but there is some possibility that crime may simply be displaced to areas where opportunity reduction measures are not implemented or to other types of crime. On the other hand there is also evidence that the benefits of crime reduction measures may be diffused to neighbouring areas (Painter and Farrington 1999). Making crime more difficult may also reduce the frequency of offending but is unlikely to cause desistance. Thus, although λ for offending might reduce as a result of opportunity reduction, λ for conviction and recidivism will almost certainly be unaffected. This is because, as we have seen, offenders are versatile and according to our theory they will continue to offend until convicted at which point a constant proportion will desist.

Also, for opportunity reduction policies to impact on overall crime, we would require reductions in the offending rate to have no effect on the rate of conviction. In particular if reducing the offending rate simply increases the inter-conviction time then criminal careers would also be lengthened and overall crime would remain the same. Conversely, over the observation period of the OI cohorts there was a consistent increase in recorded crime through to the early 1990s but both criminality and conviction rates remained substantially constant. This suggests that, within reason, the two rates are only loosely related, possibly because of the dilution of police detection efforts or increases in the numbers of crimes dealt with at individual court appearances. Opportunity reduction by target hardening and surveillance is often very effective at a local level but the impact on overall crime is difficult to assess.

Policies aimed at increasing the probability of conviction, ie increasing the probability that an offence will result in the offender being caught and formally dealt with, will tend to increase λ for convictions. In the Appendix we show that the average residual career length is inversely proportional to both λ for convictions and the probability of desistance. Thus increasing λ for convictions will have the effect of shortening the criminal career provided that the recidivism probability does not increase. A 10 per cent reduction in average inter-conviction time (increasing λ for convictions from 0.86 to 0.956 convictions per annum) for high-risk offenders would result in a 2.25 per cent reduction in overall crime.

Over the first decade of the twenty-first century a new measure of overall CJS performance was introduced[6] in which offences brought to justice (OBTJ) were counted and reported quarterly in Home Office/Ministry of Justice statistical bulletins. An offence is brought to justice if it results in a conviction, caution, fixed-penalty, or is taken into consideration in the determination of sentence. The effectiveness of increasing the OBTJ count, as a crime reducing policy, will depend on whether λ for convictions is also increased. If more offences are brought to justice as offences taken into consideration, overall crime would be unaffected. If additional offences result in a conviction, through improved policing and prosecution procedures, then overall crime is much more likely to be reduced.

The impact on overall crime of additional crimes brought to justice through police cautions will depend on the effectiveness of cautioning and any interventions which may accompany the caution ('cautioning plus'). The data available to the authors did not include any information on the subsequent criminal histories of cautioned offenders. An analysis along the lines of that in Chapters 2 and 3 of data from the Police National Computer, which includes cautioning information, would provide a very useful insight into the effectiveness of cautioning and its ability to divert offenders away from the courts. Fixed penalties are not issued for the more serious

[6] See Criminal Justice: The Way Ahead (Home Office 2001, p 21) and Narrowing the Justice Gap (Crown Prosecution Service 2002).

(standard list) crimes analysed here and are therefore unlikely to impact on the overall level of these crimes.

During the 1990s the political rhetoric in the UK, especially of Home Secretary Michael Howard, assured us that 'prison works'. Courts were encouraged to deal severely with offenders with the result that from about 1993 the prison population started to increase by about 8 per cent per year. The average prison population increased from 45,600 in 1993 to 66,300 in 2001 and over the same period according to the British Crime Survey crime reduced by around 20 per cent. Proponents of policies advocating the increased use of prison claim that the fall in crime was caused by the incapacitation of offenders and possibly the deterrent effect of the more severe punishment. In Chapter 5, in our discussion of various criminal career theories, we concluded that there was no support in the OI data for fixed career length or age-based desistance theories. Any long-term incapacitation effect relies on such theories being true. We return to this issue in greater detail in the Appendix where we show that the size of the active offender population, in the steady state, is independent of the size of the prison population. However, under the above conditions of year on year increases in the prison population we would predict a reduction in crime, but only of the order of 1.5 per cent.

Our theory also predicted a fall in crime of 12.3 per cent due to demographic changes over the six-year period up to the year 2000. We cannot explain all of the reduction in BCS crime but our theory does explain well over half of it. The observed reduction in crime also suggests that more severe punishment increases deterrence but, from our analysis, those released from prison do not appear to have been deterred any more than those sentenced to community penalties. It might of course be that general deterrence is increased but it would be very difficult to establish a causal link or even to quantify deterrence at all. There may also be 'feedback' or 'fashion' effects whereby decreased offending due to a reduced number of active offenders leads to a reduced propensity to offend in those still active. Such a 'non-linear' effect was considered by Marris and Volterra Consulting (2003).

Frequently Asked Questions

We consider here some of the objections to the arguments we have presented so far:

Q Aren't there large numbers of offenders who are never convicted?

A There are, no doubt, some offenders who never get convicted: one-off offenders or those who are effectively deterred from further offending by informal action and offenders specializing in types of crime where there are very low reporting or detection levels. However, in the major part of the analysis presented here, we are concerned with non-trivial volume crime and serious offending. Even for very low probabilities of getting caught for an individual offence, the vast majority of offenders who contribute importantly to the total level of crime, because of their repetitive offending, will be convicted at some point and thus fall within the scope of this analysis. The formulae in the Appendix show that about half of crime is committed by those who have yet to be convicted (see also Farrington et al 2006).

Q There are fewer offenders aged 30 than aged 17. How can you say that people don't grow out of crime?

A Older offenders will, on average, have been convicted more often than younger ones. As, under our theory, conviction triggers desistance, offenders are more likely to have given up lives of crime by age 30 than by age 17. Therefore there are fewer 30-year-old active offenders than 17-year-old ones. From the cohort data we know that almost half of offenders sustain their first conviction after the age of 20 and half of all convictions are of offenders over the age of 25. High-risk/high-rate (the most prolific) offenders dominate among juveniles and young adults. But, because they are convicted more often, their numbers diminish relatively quickly and less than one in ten of those active at age 17 will still be active at age 34. Of the high-risk/low-rate offenders active at age 17, 10 per cent will still be active well after retirement age and our low-risk group of offenders account for most of the convictions at ages 25 and above. In our view, it seems perverse to believe that only the most prolific offenders grow out of crime whereas age has relatively little influence on less criminal offenders. The constant probability of recidivism after conviction, independent of age, has convinced us that age is not a causal factor in desistance.

Q When someone is in prison they cannot commit a crime in the community. This must reduce the total amount of crime, mustn't it?

A For time spent in prison to reduce overall crime the sentence must either reduce the probability of recidivism or shorten the residual criminal career. Direct evidence from the cohort analysis suggests that neither outcome is achieved. After controlling for criminal history, the probability of recidivism is not significantly different after custody compared to community sentences for similar offence seriousness. There is also no significant difference in average reconviction times for these recidivists, after either custody or community penalties, who simply re-join the active offender pool with their expected residual criminal career unchanged.

Their crimes are postponed rather than averted. As soon as we release recidivists from prison they carry on committing their delayed crimes at the same rate as they would have done if given a non-custodial sentence. Unless we let the prison population increase indefinitely, for each active offender entering prison one is released and the overall level of crime stays the same. It is like putting a dam across a river. While the dam fills up there is no flow downstream but when the dam is full the flow downstream is exactly the same as it was before the dam was built. The effect on crime, of simply imprisoning offenders, is the same.

Q Conviction rates depend on the operation of the CJS. Aren't your results really just telling us about the capacity of the CJS to process people?

A It is true that the parameters describing the categories are generated by the interaction of the CJS with the offending behaviour of offenders in the categories. As the theory is based on convictions it could not be otherwise. However, it can be seen in two ways that the parameters must reflect the underlying criminal behaviour. In the first place each category has very distinct parameters. If we were just seeing the processing of the CJS, we would not expect a distinct category structure. Either all the categories should have similar parameters or there should be a continuous range. Secondly, if we were seeing artefacts of the CJS we would expect to see the number of convictions follow the capacity of the CJS to process cases. What we actually see is the annual number of convictions rising and falling in line with demographics, as predicted by the models based on our theory. The effects of CJS capacity limitations may, however, explain why the trend in the number of prosecutions instigated does not closely follow that of convictions.

9

Summary and Conclusions

Summary

In Chapter 1, we reviewed criminal career research. We pointed out that many simple theories that made quantitative predictions assumed that offences were committed at random (according to a Poisson process). We described simple theories developed by Blumstein et al (1985), Barnett and Lofaso (1985), and Barnett et al (1987, 1989) that predicted the number of offences committed at different ages, as well as the duration of criminal careers. These theories assumed that there were two groups of offenders: frequents (with a high rate of offending and a high probability of recidivism) and occasionals (with a low rate of offending and a low probability of recidivism). They also assumed that the rate of offending and the risk of recidivism were constant over age for each category of offenders.

The theories proposed in this book are based on these ideas but go beyond them in a number of ways. First, the existence of different categories of offenders is revealed by graphical methods. Second, the present analyses are based on very large longitudinal and cross-sectional samples of offenders. Third, the theories decouple rate and risk to identify a high-risk/low-rate group. Fourth, the theories account for the onset process as well as the termination of criminal careers. Fifth, attempts are made to explain the criminal careers of less serious and trivial offenders. Sixth, we show that the categories identified by our mathematical models have different psychological characteristics. Seventh, the theories are applied to explain a wide range of fundamental and applied criminological topics, including not only criminal career features but also the future prison population.

In Chapter 2 we analysed the conviction histories of a large number of offenders from cohort samples drawn from the Offenders Index (OI). Based on that analysis we showed in Chapter 3 how, by making some relatively simple assumptions concerning the process of reconviction and society's response to youthful offending, we were able to construct a theory and mathematical model which accurately replicated the age–crime curves of both the cohort samples and a 1997 cross-sectional sentencing sample.

In Chapter 4 we explored various levels of seriousness of offenders in the context of our theory and as a result a simplified model, which was mathematically more tractable, was developed. That model was shown to adequately describe serious offending and in particular those convictions leading to custodial sentences. We also investigated the versatility of offending of the various offender categories and found that consecutive convictions were more likely to be for different rather than the same offence types. On average the number of different offence types committed by offenders was found to be proportional the logarithm of their conviction counts.

By extending the analysis to include convictions for summary offences, and correcting for missing data, we showed that the overall age–conviction curve could be generated by processes consistent with our theory. The lack of detailed criminal history information on non-standard-list (SL) offenders and missing age data on about half of the non-SL convictions creates considerable uncertainty as to who commits these summary offences. A variety of possibilities were considered. Grove (2003) suggested that a group of trivial offenders committed both SL and up to half of the non-SL (mainly non-motoring) offences with high recidivism and frequency, $p = 0.955$ and $\lambda = 0.85$. As an alternative we then considered the non-SL convictions, with adjustments for missing age data. Based on the assumption that about 40 per cent of males remain totally conviction-free throughout their lives we estimated that a trivial offender category, which included the high-risk/low-rate subcategory, would have a recidivism probability $p = 0.92$ and $\lambda = 1.15$ summary convictions per year. The data suggested that juveniles were rarely convicted of summary offences possibly because many of these offences are unavailable to them and those petty offences that are, would be dealt with less formally.

In Chapter 5 we explored the implications of alternative theories which assumed that offending is directly dependent on the age of the individual. Two extreme theories were considered: the variable λ theory, and the fixed career length theory. In the first, for each individual the propensity to offend was assumed to be governed by the 'invariant' age–crime curve. An individual's rate of offending would increase during adolescence to a peak in late teens and then decline as 'self control' increased with age. The λs were assumed to vary between individuals but the variation within individuals was assumed to follow the same age–crime curve for all individuals. If this variable λ theory was correct, after age 18, we would expect to see inter-conviction times increase (λ reducing) as the conviction serial number, and age, increased. In the Offenders Index data the distributions of inter-conviction times were consistent across all conviction numbers, providing no support for variable λ theories.

The fixed career length theory considered in Chapter 5 assumed that, for an individual, λ is constant throughout the career, and that onset and termination of offending are governed by age. All individuals would have their own λ, onset and termination ages, which when aggregated over the entire population generate the age–crime curve.

Although not normally stated in this way, the existence of an incapacitative effect of average length prison sentences relies on fixed career length theories being true. 'Incapacitation strategies seek to reduce crime by interrupting or "taking a slice out of" an individual career' (Piquero and Blumstein 2007, p 267). Implicitly, for crime to be reduced, time in prison must be time out of the offending career. Some prisoners will reach their termination age whilst in prison and some after release, with a reduced residual career length. We would therefore expect a lower recidivism probability after custody compared with community sentences for similar types of offender. There was no evidence in the Offenders Index data to support either that expectation or fixed career length theories. We concluded that, if neither of these extreme age-based theories were supported by the Offenders Index data, then none but the most contrived age-based theory could explain the observed age–crime curve.

In Chapter 6 we examined data from the Offender Assessment System (OASys) database which was developed jointly by the National Probation Service and the Prison Service of England and Wales. Data from sections 7, 11, and 12, covering lifestyle and associates, thinking and behaviour, and attitudes respectively, were analysed. Initially, some 2,000 offender records from section 11 of the assessment questionnaire, obtained during the pilot study phase of the OASys implementation, were analysed. We showed that the corresponding criminal career data, from the Police National Computer (PNC), conformed to the risk model developed in

Chapter 2, but with parameter values closer to those for the serious offenders considered in Chapter 4.

In analysing the section 11 data we observed that distribution of total score was bi-modal, suggesting a mixture of two separate distributions. Guided by conviction count information we were able to partition the section 11 scores into two distributions: one a negative exponential with mean 4.23, and the other a normal distribution with mean 9.2 and standard deviation 4.8. By dichotomizing the data into subsets with total section 11 scores either 'greater than or equal to' or 'less than' 6 we showed that the former subset conformed to the high recidivism risk profile and the latter subset to a mixture of high- and low-risk in exactly the proportions expected, given the size of the left-hand tail of the normal distribution of scores. This result provides considerable support for our thesis that the risk categories have a basis in the psychological characteristics of offenders.

We then looked more closely at the individual section 11 questions and found, using a statistical technique known as non-metric multi-dimensional scaling (NMDS), that questions 5 to 10 were closely related to each other but distinct from the other questions. Interestingly, reconviction within 18 months was not strongly associated with any of the section 11 scores, suggesting that section 11 would not provide a good basis for predicting actual reconviction within this time scale. A more detailed analysis of the section 11 Q5–10 score distribution, in relation to conviction count, provided some support for the proposition that mastery of 'cognitive behavioural skills' is a protective factor against recidivism. A similar analysis of the Q1–4 scores suggested that the personality attributes measured by these questions were more independent and less amenable to change by intervention programmes.

The second part of our OASys analysis used data from the live computerized system with over 400,000 assessments on 154,000 offenders. This analysis was extended to cover sections 7, 11, and 12 of the questionnaire. The OASys data, which included the offender's previous conviction count, was again shown to be consistent with the dual-risk recidivism model of Chapter 2 and a maximum likelihood fit to the data accounted for over 99.7 per cent of the variance for both male and female subsets. The parameter values were again higher than for the cohorts because of the selection bias of OASys assessments, which include no juvenile offenders and only cases/sentences in which the probation or prison services are involved.

The scores from all the questions from sections 7, 11, and 12 were used in a principal component analysis (PCA) and the offender records were dichotomized on the basis of the 'PCA factor 1' score with a cut point of 0.9. The PCA dichotomy was found to have much greater discriminating power than the simple 'section 11 total score ≥ 6' when applied to the operational OASys data. The dual-risk recidivism model fit estimated that 119,639 of 138,615 assessed offenders were in the high-risk category. The PCA dichotomy identified 108,821 actual offenders, 91 per cent of the estimate, as members of the high-risk category without any criminal career information at all. With the addition of the constraint 'conviction count greater than 6' an additional 5,000 offenders would be identified as high-risk, in total 95 per cent of the dual-risk recidivism model estimate. These results reinforce the finding from the pilot analysis that the risk categories have a basis in the psychological characteristics of offenders. It should perhaps be stressed at this point that the PCA score is not a reconviction prediction score as we would expect some offenders from both sides of the dichotomy not to be reconvicted, but in different proportions. Thus an individual's PCA score can only be interpreted as an indication of that individual's risk category membership and hence the probability of, rather than a prediction of, reconviction.

The OASys records for offenders convicted in April 2004 were linked to an extract of PNC data for all offenders convicted in that month. The dual-risk and dual-rate models were fitted to various subsets of the April 2004 data. It was found that the high-risk parameter estimates were consistent across all subsets but that the proportion parameter[1] in the subsets varied. In the assessed offender subset there appeared to be 100 per cent high-risk offenders, but using the PCA Factor 1 dichotomy, from the OASys analysis, 4.5 per cent of the offenders were identified as low-risk. Using our theory and estimates of λ_h and λ_l, derived from the assessed offender subset, we accurately predicted, to within 1 per cent, the number of reconvictions of assessed offenders in the subsequent 15-month follow-up period. Without the PCA dichotomy, our estimate would have been over 12 per cent higher than the actual number of reconvictions. These results add considerable support to the link between the psychological characteristics of offenders and our theoretical risk categories.

[1] The proportion parameter is the proportion of high-risk offenders in the equivalent cohort, ie the number of high-risk first offenders in the subset.

In Chapter 7 we described the development and structure of the prison population projection system. The central feature is a flow model which is driven by an input stream of 'first custody' prisoners who add to the prison population and an outflow of completed sentence prisoners who are subtracted from it. A proportion of those released, having reoffended and received a further custodial sentence, return to prison and the remainder are reformed and leave the system. The approximate gamma-based models of Chapter 4, together with OPCS population data, are used to estimate the numbers of prisoners at each age and custody number entering and returning to prison. Using sentence length (time served) distribution data, the numbers released are calculated.

The results from a test version of the model for male offenders, which did not make use of actual prison data, are shown in Figures 7.2 to 7.4. The model was run with an initial condition of empty prisons in 1950 with the prison population calculated using only the offending models and population data. Three scenarios were modelled. The first assumed a constant sentencing policy (1992 custody rates) for the whole period from 1950–1993 followed by year-on-year increases in the use of custody to 1999. The second was the same as the first but used actual custody rates from 1975–1993, and the third showed what would have happened had custody rates stayed at 1992 levels through to 1999. The fit to the actual prison data in the first scenario is quite good, in the second scenario the fit is remarkable, and the third scenario demonstrates the power of political speeches. Some results from the full model, which does use prison data for calibration, are also given and discussed. The practical issues which arise, when building models used in real applications, lead to complications caused by details within the CJS procedures. What starts out as a relatively simple theory can result in a very complex model especially if a high level of disaggregation is required by the end users of the model. In the prison population model additional complications also arise because of prisoners on remand and prisoners awaiting sentence which are not covered by the general offending theory.

The theory was also used to develop models to predict the build-up and size of the DNA database. The success of that modelling is illustrated in Figure 7.10.

In Chapter 8 we identified four areas, suggested by our theory, where overall crime might be reduced. These areas are not unique to our theory but simply indicate where successful interventions would have a direct impact on the parameters of our models. We observed that the increased use of informal action and cautions over the period 1963 to 1978 did not appear to reduce criminality[2] but that the more recent 1973 cohort sample and the 1997 sentencing sample did suggest that criminality might have fallen. However for that fall to translate into a reduction in overall crime, cautions would need to be more effective than convictions in order to cause desistance at an earlier point in the offending career. If cautioning is 'as' effective as conviction at eliciting desistance then the only impact would be savings in court time and non-criminalization of some young offenders. If cautioning is less effective than convictions then overall crime would be greater.

Increasing the efficiency of convictions and reducing recidivism were also identified as potential policy levers for reducing crime. We briefly reviewed an evaluation of one intervention programme emanating from the policy document *Criminal Justice: The Way Ahead* (Home Office 2001). The Prolific and other Priority Offender (PPO) programme was intended to increase the efficiency of conviction and reduce recidivism of the target group. However, the evaluators, Dawson and Cuppleditch (2007), were unable to fully explain the results they observed. Using our theory we were able to provide a plausible counterfactual and to explain why the carefully constructed 'propensity score matching' (PSM) control sample provided an unhelpful comparison.

Applying our theory in this instance highlights the importance of understanding the impact of conditioning (sample selection criteria) on the measurements made and the interpretation of the results. Viable theories are an essential component in the evaluation of intervention programmes. Without a clear expectation it is impossible to judge whether an intervention has been successful. In the PPO case even if there had been no intervention effect there would have been an immediate 16 per cent drop in the conviction rate following the implementation, which could easily have been interpreted as caused by the programme. In the event we can see that the observed reduction in monthly convictions after the intervention is twice the size of that expected, suggesting that the PPO programme was indeed successful.

[2] We define criminality as the proportion of the population who will, at some point in their lives, receive at least one standard list conviction.

Viable theories are also important in that they can inform and influence both policy and practice. Our models enable us to calculate the potential impact of policies and quantify both the target group and the likely impact of a successful intervention. If for example we could identify potential high-risk offenders (about 5 per cent of males) and prevent just one in five of them from entering a life of crime then over a period of 20 years crime would reduce by about 10 per cent. Less focused interventions would necessarily be more costly to implement and resource constraints might limit their effectiveness. In addition, the timescale to achieve the benefits might not prove attractive to politicians. Policies to reduce recidivism, if aimed at the high-risk offender category would have a much more immediate effect. A 10 per cent reduction in the recidivism probability of all high-risk offenders would, in the long term, yield a 14 per cent reduction in crime.

Political rhetoric advocating that 'prison works' and that incapacitation reduces crime finds little support in our analysis and theory. While the prison population is increasing or decreasing, crime will certainly decrease or increase respectively, but as soon as the prison population stabilizes crime will, other things being equal, return to its former level over a period of 5 to 10 years. We estimated that the crime reduction effect of the increasing prison population in England and Wales at the end of the twentieth century was only of the order of 1.5 per cent. Our models predicted that demographic changes over the same period would have caused a 12.5 per cent reduction in crime. Together these account for 70 per cent of the crime reduction observed between 1994 and 2000 by the British Crime Survey (BCS). Our models estimate the direct effect of demographics and custody rate changes but there are clearly other processes at work: perhaps general deterrence, due to more severe punishments; target hardening; increasing police numbers; or changes in the dynamics within criminal communities. Also the BCS measures a subset of crime as experienced by the general public rather than the set of standard list crimes considered in our analysis and theory. We concluded Chapter 8 by answering some of the questions that arose when we presented and explained our theories to colleagues and at conferences.

Although not included in the main body of this book, the Appendix is perhaps the key to understanding our approach and the logic which led to the construction of the theory which underpins our models. We first show that probability is a property of populations rather than individuals and discuss how selection criteria affect the frequency distributions within sub-populations and our use of inferred subsets in the analysis of the cohort data. From the assumption of constant probability of an event in some small time interval we derive the Poisson process and show how this leads to the exponential survival time distributions used in Chapters 2 and 3. This derivation also provides the rationale for our use of survival analysis in the estimation of category λs and our suggested distribution of individual λs. We then show how the numbers of offenders in the risk/rate categories in cohorts or cross-sections are calculated from the parameters of our dual-risk and dual-rate models.

We then present an alternative approach to generating a mathematical model from the theory. By assuming that a constant proportion of active offenders reoffend in unit time and solving the differential equation for that process we show that at each offence number the age profile is described by a gamma distribution with shape parameter r, where r is the conviction, or in our Chapter 4 analysis 'conviction opportunity', number. We then show that, by solving the differential equation for the reconviction process in which recidivists are returned to the active population, the residual career length is distributed as a negative exponential distribution with parameter $(1-p)*\lambda$ where p is the reconviction probability. Shinnar and Shinnar (1975) also assumed a negative exponential residual career length distribution in their estimation of the incapacitation effect of incarceration. However, implicit in their analysis was the assumption that individual criminal careers were *fixed in time*. Our analysis of the OI data provides no evidence to support *fixed career length* theories (see Chapter 5).

By assuming that the memory-less property of the negative exponential distribution holds for residual criminal careers, we show that, in the steady state, the size of the active criminal population (and hence crime) is independent of the size of the prison population, unless of course prison sentences are long compared to prisoners' active lifetimes. There is however an incapacitation effect while the prison population is increasing but the effect would disappear quite soon after the prison population stabilized. We calculated that the 8 per cent year on year increase in the prison population which occurred at the end of the last century resulted in only a 1.5 per cent reduction in crime despite a doubling of the prison population.

We also show how our estimates of pre-conviction crime and offender population size were calculated and make estimates of the proportions of each group in both a cohort and the active population, together with the proportions of crime attributable to the risk/rate categories. We conclude the Appendix with a description of the maximum likelihood estimation of the dual-risk recidivism model parameters.

In this book we have described the results of many years work analysing large data sets collected by various criminal justice agencies. The Offenders Index cohort data provided basic criminal career information on a large number of individuals over a long period of time. This analysis enabled us to develop a theoretical understanding of the process leading to conviction and reconviction and why the age profile of offenders appears as it does. The theory is corroborated by cross-sectional data from the OI and the PNC and we have found support for our high and low-risk categorization of the criminal population from psychological assessment data collected by the prison and probation services of England and Wales.

This work has produced a very successful theory both in scientific and practical terms. In scientific terms our theory explains the age–crime curve both overall and for each individual conviction number. It explains both the distribution of inter-conviction times and of residual criminal career lengths. Practically, it has been used successfully to predict the size of the DNA database and the prison population. It has also explained why the results of the PPO evaluation control sample were unhelpful to the evaluators, yet entirely consistent with our theory. Models based on our theory were an integral part of the planning processes of the British Home Office and Ministry of Justice involving expenditure in excess of £5 billion per year from 1998 to 2010; see Councell and Simes (2002) and Ministry of Justice (2008). We know of no other quantitative criminological theory that can claim such scientific and practical success.

However, we do not claim that our theory is complete or fully developed. Following our earlier analogy of planetary motion we are still probably at the circular solar orbit stage but have moved on from geocentric or flat earth models. Just as theories of planetary motion tell us nothing about the composition of planets our theory provides no insight into why offenders start offending or why some desist after one or two convictions and others go on to 20 or 30. Our theory is quantitative and large scale, so although we can calculate how many sentenced offenders will be reconvicted within a given time from a previous conviction, or how many 60-year-old first offenders will be convicted in a given year, to remarkable accuracy, we cannot say which offenders will reoffend, only their probability of reconviction given membership of one of our categories. In the early criminal career, the correct allocation of offenders to categories is problematic. Even with psychological assessment scores providing a good indication, there is still substantial overlap of offender characteristics between the categories, making unequivocal allocation of a proportion of these offenders difficult. Critics may see this as a shortcoming of the theory but we see it as an indication of just one of the areas for future research.

Our large scale theory opens up many questions about why large scale regularities are seen in the aggregate behaviour of offenders. Some of these questions are:

- Are the origins of the categories purely psychological?
- To what extent do members of the non-criminal category have similar psychological characteristics?
- How do social factors impact on the parameters of our models and our categorizations?
- Why has criminality, the proportion of the population in each of our categories, remained substantially constant over time?
- Why is the proportion of offenders who desist after each conviction constant within the categories?
- What causes desistance?
- Why is λ, as determined from the inter-conviction time distributions, constant over time within the categories?
- What are the effects of formal cautions and warnings?
- How does our analysis and theory impact on the criminal career debate?

The Origin of the Offender Categories

In Chapter 2 we observed statistical regularities in the Offenders Index cohort data which suggested that the offender population could be divided into homogeneous categories with respect to their probability of reconviction and their inter-conviction times. In Chapter 6 we found some support for this categorization in the assessment, by the prison and probation services, of the psychological characteristics of adult offenders. However, because of their involvement with these services, the assessed offenders would necessarily have committed some of the more serious offences and thus are not typical of offenders in general.

Without full coverage of offenders (juveniles, less serious, and trivial offenders) and a proper control group of non-offenders, we cannot be certain whether psychological traits *cause* individuals to offend or are simply catalysts. One could certainly envisage individuals who might score highly on some of the attributes measured by sections 7, 11, and 12 of the OASys questionnaire who do not resort to crime. We also have good evidence to suggest that high-scoring offenders desist from crime following conviction in the same proportions as lower scoring offenders in the high-risk category. We also found no direct correlation between the OASys section 11 score and conviction serial number in either the high- or low-risk offender categories. There is clearly scope for more research into the psychological differences between offenders and non-offenders.

Criminality

In Chapter 2 we suggested that criminality (the proportion of the population in our criminal categories) was broadly constant across the cohorts but that the variation was greater than would have occurred simply by chance. We suggested a number of potential causes for the variation, including changes in policy, changes in the nature and perceptions of crime, changes in social conditions and the possibility that cohort size has an amplification effect on criminality (see Maxim 1986). Some or all of these might explain the small variations in cohort criminality observed over the period, but we still require an explanation for the relative stability of criminality over time. Is criminality changeable? Have the right policies or interventions been tried or just not been tried on a large enough scale?

There is substantial evidence that early interventions can reduce criminality (Farrington and Welsh 2007). But, over the time period covered by the OI cohorts, these programmes have not been implemented on a large enough scale in England and Wales to show up in our analysis. During the first decade of the twenty-first century, Sure Start was rolled out and by 2011 over 3,600 children's centres had been set up. However, their impact on crime and criminality could take several more decades to evaluate and even then it might be difficult to separate the effects of Sure Start from other interventions and policy initiatives.

Recidivism

In Chapter 2 we identified trends in the model parameter estimates which were accounted for by changes in the follow-up periods of the cohorts. Because the 1997 sentencing sample estimates were close to and consistent with the longest follow-up period estimates, we concluded that the proportion of offenders, recidivism, and λs in each of our categories were also substantially constant between the cohorts. The analysis in Chapter 6 suggests that the psychological characteristics of offenders are the most likely explanation for the consistency in the proportions in the risk categories. But it is not at all clear why in the 1953 cohort we are able to predict that, of the 1,000 offenders with at least seven convictions, approximately five (there were actually six) would accrue at least 37 convictions. This predictive accuracy is maintained for each conviction number in between on the basis of a constant reconviction probability.

It is even less clear why, within relatively small limits, the constant probability relationship should be replicated in all the other cohorts and consequently in cross-sectional samples. This raises the question: why do offenders desist? And why is the proportion who do, constant after each conviction? Conventional wisdom suggests that: life events such as getting married, getting a job, moving away from criminal associates or simply getting older cause desistance (Sampson and Laub 2003, 2005; Kazemian and Farrington 2010). But we believe that it is more likely that being convicted triggers a life choice decision to 'go straight' and that going straight makes the above life events, apart from getting older, more likely. It would indeed be extraordinary if life events invariably occurred in such a way as to make the reconviction probability constant.

Common sense and logic might suggest that offenders with the greatest psychological problems would be over-represented among offenders with high conviction counts. We found no correlation between the OASys section 11 score and conviction count beyond the high-/low-risk dichotomy. Although all low-risk offenders had low scores, we also identified high-risk offenders with low scores in the proportion predicted, assuming a normal distribution ($\mu = 10$, $\sigma = 4.6$) of section 11 scores for the high-risk offender category. The absence of a correlation also suggests that there are high scoring high-risk offenders who will desist from offending after only one or two convictions in line with the constant reconviction probability.

Psychological characteristics are clearly not the whole story. There are good logical arguments why reconviction probability should change as the criminal career progresses. For example, it can be argued that offenders undeterred by conviction and punishment become entrenched in the criminal lifestyle and find it progressively more difficult to rejoin mainstream society. As a result recidivism should increase as the conviction count increases. This provides a seemingly plausible explanation for increasing recidivism over the first six convictions, but not thereafter. Alternatively, it can be argued that repeated conviction and increasingly severe punishments should reduce the probability of reoffending. A constant reconviction probability however refutes all such arguments, but is in itself something of a puzzle. There is clearly a need for further research into the reasons why individuals desist from crime, whether these reasons change as the criminal career progresses and in particular why the reconviction probability is constant over time within the categories.

Conviction Rate λ

A similar puzzle is that of the constant conviction rates over time. In the Appendix we show how constant probability processes, where the probability of an event occurring in some small interval of time is constant for all such intervals, leads to both the Poisson distribution of events in a time interval 't' and the negative exponential distribution of inter-event times. Our analysis of inter-conviction survival times in Chapters 2 and 5 identified the dual-rate survival model, which is a mixture of two exponentials. This in turn suggests that conviction is a Poisson process operating on two distinct categories of offenders each with constant but different λ.

From our analysis of the April 2004 PNC assessed offender subset there did not appear to be a correlation between psychological characteristics and λ estimates for the high- and low-rate categories. Offenders on both sides of the Factor 1 dichotomy generated similar dual-rate inter-conviction time distributions, with the same λ values but different proportions of high-rate offenders. The different proportions are not surprising as we would expect more low-rate offenders in the side of the dichotomy containing low-risk offenders.

A conviction might be described as the coming together of three components: criminal propensity, opportunity, and the probability of detection or conviction (cf Cohen and Felson 1979). Criminal propensity, the willingness to commit a crime, is a similar concept to our 'risk of reconviction' and could well be associated with the offender's psychological characteristics. Criminal propensity could also explain why high-risk offenders are predominantly high-rate. Limited opportunities or low detection probabilities for some crimes might explain lower conviction rates, and higher police presence and ready identification of the 'usual suspects' might contribute to the higher conviction rates. But the puzzles remain: why are two rate categories so clearly identified by our analysis? And why have the λs, for conviction, remained substantially constant over the period of the cohorts? Over the same period, although crime, by most measures, increased, the annual conviction numbers followed demographic trends in line with our theory and the dual-rate structure and parameter values remained the same. There is clearly scope for more research relating our risk/rate categories to the sociological as well as the psychological characteristics of offenders.

The Effects of Formal Warnings and Cautions

In modelling the *age versus conviction* profile we have postulated that the rise in crime from age 10 to the late teens is due more to society's response to antisocial acts than to real changes in behaviour. Informal action by schools, parents and other agencies would dominate at age 10 with increasing recourse to the criminal justice system as age increases and offenders become capable of real harm. We showed in Chapter 3 that, even when the police became involved, the initial reaction was to issue reprimands or formal warnings to juveniles and cautions to young adults. Even at age 20, less than 40 per cent of offenders were taken to court and convicted on the first police contact. For the second and subsequent contacts, very few young juveniles appear on the PNC but the number increases steadily to age 18 and the proportion convicted also increases to almost 90 per cent convicted at age 20.

In our first attempt at modelling the age–crime curve we speculatively assumed a notional number of potential offenders at age 10 and explicitly modelled cautioning assuming that it was between 45 per cent and 80 per cent and as effective as conviction at eliciting desistance. These assumptions suggest that the majority of the male population actually fall into one of our categories with a substantial proportion ceasing to offend after informal intervention. This is consistent with a straightforward interpretation of self-report studies of offending which seem to suggest that the majority of the male population (96% in the Cambridge Study) has at some time committed a criminal act for which they could in principle have been convicted. On the other hand, there must be at least some doubt as to whether such studies are actually comparing 'like with like'. Will a member of the non-criminal group record an 'offence' with the same definitions used by the authorities for the criminal categories? One explanation of the self-report studies is that they refer to a much lower level of anti-social behaviour than we are concerned with in standard list convictions or formal police reprimands warnings, and cautions. In our age–conviction models of Chapters 3 and 4 we make no assumptions about the effectiveness of cautions, only the probability of 'conviction given age' or the number of conviction opportunities resulting in a caution, for those offenders who are eventually convicted.

The effectiveness of cautioning is however an important issue especially in view of the trend towards increasing use of cautions for the mid teens. Over the period of the cohorts the mid-point of the 'probability of conviction by age' curve increased from 14.7 in the 1953 cohort to 15.8 in the 1997 sentencing sample and the slope of the transition increased from 0.5 to 1.0. This change resulted in a significant reduction in the number of juveniles under age 16 being convicted but little change in criminality estimates between the 1953 and 1968 cohorts. The implication is that cautioning policy over that period did not reduce the number of offenders who were eventually convicted, or that cautioning did not induce desistance. The estimated criminality for the 1973 cohort is lower than the earlier cohorts but the estimate is subject to greater error because of the shorter follow-up period.

If cautioning is as effective as conviction it will reduce criminality and save some young offenders from the stigma of a criminal record and reduce court time. However for cautioning to reduce crime it would need to be more effective than conviction in reducing reoffending, but if cautioning is less effective it would delay desistance and necessarily increase overall crime. As we discussed in Chapter 8 the interventions accompanying juvenile reprimands and formal warnings are crucial in reducing offending and overall crime.

The Criminal Career Debate

At the time of writing the current criminal career debate had been ongoing for over 25 years. To what extent does our analysis and theory resolve the debated issues or simply add to the controversy? At the outset, as described in Chapter 1, the main issue of contention was between two main theoretical camps. On the one hand was the General Theory of Crime proposed by Gottfredson and Hirschi (1990), and on the other hand was the Criminal Career Paradigm stemming from the work of Blumstein et al (1985, 1988a, 1988b), and Barnett et al (1987, 1989).

Gottfredson and Hirschi (1986, 1987) strongly criticized the concept of a criminal career, the influence that the concept was having on policy, and even the value of longitudinal research to criminology. In 1990 they published their own theory in which 'self-control', or rather the lack of it, underlies criminal propensity, measured by the offending rate λ which, within all individuals, rises and falls according to the invariant age–crime curve. Serious criminals have low average self-control and as a consequence high average rates of offending. Non-criminals, on the other hand, would have high self-control and therefore very low offending rates, with all shades of criminality in between.

Greenberg (1991) modelled the distribution of offences over offenders in several cohort samples using a negative binomial (Pareto) distribution by assuming a gamma distribution of λ over the population but a constant λ over time for each individual. However, to explain the age–crime curve it was necessary to propose a uniform decline in individual λ with age. This model on the face of it supports the Gottfredson and Hirschi position. However, Barnett et al (1992) questioned the validity of this model, Greenberg (1992) defended his analysis and Land (1992, pp 149–150) tried to reconcile the two positions, stating that 'the premise that the probability of an individual … committing n offences in … time interval t … is suitably characterized by the Poisson probability distribution' is the common starting point for both modelling approaches.

As we showed in Chapter 5, there is no support for variable λ theories in the Offenders Index data. In addition the observed heterogeneity in λ, as estimated from inter-conviction time distributions, in the OI data is adequately described by our dual-rate mixed exponential model rather than any continuous distribution of λ

over offenders. There is certainly no evidence in the OI data to suggest that any, or even the most prolific, offenders slow down as the career progresses. We find no support for Gottfredson and Hirschi's (1990) General Theory of Crime which requires a declining λ with age and a continuous distribution of λ across individuals.

Our analysis has many similarities with the five parameter model of Barnett et al (1987) and may be regarded as an extension of their model development. With the benefit of a much larger data set, covering criminal careers from age 10 to 46, we have adopted rather different estimation procedures. Similar to Barnett et al (1987), our recidivism analysis identifies two distinct categories of offenders with different but constant recidivism probability. We also identify two categories with different but constant conviction rates. In their analysis, offenders are divided into two categories in which a high recidivism probability coincides with a high rate of offending and a low recidivism probability coincides with a low rate of offending. The two categories were designated *frequents* and *occasionals* which corresponded, approximately, to the *persisters* and *desisters* of Blumstein et al (1985) and our high- and low-risk categories. Offenders were allocated to the *frequent* and *occasional* categories using a quite complex procedure involving their individual conviction history on a likelihood ratio basis.

In our analysis, in Chapter 2, the dual-risk recidivism and dual-rate inter-conviction time models emerge naturally from the data (and can be discovered graphically) without any prior assumptions. The models are simply a very accurate mathematical description of the data. In generating our theory, in Chapter 3, we make a number of assumptions about the process of offending and conviction which generate the same mathematical models. Our analysis validates both the constant desistance probability and Poisson process assumptions made by Barnett et al (1987). However, we found that their two group model was inconsistent with our data, in that there were too few inter-conviction times, in the high-rate part of the distribution, for the estimated number of high-risk reconvictions. We therefore introduced a third group of low-rate *persisters*.

Later criminal career researchers (eg Moffitt 1993; Nagin and Land 1993; Nagin, Farrington, and Moffitt 1995; Sampson and Laub 2003, 2005) have analysed criminal careers in terms of life-course trajectories, linking early childhood characteristics and adolescent developmental factors to involvement in crime over the life course. Moffitt (1993) identified two criminal categories, designated *life-course-persistent* (LCP) and *adolescence-limited* (AL). The former were a small group who had early neuropsychological deficit, life disadvantage and high levels of antisocial behaviour in childhood. The latter had more normal early childhood characteristics, joined in with delinquent behaviour during adolescence but had shorter periods of involvement in crime, desisting in early adulthood. Moffitt (1993) suggested that the age–crime curve reflected the build-up and decline of participation of the adolescence limited group of offenders.

Nagin and Land (1993) identified three criminal categories in panel data from the Cambridge Study which were designated *High-Rate Chronics*, *Adolescence-Limited*, and *Low-Rate Chronics*. The categories were identified using complex modelling procedures in which λ and *intermittency in offending* were assumed to vary within individuals according to a quadratic function of age. Both intermittency and λ were also assumed to vary across the population depending on both observed early life characteristics and unobserved sources of heterogeneity. In all, their modelling involved the estimation of some 19 parameters. They concluded that their analysis supported elements of both criminal propensity theory and criminal career theory. Nagin et al (1995) extended this study to include self-reports of offending and other life-course outcomes. They found that the adolescence limited group tended to continue with their antisocial activities but without sustaining further convictions up to age 32.

Sampson and Laub (2003, 2005), in their follow-up of the Glueck and Glueck (1950) offender sample through to age 70, modelled the age–crime profiles for three crime types, using a Poisson regression model with a best fit cubic polynomial in age. The data was then dichotomized on the basis of a raft of childhood delinquency measures and the trajectory profiles recalculated. They concluded that 'the aggregate age–crime curve is not the same as individual trajectories' and 'although childhood prognoses are reasonably accurate in terms of predicting levels of crime between individuals, they do not yield distinct groupings that are valid prospectively in a straightforward test' (Sampson and Laub 2003, p 525). They retrospectively identified categories, or latent classes, corresponding to different trajectories of offending, but these categories were not readily identifiable prospectively. They also found single peak trajectories and a consistent decline in offending with increasing age for all crime types and latent classes. However, they did not measure the individual frequency of offending by active offenders; rather, they measured the offending rate over all offenders and non-offenders.

On the face of it, our analysis and theory are at odds with these life-course trajectory interpretations of the criminal career paradigm. Our models appear simplistic and certainly ignore all the early life correlates of crime. Yet they have also much in common with the offender groupings identified in the life-course trajectories. Moffitt's life-course-persistent offenders and Nagin's chronics are in many respects similar to our high-risk offenders. Adolescence-limited offenders might also have much in common with our low-risk offenders. In particular the proportions of the male population in the corresponding Moffitt (1993) categories are identical to ours. Both Moffitt's taxonomy and our theory regard criminal activity as a continuation of pre-existing antisocial tendencies. We would expect such tendencies to be more obvious in early childhood in the LCP/high-risk than in the AL/low-risk categories. Nagin's high- and low-rate chronics chime well with our high- and low-rate/high-risk offender categories.

Our main points of difference from other theories involve the modelling of the process, the interpretation of the observations and the estimation procedures for the model parameters. The use of polynomial models to describe the age–crime curve is atheoretical, in that there is no logical or criminological justification for offending rates (and intermittency in the Nagin model) to depend on arbitrary powers of age other than this approximates the shape of the curve. Indeed polynomials can be made to fit any curve. The offending rates in both models are calculated as the average number of offences (convictions) in given time periods and the divisors for the averages would appear to be the group sizes, resulting in different λs in each of the age bands considered. Although desistance is discussed it is not specifically modelled in either Nagin's or Sampson and Laub's theories.

In contrast we estimate our λs directly from the inter-event time distribution, as Nagin and Land (1993, p 333, footnote 5) would have preferred to do, thus providing life-course estimates. The negative exponential survival time distributions identified in our analysis are evidence of a Poisson processes and the observed frequencies of inter-conviction times, from close to zero to 30 years or more, are entirely consistent with the estimates of the λs. Apparent intermittency in offending is thus a natural consequence of the Poisson process and needs no separate modelling. Apparent 'crime sprees' also occur naturally as shorter inter-conviction times are more likely than longer ones and consecutive convictions are more likely to be close together than far apart. This effect is more noticeable after a long gap or when samples are conditioned on a conviction at time $t = 0$.

Our definition of an active offender is therefore: an individual who is willing to commit a *standard list* offence given the right circumstances, rather than one who has actually been convicted. The potential for long inter-conviction times,[3] compared with observation periods, makes estimation of λ, from conviction counts in a short period, problematic, especially when there are two processes operating. In a one-year time interval 37 per cent of high-rate and 78 per cent of low-rate active offenders would not be expected to sustain a conviction. Also the estimate of λ would depend on the divisor, the definition of active, and the conditioning of the sample. In using inter-conviction times our sample is conditioned on (selected according to) *more than one conviction over the whole observation period of 35 years*, and includes only offenders who are active at the time of measurement. Although there may be a small number of active offenders yet to reoffend whose next inter-conviction time is not included, our estimates are not influenced by the large number of offenders who have desisted.

It is clear from our analysis that virtually all offenders eventually desist from crime. Our dual-risk recidivism model suggests that, within our risk categories, irrespective of age and previous conviction history, the probability of desistance after the next conviction is constant. Offending is correlated with age simply because offenders take time to accumulate convictions and only a proportion make the life-choice decision to 'go straight', or at least to modify their behaviour so as not to risk reconviction, at each conviction. For active offenders the residual career length is distributed as a negative exponential with mean $1/(q*\lambda)$ where q is the probability of desistance and λ is the expected time to the next conviction.

Desistance can occur at any age and in both risk categories is skewed towards younger offenders simply because of the negative exponential distribution. It is therefore not difficult to find a substantial group

[3] The time to the next conviction has the same distribution as the inter-conviction time because of the memory-less property of the negative exponential distribution.

of adolescence-limited offenders retrospectively. Our analysis would also suggest that a significant proportion of the individuals identified as AL, at age 32, would in fact be convicted again later in life. Sampson and Laub's (2003) finding that early risk factors predicted levels of crime but could not identify trajectories, is again consistent with our process driven theory and their suggestion of *life-course desisters* is perhaps a better description than *life-course persisters*.

In our theory the age–crime curve is an artefact of the (re)conviction process and is fully explained by it. The theory is consistent with and indeed extends the early criminal career work of Barnett et al (1987) but leads to different explanations of the life-course trajectory observations of later research. We believe that the life-course risk factors, like the OASys assessments, would correlate with our risk categories and might improve the discrimination between categories. Our analysis has identified and our theory predicts a significant group of late onset offenders, an area of criminal career research which has received little attention up to now, in part because the focus has been on youth crime (but see Zara and Farrington 2009).

Conclusions

We have now come to the end of our journey. We have proposed a simple theory that there are three categories of offenders: high-risk/high-rate, high-risk/low-rate, and low-risk/low-rate. Each category has a constant risk of reconviction and a constant rate of offending. Like many other scholars, we have assumed that crimes occur at random over time, according to a Poisson process. This simple theory makes exact quantitative predictions, and we have shown that it can explain a wide range of criminal career findings, for example concerning the age–crime curve. The categories of offenders were originally revealed by plotting graphs, and we have shown that they have different psychological characteristics. We have shown that individual age–crime curves are very different from the aggregate curve. We have also explained the onset of offending by reference to how official reactions to offending change during the juvenile years, and we have extended our theory to explain the criminal careers of less serious and trivial offenders.

Our theory has many policy implications. We have estimated that there are about 100,000 prolific offenders in England and Wales at any given time. We have shown that custodial and non-custodial sentences have no differential effects on criminal careers and that on release from prison the expected duration of the residual criminal career is the same as after a non-custodial sentence (and hence there is no incapacitative effect). The most important influence on desistance is getting convicted. We have shown that the increasing use of cautions did not cause a decrease in the life-time prevalence of convictions (which is generally constant over time) and we have applied our theory to predict the prison population and the number of offenders in the DNA database.

We believe that more criminal career research is needed based on longitudinal self-reports of offending. In the Cambridge Study, Farrington et al (2006) estimated that there were on average 39 self-reported offences for every conviction occasion. It is important to estimate the scaling-up factor from convictions to offences. We also believe that more research is needed on the early prediction of different categories of offenders and on predicting the residual length of criminal careers. We hope that our work will inspire others to build on our theory to make more wide-ranging quantitative predictions, especially about the influence of risk and protective factors, and life events, at different ages and stages of criminal careers. This is the new frontier.

Appendix
Mathematical Notes

Introduction

In the main body of this book we have described a quantitative theory of crime. The theory is based on extensive data collected by criminal justice agencies and as a result it might more accurately be described as a theory of *conviction and reconviction*, or *crime as it is experienced by the criminal justice system*. We have tried to make our description non-technical, relying mainly on graphical representations of both the data and our models to support our arguments. Inevitably we have had to include mathematical equations where necessary but have not fully explained the link between our basic assumptions stated in Chapter 3 and the mathematical formulation of the theory. If the theory is to be used in practical applications, like prison population forecasting or estimating the impact of policy, a more detailed exposition of the mathematics is needed. This Appendix is intended to provide the mathematical and statistical logic and understanding necessary to develop the theory and apply it.

The theory developed in Chapters 2 and 3, and in particular the mathematics of the theory, is based on the concept of constant probabilities. It is important therefore for us to make clear what we understand by probability. There are two schools of thought on probability: the Bayesian School and the Frequentist School. Bayesians see probability as a reflection of the state of knowledge concerning some future event, which is updated in the light of experiment or experience. In the absence of any empirical evidence a purely subjective probability is assigned as a prior probability which is then updated to form a posterior probability in the light of experience. This approach is ideally suited to activities like horse racing or stock market analysis but, in our view is less useful when studying the random events occurring in stable stochastic systems, for example in physics (radioactive decay), or in criminology (the large-scale behaviour of criminals in the population). Frequentists, on the other hand, define probability in terms of relative frequencies. Probabilities cannot be assigned to events without some pre-existing data or well founded theoretical reasoning concerning the system or population in which the event might occur. In practice Bayesians effectively use the Frequentist's methods where the data is available.

Constant Probability Systems

In the context of our theory, among the events that we consider is 'one or more criminal convictions in a life time'. If we select an individual at random from the entire population, we define the probability of that individual being convicted within their lifetime as the ratio of the number of individuals who have been or will be convicted to the total number of individuals in the population. There is clearly a problem doing the calculation as we do not know the number of individuals who will be convicted in the future. We must therefore estimate this probability from the information that we do have. Our data source, the Offenders Index, enabled the selection of cohort samples of individuals born in one of four weeks in selected years, 1953, 1958, 1963, 1968, and 1973. In Chapter 2 we made estimates of the whole life conviction probability (the cohort criminality) for each of the cohorts. The whole life criminality was calculated using the age–crime model of Chapter 3 to estimate the number who had or would be convicted.

The criminality estimate was found to vary between the cohorts by more than could be accounted for simply by chance, suggesting that there is also some additional stochastic variation in criminality over time. It is also clear from Chapter 2 that male and female criminalities are very different both from each other and from the overall value. Thus we can only estimate the probability of an event for an individual in the context of the population to which that individual belongs. Probability is a property of the population and not of the individual. To some extent this chimes with the Bayesian view. If we do not know the gender of the individual we would assign the whole population probability and update that when the gender was known.

In developing our theory we make use of the concept of randomness. A random selection is made on the basis of no prior knowledge, except that the selection is from a known parent population. A random selection is assumed to have the same statistical properties as the parent population. Selecting on the basis of some property or characteristic would not be random, but having made the selection a new parent population would be defined from which a random selection could then be made. In the main text we frequently make non-random selections to create subsets (categories) of offenders with specific characteristics: males/females, serious/less serious offenders, etc. In these subsets the statistical structure is often similar but with different parameters, but not necessarily as both will depend on the selection criterion (conditioning).

We also make use of inferred subsets where collectively the subset (group or category) exhibits a frequency distribution which infers that the members of the subset share a common parameter value for the property that generates the distribution. The main examples of inferred categories are those with a common constant probability of reconviction (or desistance) or a constant probability of offending (being convicted) in a given time interval. These inferred categories are said to be homogeneous with respect to the specified property. Moving up a level, where the parent population contains two or more of these inferred categories it is said to be heterogeneous with respect to the specified property.

In our analysis of recidivism, for each cohort, the parent population was the set of individuals born in one of four weeks in the cohort year who were convicted of one or more offences in the follow-up period. Recidivism is defined as the proportion of offenders with at least n convictions who are reconvicted. In the parent population the distribution of offence number was found to be heterogeneous with respect to recidivism probability. However we were able to create two inferred subsets (categories) that were homogeneous with respect to recidivism probability p, which was constant for all conviction numbers. Within the inferred categories the probability of at least n convictions was simply $p^{(n-1)}$.

In our analysis of reconviction times it is not immediately obvious that we are again dealing with a constant probability process, or why we can infer this from the data. By way of explanation, let us assume that the probability p of an event (say an offender committing a crime) is constant in any/all small interval/s of time and on average there are λ events in unit time (say crimes per year). In a time interval t (years) there will on average be $\lambda * t$ events. If there are n of our small time intervals in time t: then $\lambda * t = n * p$. By considering each of the n intervals as an independent opportunity for the event to occur we can calculate the probability of exactly zero, one, two etc events occurring in time t simply by using the binomial expansion:

$$(q+p)^n = q^n + n \cdot p \cdot q^{n-1} + \frac{n \cdot (n-1)p^2 \cdot q^{n-2}}{2!} + \frac{n \cdot (n-1) \cdot (n-2) \cdot p^3 \cdot q^{n-3}}{3!} + \dots \tag{A.1}$$

where: $q = 1-p$

If we now assume that our small time intervals get smaller and smaller so that n tends to ∞ and p tends to zero and that this happens in such a way that $n*p = \lambda*t$ remains true and $n*(n-1)*p^2 = (n*p)^2$ etc then in the limit the right-hand side of Equation A.1 becomes:

$$1 + \lambda \cdot t + \frac{(\lambda \cdot t)^2}{2!} + \frac{(\lambda \cdot t)^3}{3!} + \dots + \frac{(\lambda \cdot t)^r}{r!} + \dots \tag{A.2}$$

But this is the series expansion of $e^{\lambda * t}$ and, as this is a probability distribution, the sum should be equal to 1. Dividing each term by $e^{\lambda * t}$ satisfies this requirement, and successive terms in the expansion give the probability of 0, 1, 2, 3 or in general r events in the time interval t. The probability of exactly r events in a time interval t is given by:

$$P(r,t) = e^{-\lambda \cdot t} \frac{(\lambda \cdot t)^r}{r!} \qquad \text{(A.3)}$$

The right hand side of Equation A.3 is the general term in the Poisson distribution.

Of particular interest in studying the Poisson process is the time interval between successive events or put another way the probability of no events in the time interval t expressed as a function of t. Putting $r = 0$ in Equation A.3 gives the probability that the inter-event time is greater than t:

$$P(\mathit{time\ to\ next\ event} > t) = e^{-\lambda \cdot t} \qquad \text{(A.4)}$$

Equation A.4 is of the form of the survival time distributions used in the analyses of Chapter 2 with average survival time $1/\lambda$. If in the above derivations we assumed that we selected events at random with probability p_s then the average number of selected events in time interval t would become $\lambda_s * t = p_s * \lambda * t$, ie $\lambda_s = p_s * \lambda$ and, substituting λ_s for λ in Equations A.2 to A.4, the derivation would proceed in exactly the same way, resulting in a further Poisson process with parameter λ_s.

We use this result in Chapter 3 to account for the apparent disparity between the time to first conviction and the inter-conviction time distributions.[1] This result also implies that convictions are in effect a random selection from crimes committed which also occur as random events in a Poisson process. It should be noted here that any one of the characteristics of the Poisson process implies the others. A negative exponential distribution of inter-event times implies a Poisson distribution of events in any given time interval which in turn implies a constant probability of an event occurring in any small interval of time within the observation period.

The Poisson process is a common feature of criminal career models (see eg Barnett et al 1987; Canela-Cacho et al 1997; Greenberg 1991; Maltz 1996). In criminal career research the rate of offending λ is often estimated from surveys of individuals which are heavily conditioned by the target sample of the survey, which could be anything from the general population to prison inmates. Piquero and Blumstein (2007) in their discussion of incapacitation make many references to λ. They suggest that 'Rather than focusing on individual-level measurement of λ, it is more reasonable to direct attention to the distribution of λ among various populations'.

[1] In Chapter 3 we use this result in the form of the inter-event time T which is equal to $1/\lambda$. ie selecting events at random with probability p results in a stream of random events with inter-event time $1/p * \lambda = T/p$.

In estimating the distribution of λ for offenders in general, Greenberg (1991) assumed that the population was heterogeneous with respect to λ and that λ was distributed as a gamma variate leading to a Pareto distribution for the number of crimes in time t. Canela-Cacho et al (1997) also assumed heterogeneity for λ in the offender population. They assumed that the distribution of λ was the sum of r exponential distributions and r equal to 3 was required to fit data from the Rand surveys of prison inmates in the late 1970s.

In our model we also assume heterogeneity, dividing our parent population into just two categories which are homogeneous with respect to λ. This implies that individuals in our inferred categories commit crimes as a Poisson process. We estimate the Poisson rate λ from inter-conviction survival times. This estimation technique has a number of advantages. It automatically accommodates low individual λs, which is very important when we analyse first convictions. The 'too many zeros' problem (Chaikin and Rolph 1981) encountered when counting convictions in some short time period does not occur; desistance from crime does not influence the estimation of λ; and censorship, caused by the limit of the observation period, is clearly identifiable on the survival plot and can be compensated for.

However, we can derive a distribution for individual λs. An individual measurement of the number, r, of offences committed in unit time, say one year, by an individual offender can be considered as a random instance from the Poisson distribution of Equation A.3, with $t = 1$. The estimate of individual λ from that instance is simply r. Therefore Equation A.3 (with $t = 1$) gives the probability distribution of individual λs, ie a Poisson distribution of r with mean λ. Estimating λ from one year sub-samples for a birth cohort would of course involve the too many zeroes problem caused by desistance and, unless the one year samples were drawn from the whole observation period, the estimation process would also suffer from selection bias induced by the age–crime curve. To avoid these problems we have contented ourselves with the inter-conviction survival time method of estimation.

Allocation of Offenders to the Risk/Rate Categories

In Chapter 2 we derived the dual-risk recidivism model and the dual-rate survival time model, Equations 2.4 and 2.8 respectively. We repeat them here for ease of reference:

The risk equation

$$Y(n) = A \cdot \left(a \cdot p_h^{(n-1)} + (1-a) \cdot p_l^{(n-1)}\right) \tag{A.5}$$

The rate equation

$$S(t) = B \cdot \left(b \cdot e^{-\lambda_h \cdot t} + (1-b) \cdot e^{-\lambda_l \cdot t}\right) \tag{A.6}$$

Where:

- **N** is the conviction (court appearance) number,
- **$Y(n)$** is the number of offenders in a cohort or cross-section sample with at least **n** convictions,
- **A** is the number of convicted offenders in the cohort or cohort equivalent,
- **P_h** is the probability that a high-risk offender will reoffend,
- **P_l** is the probability that a low-risk offender will reoffend,
- **A** is the proportion of high-risk offenders,
- **$S(t)$** is the number of reconvictions of offenders surviving **t** years from their previous conviction,
- **B** is the total number of reconvictions in the sample,
- **λ_h** is 1/(mean time to next conviction) for high-rate offenders,
- **λ_h** is 1/(mean time to next conviction) for low-rate offenders,
- **b** is the proportion parameter for rate.

From Equation A.5 the total number of convictions (court appearances) sustained for a cohort is given by:

$$Y_{total} = \sum_{n=1}^{\infty} Y(n) \qquad \text{(A.7)}$$

This is expanded to:

$$Y_{total} = \sum_{n=1}^{\infty} \left(A \cdot a \cdot p_h^{(n-1)}\right) + \sum_{n=1}^{\infty} \left(A \cdot (1-a) \cdot p_l^{(n-1)}\right) \qquad \text{(A.8)}$$

For a cross-section, Equation, A.7 represents the total number of offenders in the sample. Equation A.8, summing over the range of **n** = 2 to ∞, gives the number of reconvictions for the cohort or the number of offenders with more than one conviction for the cross-section. The summations in Equation A.8 separately provide the estimates for the high- and low-risk offender categories. It is assumed that all low-risk offenders are low-rate but that high-risk offenders can be either high or low-rate. These assumptions lead to the following relationships:

The total number of reconvictions:

$$S_{total} = \sum_{n=2}^{\infty} \left(A \cdot a \cdot p_h^{(n-1)}\right) + \sum_{n=2}^{\infty} \left(A \cdot (1-a) \cdot p_l^{(n-1)}\right) \qquad \text{(A.9)}$$

The number of high-risk/low-rate reconvictions:

$$S_{hl} = A \cdot a \cdot \sum_{n=2}^{\infty} p_n^{(n-1)} - b \cdot S_{total} \qquad \text{(A.10)}$$

The number of low-risk/low-rate reconvictions:

$$S_{ll} = A \cdot (1-a) \cdot \sum_{n=2}^{\infty} \left(p_l^{(n-1)}\right) \qquad \text{(A.11)}$$

And the number of high-risk/high-rate reconvictions:

$$S_{hh} = b \cdot S_{total} \tag{A.12}$$

For a cohort these can be translated into numbers of offenders as follows.

In the low-risk/low-rate category:

$$N_{ll} = Y(1) \cdot (1 - a) \tag{A.13}$$

In the high-risk/high-rate category:

$$N_{hh} = Y(1) \cdot a \cdot \frac{S_{hh}}{S_{hh} + S_{hl}} \tag{A.14}$$

In the high-risk/low-rate category:

$$N_{hl} = Y(1) \cdot a \cdot \left(\frac{S_{hl}}{S_{hh} + S_{hl}} \right) \tag{A.15}$$

An Alternative Modelling Approach

In Chapter 3 we derived equations for the age–crime (conviction) curve in which we explicitly modelled the apparent rise in crime between the ages of 10 and 18. This approach worked well for first convictions but led to equations requiring numerical rather than analytic solutions for subsequent convictions. The problem was caused by the explicit modelling of the rise in crime. We now consider a system in which we assume that crime itself does not vary with age and in which crimes are committed randomly and in direct proportion to the number of active offenders. In what follows, an 'offence' refers to 'a conviction opportunity', ie where the offender is caught and could be, but isn't necessarily, convicted. We also assume that the population is homogeneous with respect to offending.

Let $\mathbf{N}_r(t)$ be the number of offenders in the population responsible for r offences in the period up to time t. We start our process at time $t = 0$ with $\mathbf{N}_0(0)$ potential offenders who have no previous offences, thus $\mathbf{N}_r(0) = 0$ for all non-zero r. This is the situation for all potential offenders on their 10th birthday as, by definition, under-10s cannot commit crime. As offenders commit each offence they move from the sub-population with r offences to that with $r + 1$ offences and this occurs at rate $\boldsymbol{\lambda} * \mathbf{N}_r(t)$. This system can be described as an infinite series of first order linear differential equations:

$$\frac{dN_r(t)}{dt} = \lambda \cdot N_{r-1}(t) - \lambda \cdot N_r(t) \qquad r \geq 0 \tag{A.16}$$

The general solution to this equation is:

$$N_r(t) = N_r(0) \cdot e^{-\lambda \cdot t} + \lambda \cdot e^{-\lambda \cdot t} \cdot \int_0^t e^{\lambda \cdot \tau} \cdot N_{r-1}(\tau) \cdot d\tau \qquad \text{(A.17)}$$

Now for $r = 0$ the term $N_{r-1}(t)$ is undefined in the system and does not exist, thus:

$$N_0(t) = N_0(0) \cdot e^{-\lambda \cdot t} \qquad \text{(A.18)}$$

For $r > 0$, $N_r(0) = 0$, and the integral term in Equation A.17 evaluates to:

$$N_1(t) = N_0(0) \cdot \lambda \cdot t \cdot e^{-\lambda \cdot t} \quad \text{for } r = 1 \qquad \text{(A.19)}$$

and:

$$N_2(t) = \frac{1}{2} N_0(0) \cdot (\lambda \cdot t)^2 \cdot e^{-\lambda \cdot t} \quad \text{for } r = 2 \qquad \text{(A.20)}$$

and in general:

$$N_r(t) = N_0(0) \cdot \frac{(\lambda \cdot t)^r \cdot e^{-\lambda \cdot t}}{r!} \qquad \text{(A.21)}$$

Thus the number of offenders with exactly r offences at time t is the product of the total number of potential offenders in the population, $N_0(0)$, and the probability of r events in time t in a Poisson process with mean λ (see Equation A.3). We can now derive an expression for the rate of first offences (equal to the rate of decline in the number of offenders with no offences) as a function of t (age), either by substituting for $N_0(t)$ from Equation A.18 into Equation A.16 with $r = 0$, or by differentiating A.18 to give:

$$-\frac{dN_0(t)}{dt} = \lambda \cdot N_0(0) \cdot e^{-\lambda \cdot t} \qquad \text{(A.22)}$$

But this suggests that at $t = 0$ the offending rate is $\lambda * N_0(0)$ whereas we know that at age 10 ($t = 0$) the offending rate should be very close to zero. However, if we assume that early conviction opportunities are ignored and do not result in conviction, the probability distribution of the first recorded offence/conviction as a function of time would be some combination of the probability distributions of the second, third, etc offences as functions of time. The probability density of the rth offence occurring at time t is simply derived from the probability of $r - 1$ offences in time t giving:

$$Pdf(offence(r)@time(t)) = \lambda \cdot \frac{(\lambda \cdot t)^{r-1} \cdot e^{-\lambda \cdot t}}{(r-1)!} = \frac{\lambda \cdot (\lambda \cdot t)^{r-1} \cdot e^{-\lambda \cdot t}}{\Gamma(r)} \tag{A.23}$$

For integer values of r: $\Gamma(r) = (r-1)!$

This is the gamma distribution, which we introduced in Chapter 4 as an approximation to account for the rise in crime in the early part of the criminal career.

Incapacitation

The negative exponential distribution has the property of being *memory-less*, in the sense that what happens after time t is independent of what happened before. We can therefore choose to start our (re-) conviction process at any time. If in Equation A.16 we assume that, instead of moving offenders on into the next offence-count subset, we return recidivists into the active offender pool and move the desisters into a non-offender pool then the differential equation becomes:

$$\frac{dN(t)}{dt} = -\lambda \cdot N(t) + p \cdot \lambda \cdot N(t) = -\lambda \cdot (1-p) \cdot N(t) \tag{A.24}$$

This has the solution:

$$N(t) = N(0) \cdot e^{-\lambda \cdot (1-p) \cdot t} \tag{A.25}$$

Where $N(t)$ is the number of (*active*) offenders still offending at time t and $N(0)$ is the number who will offend at some time after we choose to start the process. From this we can see that the average residual career length of active offenders, from our arbitrary start time, is $1/(\lambda*(1-p))$. In this last expression, the operative word is *active* and this is very important when considering incapacitation. Avi-Itzhik and Shinnar (1973) and Shinnar and Shinnar (1975) in their models of crime made many basic assumptions in common with us. However, in estimating incapacitation, like us they assumed that criminal career length is exponentially distributed, but they also implicitly assumed that for an individual the career is *fixed in time*, which implies that offenders could terminate their careers whilst incarcerated and those still active on release would have a reduced residual career length (ie active offending time = career length – time in prison). Their result that incapacitation reduces crime relies on this assumption; the dependency on the invariance of criminal career length with respect to CJS interventions is not made explicit in their analysis.

Using their formulation and parameter estimates from UK data, Tarling (1993, pp 143–146) estimated that the extant prison populations in England and Wales in 1975, 1980, and 1986 had reduced recorded crime by between 5.8 per cent and 9 per cent. But as we show below even these modest estimates would appear to be gross exaggerations.

As reported in Chapter 5, from the 1953 cohort, for high-risk offenders with at least one custodial sentence and more than four convictions, the proportion of reconvictions after custody was 84.8 per cent compared with 83.1 per cent after non-custodial disposals. Similarly, from Table 5.2 the four year reconviction proportions after custody and supervision were 64.4 per cent and 62.5 per cent respectively. In both of these situations, where recidivism risk and seriousness is controlled for, we would have expected some 11 per cent fewer reconvictions after custodial, compared with non-custodial, sentences for *fixed in time* careers. This is because, for high-rate offenders our estimated residual career length would be about five years and average prison time served about seven months during which time 11 per cent of offenders, who otherwise would have reoffended, should desist and not reoffend on release, which should result in 11 per cent fewer reconvictions than for non-custodial disposals. Tarling's shorter residual career length estimates would result in even higher reductions in recidivism. What was actually observed is that recidivism tends to be higher following custody than for non-custodial sentences. There is therefore no evidence in these data that criminal careers terminate during incarceration rather than at the point of conviction, in fact to the contrary. We therefore conclude that there is no overall crime reduction brought about by incapacitation except where offenders are incarcerated for a large proportion of their active lives.

In our theory we assume that the career termination decision is made at the time of, and as a result of, conviction. This assumption implies that on release from prison the proportion p, destined to reoffend, is the same as for any other disposal, as is the residual career length. Released prisoners simply rejoin the active offender pool in which the residual career length is distributed exponentially with the same constant parameter value. We now consider incapacitation from the viewpoint of our theory. In a simplified situation where the birth rate is constant over time and there is a single offender group in which criminality = c, incarceration probability = p_c, and conviction rate = λ are also all constant, we can create a simple model of the impact of prison on crime.

In our theory crime is proportional to the active criminal population and we therefore need to calculate the impact of prison on the number of active offenders. With a constant birth rate, the age–crime curve for all cohorts is the same. If for the moment we ignore crimes committed prior to the first conviction opportunity and start our process at age 10 or at the conviction opportunity before the first conviction, whichever is later, we can calculate, using Equation A.25, the rate of conviction for the cohort at time t. As all of the cohorts have identical rate of conviction profiles, we can use this to calculate the overall number of convictions by integrating A.25 over $t = 0$ to ∞:

$$N(\infty) = N(0) \cdot \int_0^{\infty} e^{-\lambda \cdot (1-p) \cdot t} dt = \frac{N(0)}{\lambda \cdot (1-p)} \tag{A.26}$$

Here $N(0)$ is the number of offenders in one homogeneous category of a cohort sample and $N(\infty)$ is the lifetime total number of convictions sustained by the category, but, because all cohorts are equivalent, $N(0)$ and $N(\infty)$ are also equal to the number of new, $N_N(t)$, and active, $N_A(t)$, offenders respectively in the equivalent category of active offenders at time t. If the system is in equilibrium, the number of offenders giving up crime, $N_A(t)*(1-p)$, will be balanced by the number of new offenders, $N_N(t)$, being convicted for the first time and hence entering the system ($N_N(t)$ is a constant because birth rate is assumed constant). This is trivially true for empty prisons. If we now incarcerate a proportion p_c of those convicted and sentence them to an average time served $1/\lambda_s$ then the prison population $N_p(t)$ would build up until the prison element of the system was also in equilibrium, thus the rate of change in the active offender population is given by:

$$\frac{dN_A(t)}{dt} = [N_N(t) - \lambda \cdot (1-p) \cdot N_A(t)] + p \cdot [\lambda_s \cdot N_p(t) - p_c \cdot \lambda \cdot N_A(t)] \tag{A.27}$$

During the build-up of the prison population the right hand bracketed (prison) term in A.27 will become negative as more individuals enter prison than leave; this will cause the active population $N_A(t)$ to reduce, causing the left hand bracketed (active) term to become more positive; this will cause the rate of decrease of $N_A(t)$ over time to slow down and change sign to become an increase; eventually the prison population will stabilize and the prison and active terms will both return to zero. In the steady state the active population is given by:

$$N_A(t) = \frac{N_N(t)}{\lambda \cdot (1-p)} \tag{A.28}$$

But, remembering that in a stable population $N_A(t) \equiv N(\infty)$ and $N_N(t) \equiv N(0)$, this is the same situation as existed when the prisons were empty; see Equation A.26. Thus, in the steady state, the active population, $N_A(t)$, and by inference crime, is independent of the actual prison population. However, following a step change in custodial sentencing policy, both the active population and crime will reduce if the prison population is increasing and increase if it is reducing. The changes in active population (crime rate) are transient but the changes in prison population persist, unless of course the prison population increases/decreases indefinitely. In the steady state the prison population, $N_p(t)$ is given by:

$$N_p(t) = \frac{p_c \cdot \lambda}{\lambda_s} \cdot N_A(t) \tag{A.29}$$

The steady state prison population is therefore proportional to the product of the probability of a custodial sentence and sentence length (time served).

If we now assume that the prison population is increased at a constant linear rate r (extra inmates per year) then Equation A.27 would become:

$$\frac{dN_A(t)}{dt} = \left[N_N(t) - p \cdot r - \lambda \cdot (1-p) \cdot N_A(t)\right] \tag{A.30}$$

Which has the solution:

$$N_A(t) = \frac{N_N(t) - p \cdot r}{\lambda \cdot (1-p)} \cdot \left(1 - e^{-\lambda \cdot (1-p) \cdot t}\right) \tag{A.31}$$

Over time the exponential term tends to zero, thus in the steady state:

$$N_A = N_A(0) - \frac{p \cdot r}{\lambda \cdot (1-p)} \tag{A.32}$$

The right hand side of Equation A.32 is independent of t and therefore constant, thus there is an ongoing reduction in the active population of:

$$\Delta N_A = \frac{p \cdot r}{\lambda \cdot (1-p)} \tag{A.33}$$

The constant rate of increase in prison population can be expressed as:

$$r = \lambda \cdot N_A(0) \cdot \Delta p_c \tag{A.34}$$

Giving the proportionate change in the active population of:

$$\frac{\Delta N_A}{N_A(0)} = \frac{p \cdot \Delta p_c}{1-p} \tag{A.35}$$

If the probability of custody, p_c, is increased in such a way as to result in a constant annual increase in the prison population then the active population will be reduced by a steady state constant proportion.

Although the derivations above assume only one risk category, we can accommodate different risk/rate categories by simply summing the results over all homogeneous categories. Also the real situation is more complicated, the active population is determined by demographics (the birth rate at each age weighted by the normalized age–crime curve) and policies are subject to change over time potentially influencing any or all of the parameters. But the principles still hold.

Over the six-year period from 1993 to 1999 the prison population in England and Wales increased by about 50 per cent, a linear change of 8.3 per cent, of the initial value per year. With an overall custody rate of 14 per cent this results in a steady state $\Delta p_c = 0.012$, and a change in active high and low-risk populations of –6.6 per cent and –0.6 per cent respectively. Our analysis suggests that overall about half of crime is committed prior to the first conviction and that the risk group proportions in the offender population are 43 per cent high-risk and 57 per cent low-risk. From these estimates and Equation A.34 the percentage change in recorded crime, due to increasing the prison population, during period 1993–1999 would have been in the region of –1.5 per cent.

Steady State Solutions

The derivations above, concerning constant probability systems and the alternative approach to generating the models, demonstrate that, for homogeneous categories of offenders, the models derived in Chapters 3 and 4 follow directly from the basic assumptions of our theory. The distribution fitting and the goodness of fit achieved in Chapter 2 strongly support our assumptions of combinations of homogeneous categories in both recidivism probabilities and offending rates. The Poisson processes derived above (from both constant probability processes and proportional offending approaches) implicitly assume 100 per cent recidivism but we can incorporate recidivism probabilities less than one simply by multiplying the distributions for the rth offences by $p^{(r-1)}$ leading to the age–crime models of Chapters 2 and 3. Recidivism was also incorporated in our simplified model of active and incarcerated populations derived above in our discussion of incapacitation.

Of interest to planners and policy makers are estimates of overall crime/conviction rates and which aspects of the process are amenable to policy interventions. Equation A.28 showed that the size of the active population is proportional to the number of first convictions and inversely proportional to the rate of desistance $\lambda * (1-p)$. First convictions at time t are proportional to the weighted sum of birth rates for each age at time t. In A.28 λ is the conviction rate and, as discussed earlier, convictions are a sample of offences committed. Thus doubling the probability of conviction given an offence should halve crime if (cumulatively) conviction truly is the cause of desistance. The factor $1/(1-p)$ which occurs in A.28, and other formulae, is simply the sum of the series $\sum_{n=0}^{\infty} p^n$ and is the average number of convictions for members of the risk category with reconviction probability $\boldsymbol{p}$.

Thus reducing $\boldsymbol{p}$ for the high-risk category by 10 per cent from 0.84 to 0.76 would reduce the future crime of those offenders by about 40 per cent and crime overall by about 13 per cent. Reducing recidivism for low-risk offenders would have a much smaller impact as relatively few are convicted more than once or twice. The number of first convictions, $\boldsymbol{N_N(t)}$ is proportional to the birth rate, $\boldsymbol{B(t, age)}$, and for each group $\boldsymbol{N_{Ng}(t) = B(t, age)*c*q_g}$. The proportionality parameter is made up of population criminality $\boldsymbol{c}$ and the proportion of offenders in each category $\boldsymbol{q_g}$. Overall crime can potentially be reduced by reducing criminality and/or moving offenders from high recidivism to low-recidivism risk categories. Early intervention programmes and more effective informal and pre-conviction disposals could possibly make these changes.

In the above we have assumed that criminal careers start at the first conviction. Although our estimates of crime will implicitly include some offences prior to the first conviction, the majority of early offences will be excluded. From our two modelling approaches we can estimate the extent of crime by unconvicted offenders as follows: by numerically integrating Equation 3.4, with $\boldsymbol{C}$ set equal to 1, over the age range 10 to 70 we obtain an estimate of the average number of offender years between age 10 and the first conviction for each of the rate categories. Multiplying this by $\boldsymbol{\lambda}$ for the category results in an estimate of the average number of conviction opportunities which have been ignored, otherwise dealt with, or missed due to the reduced probability of detection prior to being known to the police. Table A.1 gives estimates from the three category model of Chapters 2 and 3.

Our approximate model explicitly assumes that early conviction opportunities are ignored and the numbers of these ignored opportunities are estimated in the fitting process. Average values over all cohorts are quoted in Table 4.5 for males and females separately. These approximate model estimates suggest that about 42 per cent of crime is committed by offenders prior to their first convictions for males and about 38 per cent for females.

The three category model of Chapter 3 is likely to overestimate crimes because, for example, acts like playground fights, although strictly assaults, would not generally be regarded as crime but may be the forerunner of more serious violence. The approximate model estimates, on the other hand, are likely to be underestimates as crimes committed by 10-year-olds are omitted completely and the *gamma approximation* for the high category requires a lower $\boldsymbol{\lambda}$, to achieve the fit, which is corrected for by the temporal adjustment δ for actual convictions but not for the ignored conviction opportunities. Both estimates are, however, speculative, as we have very limited information on unsolved crimes and who has committed them. We do

Table A.1 Estimates of the number of conviction opportunities and the proportion of crime committed prior to the first conviction, three group model

Integral of Equation 3.4

$$\int_{10}^{70} (1+e^{\alpha\cdot(t-c)})^{\frac{P_f \cdot \lambda}{\alpha}} \cdot dt$$

	q_g	Average No. of convictions	$\frac{P_f \cdot \lambda}{\alpha}$	Average offending years prior to 1st conviction	Conviction opportunities prior to 1st conviction	Proportion of crime prior to 1st conviction
High-rate high-risk	0.17	6.25	0.8	5.5	4.8	43%
Low-rate low-risk	0.76	1.40	0.2	13.2	2.9	67%
Low-rate high-risk	0.07	6.25	0.2	13.2	2.9	47%
Overall						55%

Note: Estimates are for the 1953 cohort from the Offenders Index.

know that clear-up rates over the period of the cohort samples have been between 35 per cent and 20 per cent and that a significant proportion of crime remains unreported. Also our analysis assumes that most crime is committed by offenders who are eventually convicted. For the purpose of making conservative estimates of the impact of offender based crime reduction policy initiatives, we assume that about 50 per cent of crime is committed by unknown/unconvicted offenders at the time of commission.

Estimating the Active Offender Population Size

The definition of an active offender used in our theory differs from that used in most criminal career research, in that our offenders are active from the age of 10 until they desist. We have no intermittency because being active is defined by the *constant* probabilities of continuing to offend at the *constant* Poisson rate. Our analysis suggests that offenders do actually desist. This is because, for many offenders, the time between their last recorded conviction and the end of the observation period is long compared with the average inter-conviction time. If these offenders had continued to offend as before, the proportion caught and convicted would have approached 1. Also, offenders who are reconvicted appear in precisely the numbers and at the age predicted by the recidivism and rate parameters. Occam's razor favours this simple explanation over the rather convoluted changes in λ that would otherwise be required. Such convoluted changes are also not supported by the data.

In a cross-section sample, like the 1997 sentencing sample of Chapter 3, we can estimate the high and low-rate parameters, λ_h and λ_l from an analysis of time since the previous conviction. And from the conviction number frequencies we can estimate p_h, p_l and the proportions of offenders in the risk/rate categories. For each homogeneous category of offenders with rate parameter λ and reconviction probability p: we can calculate the cohort equivalent category size in the sample, N_S, and therefore the total convictions, $N_S/(1-p)$, for the category. We now apply this calculation to the offender categories in the 1997 sentencing sample. This sample was in fact six one-week samples from across the year, so the average total convictions for one group in one week is given by $N_S/(6*(1-p))$. Now the expected number of convictions, N_E, in a week for a single category is given by:

$$N_E = N_A \cdot \left(1 - e^{-\frac{\lambda}{52}}\right)$$

giving:

$$N_A = \frac{N_E}{\left(1 - e^{-\frac{\lambda}{52}}\right)} \qquad \text{(A.36)}$$

where N_A is the size of the active offender population.

Substituting parameter estimates from the 1997 sentencing sample into A.36 gives estimates of:

- 156,800 active (in the sense that they will be convicted of one or more offences at some time in the future) high-risk/high-rate offenders of whom approximately 133,700 would have been convicted in 1997;
- 604,700 active low-risk/low-rate offenders but only approximately 127,400 would have been convicted in 1997;
- 438,900 active high-risk/low-rate offenders of whom only approximately 92,400 would have been convicted in 1997.

In 1997 we estimate that there were just under 1,200,000 individuals in England and Wales who would commit and be convicted of relatively serious (standard list) crime if appropriate opportunities presented themselves and who would do so at least once in the remainder of their lives. Almost 30 per cent of these individuals would have been convicted within 12 months. Not surprisingly the most active offenders are disproportionately responsible for convictions; the high-risk/high-rate offenders represent 17 per cent of a cohort and 13 per cent of active offenders. They are responsible for 38 per cent of annual convictions and, if clear-up rates are the same for all categories, the same proportion of crime. The low-risk low-rate offenders make up 76 per cent of a cohort, 50 per cent of the active offender population and accrue only 36 per cent of annual convictions. The high-risk/low-rate group make up only 7 per cent of a cohort but 37 per cent of active offenders and 26 per cent of annual convictions. In these calculations we have taken no account of early career offending prior to (and including) the last conviction opportunity before the first actual conviction. Including early offending would almost certainly increase the disproportionality of crime committed by high-risk/high-rate offenders.

If offender population estimates are required for specific crime types, drug dealing or burglary for example, then these can be obtained by substituting parameter values for specific crime types into Equation A.36.

Maximum Likelihood Estimation of the Recidivism Parameters

In Chapter 2 we derived an equation for the dual-risk recidivism model. Initially we used a graphical technique which fitted a straight line to the log of the *conviction number frequency* data ($\boldsymbol{n} > 6$) from the 1953 cohort, subtracted the fitted line from the data to obtain the residuals and fitted a second straight line to these residuals. This procedure provided us with a good structural model of the data but it was unclear how well the model fitted. Visually the fit was almost unbelievably good but there was no direct measure of the sensitivity of the fit to the parameter values. It is also clear that the parameters are not independent of each other. A small change in $\boldsymbol{p}_h$ would give rise to changes in both $\boldsymbol{a}$ and $\boldsymbol{p}_l$. The parameters quoted in

Chapter 2 were in fact jointly estimated using a maximum likelihood objective function in an iterative curve fitting procedure. The objective function was derived as follows:

In the cohort datasets there is one record for every conviction (court appearance) of each offender in the cohort sample. For each offender the convictions are numbered from 1, the first conviction, to the last conviction in the observation period. The likelihood of a record having conviction number $\boldsymbol{n}$ is simply the probability of $\boldsymbol{n}$ under our dual-risk recidivism model:

$$P(n) = \frac{1}{C} \cdot \left[a \cdot p_h^{n-1} + (1-a) \cdot p_l^{n-1} \right] \tag{A.37}$$

Where:

$$C = \sum_{1}^{\infty} \left[a \cdot p_h^{n-1} + (1-a) \cdot p_l^{n-1} \right] = \frac{1 - p_h + a \cdot (p_h - p_l)}{(1-p_h) \cdot (1-p_l)}$$

In a cohort dataset, $\boldsymbol{x_n}$ records have conviction number $\boldsymbol{n}$ and the likelihood of this is:

$$likelihood(x_n) = P(n)^{x_n}$$

The likelihood of the whole dataset is given by the product of the likelihoods of the $\boldsymbol{x_n}$s for each conviction number. Therefore:

$$likelihood(data) = \prod_{n-1}^{N} \left(P(n)^{x_n} \right)$$

where: $\boldsymbol{N}$ is the highest recorded conviction number in the data set.
and:

$$\log \boldsymbol{lik}(data) = x_n \cdot \sum_{1}^{N} \left[\begin{array}{l} Ln\left(\dfrac{(1-p_h) \cdot (1-p_l)}{1 - p_h + a \cdot (p_h - p_l)} \right) \\ + Ln\left(a \cdot p_h^n + (1-a) \cdot p_l^n \right) \end{array} \right] \tag{A.38}$$

The parameters $\boldsymbol{p_h}$, $\boldsymbol{p_l}$ and $\boldsymbol{a}$ were estimated by minimizing –log$\boldsymbol{lik}$($\boldsymbol{data}$) in the fitting procedure. The proportion of variance accounted for by the model was over 99.9 per cent, an extremely high correlation between the model and the data. For the 1953 cohort data the maximum likelihood estimates were $\boldsymbol{p_h} = 0.840$, $\boldsymbol{p_l} = 0.313$ and $\boldsymbol{a} = 0.237$. Because the parameters are jointly estimated, conventional confidence intervals for individual parameters are misleading as such intervals would represent a rectangular box around the maximum likelihood estimate (see Figure A.1). The true

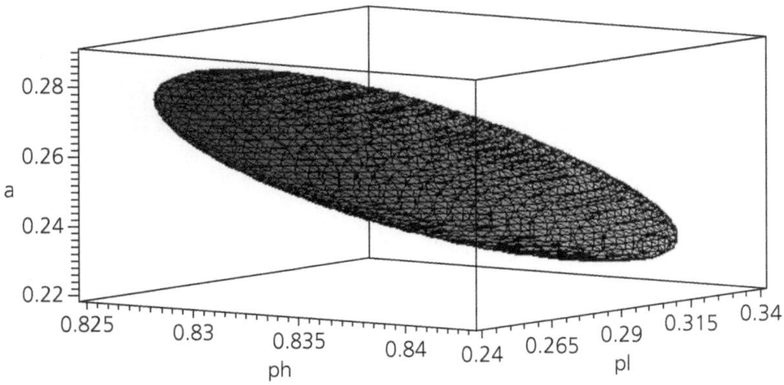

Figure A.1 Likelihood surface for dual-risk recidivism model

Source: Parameter estimates for the 1953 cohort, Offenders Index.
Note: The surface is equivalent to the more conventional 95% confidence intervals for the parameters.

confidence interval is represented by the surface contained within the box which is defined by parameter triplets (points) resulting in the likelihood ratio (*likelihood of (triplet) point on surface/maximum likelihood*) = 0.05 (ie 20 times less likely than the estimate),[2] points outside the surface are even less likely.

[2] This might be considered similar to a 95 per cent 'confidence interval' and indeed would be exactly equivalent if we were dealing with a two parameter multivariate normal distribution.

Bibliography

Andrade, J.T. (ed),(2009). *Handbook of Violence Risk Assessment and Treatment*. New York: Springer.

Atkinson, R.C. Bower, G.H. and Crothers, E.J. (1965). *An Introduction to Mathematical Learning Theory*. London: Wiley.

Avi-Itzhik, B. and Shinnar, R. (1973). 'Quantitative models in crime control'. *Journal of Criminal Justice*, 1, 85–217.

Barnett, A., Blumstein, A., Cohen, J. and Farrington, D.P. (1992). 'Not all criminal career models are equally valid'. *Criminology*, 30, 133–140.

—— —— and Farrington D.P. (1987). 'Probabilistic models of youthful criminal careers'. *Criminology*, 25, 83–107.

—— —— and Farrington, D.P. (1989). 'A prospective test of a criminal career model'. *Criminology*, 27, 373–388.

—— and Lofaso, A.J. (1985). 'Selective incapacitation and the Philadelphia Cohort data'. *Journal of Quantitative Criminology*, 1, 3–36.

Beelmann, A. and Raabe, T. (2009). 'The effects of preventing antisocial behaviour and crime in childhood: Results and implications of research reviews and meta-analyses'. *European Journal of Developmental Science*, 3, 260–281.

Belkin. J., Blumstein, A. and Glass, W. (1971). *JUSSIM: An Interactive Computer Program for Analysis of Criminal Justice Systems*. Pittsburgh, PA: Urban Systems Institute, Carnegie-Mellon University.

—— —— and—— (1973). 'Recidivism as a feedback process: An analytical model and empirical validation'. *Journal of Criminal Justice*, 1, 7–26.

Bernburg, J.G. and Krohn, M.D. (2003). 'Labelling, life chances, and adult crime: The direct and indirect effects of official intervention in adolescence on crime in early adulthood'. *Criminology*, 41, 1287–1318.

Bernfeld, G.A., Farrington, D.P. and Leschied, A.W. (eds) (2001). *Offender Rehabilitation in Practice: Implementing and Evaluating Effective Programs*. Chichester: Wiley.

Blumstein, A. and Cohen. J. (1979). 'Estimation of individual crime rates from arrest records'. *Journal of Criminal Law and Criminology*, 70, 561–585.

—— —— and Farrington, D.P. (1988a). 'Criminal career research: Its value for criminology'. *Criminology*, 26, 1–35.

—— —— and —— (1988b). 'Longitudinal and criminal career research: Further clarifications'. *Criminology*, 26, 57–74.

Blumstein, A., Cohen, J., Piquero, A.R. and Visher, C.A. (2010). 'Linking the crime and arrest processes to measure variation in individual arrest risk per crime'. *Journal of Quantitative Criminology*, 26, 533–548.

—— —— Roth, J.A. and Visher, C.A. (eds) (1986). *Criminal Careers and "Career Criminals"*. Washington, DC: National Academy Press.

—— Farrington, D.P. and Moitra, S. (1985). 'Delinquency Careers: Innocents, Desisters, and Persisters'. In M. Tonry and N. Morris (eds), *Crime and Justice* Vol. 6 (pp 187–222). Chicago: University of Chicago Press.

—— and Larson, R. (1969). Models of a total criminal justice system. *Operations Research*, 17, 199–232.

—— and Moitra, S. (1980). 'The identification of "career criminals" from "chronic offenders" in a cohort'. *Law and Policy Quarterly*, 2, 321–334.

—— and Nakamura, K. (2009). 'Redemption in the presence of widespread criminal background checks'. *Criminology*, 47, 327–359.

Bottoms, A., Shapland, J., Costello, A., Holmes, D. and Muir, G. (2004). 'Towards desistance: Theoretical underpinnings for an empirical study'. *Howard Journal of Criminal Justice*, 43, 368–389.

Burnett, R. and Maruna, S. (2004). 'So "Prison Works", Does It? The criminal careers of 130 men released from prison under Home Secretary Michael Howard'. *Howard Journal of Criminal Justice*, 43, 390–404.

Bushway, S.D., Piquero, A.R., Broidy, L.M., Cauffman, E. and Mazerolle, P. (2001). 'An empirical framework for studying desistance as a process'. *Criminology*, 39, 491–515.

—— Thornberry, T.P. and Krohn, M.D. (2003). 'Desistance as a developmental process: A comparison of static and dynamic approaches'. *Journal of Quantitative Criminology*, 19, 129–153.

Canela-Cacho J.A., Blumstein A. and Cohen, J. (1997). 'Relationship between frequency (λ) of imprisoned and free offenders'. *Criminology*, 35, 133–175.

Carr-Hill, G.A. and Carr-Hill, R.A. (1972). 'Reconviction as a process'. *British Journal of Criminology*, 12, 35–43.

Cassidy, R.G. (1985). 'Modelling a Criminal Justice System'. In D.P. Farrington and R. Tarling (eds), *Prediction in Criminology* (pp 193–207). Albany, NY: State University of New York Press.

Chaikin J M. and Rolph, J.E. (1981). *Methods of Estimating Crime Rates of Individuals*. Santa Monica, CA: Rand Corporation.

Cohen, L. and Felson, M. (1979). 'Social change and crime rate trends: A routine activity approach'. *American Sociological Review*, 44, 588–608.

Cohen, M.A. and Piquero, A.R. (2009). 'New evidence on the monetary value of saving a high-risk youth'. *Journal of Quantitative Criminology*, 25, 25–49.

Copas, J. and Marshall, P. (1998). 'The Offender Group Reconviction Scale: A statistical reconviction score for use by probation officers'. *Applied Statistics*, 47, 159–171.

Councell, R. and Simes, J. (2002). *Projections of the long term trends in the prison population to 2009*. London: Home Office (Statistical Bulletin 14/02).

Crown Prosecution Service (2002). *Narrowing the justice gap*. London: CPS.

Davies, P.M. and Coxon, A.P.M. (1982). *Key Texts in Multidimensional Scaling*. London: Heinemann.

Dawson, P. and Cuppleditch, L. (2007). *An impact assessment of the prolific and other priority offenders programme*. London: Home Office (Online Report 08/07).

Delisi, M. and Piquero, A.R. (2011). 'New frontiers in criminal careers research, 2000–2011: A state-of-the-art review'. *Journal of Criminal Justice*, 39, 289–301.

Edwards, A.W.F. (1972). *Likelihood*. Cambridge: Cambridge University Press.

Farrington, D.P. (1977). 'The effects of public labelling'. *British Journal of Criminology*, 17, 122–135.

——(1979). 'Longitudinal Research on Crime and Delinquency'. In N. Morris and M. Tonry (eds) *Crime and Justice*, Vol. 1 (pp 289–348). Chicago: University of Chicago Press.

—— (1986). 'Age and Crime'. In M. Tonry and N. Morris (eds), *Crime and Justice*, Vol. 7 (pp 198–250). Chicago: University of Chicago Press.

—— (1987). 'Predicting Individual Crime Rates'. In D.M. Gottfredson and M. Tonry (eds), *Prediction and Classification: Criminal Justice Decision Making* (pp 53–101). Chicago: University of Chicago Press.

—— (1988). 'Studying Changes Within Individuals: The Causes of Offending'. In M. Rutter (ed), *Studies of Psychosocial Risk: The Power of Longitudinal Data* (pp 158–183). Cambridge: Cambridge University Press.

—— (1990). 'Age, Period, Cohort, and Offending'. In D.M. Gottfredson and R.V. Clarke (eds), *Policy and Theory in Criminal Justice: Contributions in Honour of Leslie T. Wilkins* (pp 51–75). Aldershot: Avebury.

—— (1997). 'Human Development and Criminal Careers'. In M. Maguire, R. Morgan and R. Reiner (eds), *The Oxford Handbook of Criminology* (2nd edn, pp 361–408). Oxford: Clarendon Press.

—— (2000). 'Explaining and preventing crime: The globalization of knowledge—The American Society of Criminology 1999 Presidential Address'. *Criminology*, 38, 1–24.

—— (2002). 'Developmental Criminology and Risk-focussed Prevention'. In M. Maguire, R. Morgan and R. Reiner (eds), *The Oxford Handbook of Criminology* (3rd edn, pp 657–701). Oxford: Oxford University Press.

Farrington, D. P. (2003). 'Key Results from the First Forty Years of the Cambridge Study in Delinquent Development'. In T.P. Thornberry and M.D. Krohn (eds), *Taking Stock of Delinquency: An Overview of Findings from Contemporary Longitudinal Studies* (pp 137–183). New York: Kluwer/Plenum.

—— (2007). 'Childhood risk factors and risk-focussed prevention'. In M. Maguire, R. Morgan and R. Reiner (eds), *The Oxford Handbook of Criminology* (4th edn, pp 602–640). Oxford: Oxford University Press.

—— (2010). 'The Developmental Evidence Base: Psychosocial Research'. In G.J. Towl and D.A. Crighton (eds), *Forensic Psychology* (pp 113–132). Oxford: Blackwell Publishing.

—— and Bennett, T.H. (1981). 'Police cautioning of juveniles in London'. *British Journal of Criminology*, 21, 123–135.

—— Coid, J.W., Harnett, L., Jolliffe, D., Soteriou, N., Turner, R. and West, D.J. (2006). 'Criminal careers up to age 50 and life success up to age 48: New findings from the Cambridge Study in Delinquent Development'. London: Home Office (Research Study No. 299).

—— ——and West, D.J. (2009). 'The development of offending from age 8 to age 50: Recent results from the Cambridge Study in Delinquent Development'. Monatsschrift fur Kriminologie und Strafrechtsreform (Journal of Criminology and Penal Reform). 92, 160–173.

—— Gallagher, B., Morley, L., St Ledger, R.J. and West, D.J. (1986). 'Unemployment, school leaving and crime'. *British Journal of Criminology*, 26, 335–356.

——and Hawkins, J.D. (1991). 'Predicting participation, early onset, and later persistence in officially recorded offending'. *Criminal Behaviour and Mental Health*, 1, 1–33.

—— and Jolliffe, D. (2004). 'England and Wales'. In D.P. Farrington, P.A. Langdon, and M. Tonry (eds), *Cross-national Studies of Crime and Justice* (pp 1–38). Washington, DC: US Bureau of Justice Statistics.

—— and —— (2005). 'Cross-national Comparisons of Crime Rates in Four Countries, 1981–1999'. In M. Tonry, and D.P. Farrington (eds), *Crime and Punishment in Western Countries, 1980–1999* (pp 377–397). Chicago: University of Chicago Press.

—— —— Hawkins, J.D., Catalano, R.F., Hill, K.G. and Kosterman, R. (2003). 'Comparing delinquency careers in court records and self-reports'. *Criminology*, 41, 933–958.

—— and Maughan, B. (1999). 'Criminal careers of two London cohorts'. *Criminal Behaviour and Mental Health*, 9, 91–106.

—— Ohlin, L.E. and Wilson, J.Q. (1986). *Understanding and Controlling Crime: Toward a New Research Strategy*. New York: Springer.

Farrington, D.P., Snyder, H.N. and Finnegan, T.A. (1988). 'Specialization in juvenile court careers'. *Criminology*, 26, 461–487.

—— and Welsh, B.C. (2007). *Saving Children from a Life of Crime: Early Risk Factors and Effective Interventions*. Oxford: Oxford University Press.

—— and West, D.J. (1993). 'Criminal, penal and life histories of chronic offenders: Risk and protective factors and early identification'. *Criminal Behaviour and Mental Health*, 3, 492–523.

—— and —— (1995). 'Effects of Marriage, Separation and Children on Offending by Adult Males'. In J. Hagan (ed) *Current Perspectives on Aging and the Life Cycle*, Vol. 4: *Delinquency and Disrepute in the Life Course* (pp 249–281). Greenwich, CT: JAI Press.

—— and Wikström, P.-O.H. (1994). 'Criminal Careers in London and Stockholm: A Cross–national Comparative Study'. In E.G.M. Weitekamp and H.-J. Kerner (eds) *Cross-national Longitudinal Research on Human Development and Criminal Behaviour* (pp 65–89). Dordrecht, Netherlands: Kluwer.

Flood-Page, C., Campbell, S., Harrington, V. and Miller, J. (2000). *Youth crime: Findings from the 1998/99 Youth Lifestyles Survey*. London: Home Office.

Francis, B. and Crosland, P. (2002). *The Police National Computer and the Offenders Index: Can they be combined for research purposes?* London: Home Office.

—— Liu, J. and Soothill, K. (2010). 'Criminal lifestyle specialization: Female offending in England and Wales'. *International Criminal Justice Review*, 20, 188–204.

—— Soothill, K. and Ackerley, E. (2004). 'Multiple cohort data, delinquent generations, and criminal careers'. *Journal of Contemporary Criminal Justice*, 20, 103–126.

—— —— and Fligelstone, R. (2004). 'Identifying patterns and pathways of offending behaviour: A new approach to typologies of crime'. *European Journal of Criminology*, 1, 48–87.

—— —— and Piquero, A. R. (2007). 'Estimation issues and generational changes in modelling criminal career length'. *Crime and Delinquency*, 53, 84–105.

Glueck, S. and Glueck, E. (1950). *Unravelling Juvenile Delinquency*. New York: Commonwealth Fund.

Goldblatt, P. and Lewis, C. (eds). (1998). *Reducing offending: An assessment of research evidence on ways of dealing with offending behaviour*. London: Home Office (Research Study No. 187).

Gottfredson, M.R. and Hirschi, T. (1986). 'The true value of Lambda would appear to be zero: An essay on career criminals, criminal careers, selective incapacitation, cohort studies, and related topics'. *Criminology*, 24, 213–234.

Gottfredson, M. R. and Hirschi, T. (1987). 'The methodological adequacy of longitudinal research on crime'. *Criminology*, 25, 581–614.

—— and —— (1990). *A General Theory of Crime*. Stanford, CA: Stanford University Press.

Greenberg, D.F. (1979). *Mathematical Criminology*. New Brunswick, NJ: Rutgers University Press.

—— (1991). 'Modelling Criminal Careers'. *Criminology*, 29, 17–46.

—— (1992). 'Comparing criminal career models'. *Criminology*, 30, 141–148.

Greenwood, P.W. and Abrahamse, A. (1982). *Selective Incapacitation*. Santa Monica, CA: Rand Corporation (Report no. R-2815-NIJ).

Grove, P.G. (2003). 'Developments and Applications of MacLeod's Hypothesis'. In R. Morris et al, *Modelling Crime and Offending: Recent Developments in England and Wales*. London: Home Office (Occasional Paper No.80), section D.

—— Macleod, J.F. and Godfrey, D. (1998). 'Forecasting the prison population: Predicting the consequences of sentencing policy. *Operations Research Insight*', 11 (1), 3–9.

Haapanen, R. (1990). *Selective Incapacitation and the Serious Offender: A Longitudinal Study of Criminal Career Patterns*. New York: Springer.

Hirschi, T. (1969). *Causes of Delinquency*. Berkeley, CA: University of California Press.

Home Office (1991). *National prison survey, main findings*. London: Home Office.

—— (1998a). *The offenders index: A user's guide*. London: Home Office.

—— (1998b). *The offenders index: Codebook*. London: Home Office.

—— (2001). *Criminal justice: The way ahead*. London: Home Office (CM5074).

—— (2002). *OASys handbook*. London: Home Office.

—— (2003). *OASys pilot study report*. London: Home Office.

Jolliffe, D. and Farrington, D.P. (2010). 'Individual Differences and Offending'. In E. McLaughlin and T. Newburn (eds), *The Sage Handbook of Criminological Theory* (pp 40–55). London: Sage.

Kazemian, L and Farrington, D.P. (2006). 'Exploring residual career length and residual number of offences for two generations of repeat offenders'. *Journal of Research in Crime and Delinquency*, 43, 89–113.

—— and —— (2010). 'The Developmental Evidence Base: Desistance'. In G.J. Towl and D.A. Crighton (eds), *Forensic Psychology* (pp133–147). Oxford: Blackwell.

Kershaw, C. (1999). *Reconviction of offenders sentenced or discharged from prison in 1995, England and Wales*. London: Home Office (Statistical Bulletin 5/1999).

Killias, M., Gillieron, G., Villard, F., and Poglia, C. (2010). 'How damaging is imprisonment in the long-term? A controlled experiment comparing long-term effects of community service and short custodial sentences on reoffending and social integration'. *Journal of Experimental Criminology*, 6, 115–130.

Kurlychek, M.C., Brame, R. and Bushway, S.D. (2007). 'Enduring risk? Old criminal records and predictions of future criminal involvement'. *Crime and Delinquency*, 53, 64–83.

Laming, D. (1973). *Mathematical Psychology*. London: Academic Press.

Land, K.C. (1992). 'Models of criminal careers: Some suggestions for moving beyond the current debate'. *Criminology*, 30, 149–155.

Laub, J.H. and Sampson, R.J. (2001). 'Understanding Desistance from Crime'. In M. Tonry (ed), *Crime and Justice,* Vol. 28 (pp 1–69). Chicago: University of Chicago Press.

LeBlanc, M. and Frechette, M. (1989). *Male Criminal Activity from Childhood through Youth: Multilevel and Developmental Perspectives*. New York: Springer-Verlag.

Lipsey, M.W. and Landenberger, N.A (2006). 'Cognitive-behavioural interventions'. In B.C. Welsh and D.P. Farrington, (eds) *Preventing Crime: What Works for Children, Offenders, Victims, and Places* (pp 57–71). Dordrecht: Springer.

Liu, J., Francis, B. and Soothill, K. (2011). 'A longitudinal study of escalation in crime seriousness'. *Journal of Quantitative Criminology*, 27, 175–196.

Loeber, R. and Snyder, H.N. (1990). 'Rate of offending in juvenile careers: Findings of constancy and change in Lambda'. *Criminology*, 28, 97–110.

—— Stouthamer-Loeber, M., Van Kammen, W.B. and Farrington, D.P. (1991). 'Initiation, escalation, and desistance in juvenile offending and their correlates'. *Journal of Criminal Law and Criminology*, 82, 36–82.

MacLeod, J. (2003). 'A Theory and Model of the Conviction Process'. In R. Morris et al., *Modelling Crime and Offending: Recent Developments in England and Wales*. London: Home Office (Occasional Paper No.80).

Maltz, M.D. (1996). 'From Poisson to the present: Applying operations research to problems of crime and justice'. *Journal of Quantitative Criminology*, 12, 3–61.

Marris, R. and Volterra Consulting. (2003). 'Survey of the Research Literature on the Criminological and Economic Factors Influencing Crime Trends'. In R. Marris et al (eds), *Modelling Crime and Offending: Recent Developments in England and Wales*. London: Home Office (Occasional Paper No. 80).

Maxim, P.S. (1986). 'Cohort size and juvenile delinquency in England and Wales'. *Journal of Criminal Justice*, 14, 491–499.

McGloin, J.M., Sullivan, C.J. and Piquero, A.R. (2009). 'Aggregating to versatility? Transitions among offender types in the short term'. *British Journal of Criminology*, 49, 243–264.

McGuire, J. (ed) (1995). *What Works: Reducing Reoffending: Guidelines from Research and Practice*. Chichester: Wiley.

Melhuish, E, Belsky, J., Leyland, A.H., Barnes, J. and the National Evaluation of Sure Start Research Team (2008). Effects of fully-established Sure Start local programmes on 3-year-old children and their families living in England: A quasi-experimental observational study. *Lancet*, 372, 1641–1647.

Ministry of Justice (2008). *Prison population projections 2008–2015, England and Wales*. London: Ministry of Justice (Statistical Bulletin).

—— (2010). *Conviction histories of offenders between the ages of 10 and 52*. London: Ministry of Justice (Statistics Bulletin).

—— (2010). *Offences brought to justice*. London: Ministry of Justice.

Moffitt, T.E. (1993). 'Adolescence-limited and life-course persistent anti-social behaviour: A developmental taxonomy'. *Psychological Review*, 100, 674–701.

Mott, J. (1983). 'Police decisions for dealing with young offenders'. *British Journal of Criminology*, 23, 249–262.

Nagin, D.S. (1999). 'Analysing developmental trajectories: A semi-parametric, group-based approach'. *Psychological Methods*, 4, 39–77.

—— (2005). *Group-Based Modelling of Development*. Cambridge, MA: Harvard University Press.

—— and Farrington, D.P. (1992a). 'The onset and persistence of offending'. *Criminology*, 30, 501–523.

—— —— (1992b). 'The stability of criminal potential from childhood to adulthood'. *Criminology*, 30, 235–260.

—— —— and Moffitt, T.E. (1995). 'Life-course trajectories of different types of offenders'. *Criminology*, 33, 111–139.

—— and Land, K.C. (1993). 'Age, criminal careers, and population heterogeneity: Specification and estimation of a nonparametric, mixed Poisson model'. *Criminology*, 31, 327–336.

—— and Paternoster, R. (1991). 'On the relationship of past and future participation in delinquency'. *Criminology*, 29, 163–190.

—— and —— (2000). 'Population heterogeneity and state dependence: State of the evidence and directions for future research'. *Journal of Quantitative Criminology*, 16, 117–144.

—— and Tremblay, R.E. (1999). 'Trajectories of boys' physical aggression, opposition, and hyperactivity on the path to physically violent and non-violent juvenile delinquency'. *Child Development*, 70, 1181–1196.

Otto, R.K. and Douglas, K.S. (eds) (2010). *Handbook of Violence Risk Assessment and Treatment*. New York: Routledge.

Painter, K.A. and Farrington, D.P. (1999). 'Street Lighting and Crime: Diffusion of Benefits in the Stoke-on-Trent Project'. In K.A. Painter and N. Tilley (eds), *Surveillance of Public Space: CCTV, Street Lighting and Crime Prevention* (pp 77–122). Monsey, NY: Criminal Justice Press.

Paternoster, R., Brame, R. and Farrington, D.P. (2001). 'On the relationship between adolescent and adult conviction frequencies'. *Journal of Quantitative Criminology*, 17, 201–226.

Piquero, A.R. (2008). 'Taking Stock of Developmental Trajectories of Criminal Activity over the Life Course'. In A. Liberman (ed), *The Long View of Crime: A Synthesis of Longitudinal Research* (pp 23–78). New York: Springer.

—— and Blumstein, A. (2007). 'Does incapacitation reduce crime?' *Journal of Quantitative Criminology*, 23, 267–285.

—— Farrington, D.P. and Blumstein, A. (2003). 'The Criminal Career Paradigm'. In M. Tonry (ed), *Crime and Justice,* Vol. 30 (pp 359–506). Chicago: University of Chicago Press.

—— —— and Blumstein, A. (2007). *Key Issues in Criminal Career Research: New Analyses of the Cambridge Study in Delinquent Development.* Cambridge: Cambridge University Press.

—— and Weisburd, D. (eds) (2010). *Handbook of Quantitative Criminology*. New York: Springer.

Piquero, N.L. and Benson, M.L. (2004). 'White-collar crime and criminal careers: Specifying a trajectory of punctuated situational offending'. *Journal of Contemporary Criminal Justice*, 20, 148–165.

Prime, J., White, S., Liriano, S. and Patel, K. (2001). *Criminal careers of those born between 1953 and 1978*. London: Home Office (Statistical Bulletin 4/01).

Reiss, A.J. and Farrington, D.P. (1991). 'Advancing knowledge about co-offending: Results from a prospective longitudinal survey of London males'. *Journal of Criminal Law and Criminology*, 82, 360–395.

Roberts, B. and DelVecchio, W. (2000). 'The rank-order consistency of personality traits from childhood to old age: A quantitative review of longitudinal studies'. *Psychological Bulletin*, 126 (1), 3–25.

Sampson, R.J. and Laub, J.H. (2003). 'Life-course desisters? Trajectories of crime among delinquent boys followed to age 70'. *Criminology*, 41, 301–339.

—— and —— (2005). 'A life-course view of the development of crime'. *Annals of the American Academy of Political and Social Science*, 602, 12–45.

Shinnar, S. and Shinnar, R. (1975). 'The effects of the criminal justice system on the control of crime: A quantitative approach'. *Law and Society Review*, 9, 581–612.

Soothill, K., Ackerley, E. and Francis, B. (2008). 'Criminal convictions among children and young adults: Changes over time'. *Criminology and Criminal Justice*, 8, 297–315.

—— Fitzpatrick, C. and Francis, B. (2009). *Understanding Criminal Careers*. Cullompton, Devon: Willan.

Soothill, K., Francis, B., Ackerley, E. and Humphreys, L. (2008). 'Changing patterns of offending behaviour among young adults'. *British Journal of Criminology*, 48, 75–95.

—— and —— (2009). 'When do ex-offenders become like non-offenders?' *Howard Journal of Criminal Justice*, 48, 373–387.

Stander, J., Farrington, D.P., Hill, G. and Altham, P.M.E. (1989). 'Markov chain analysis and specialization in criminal careers'. *British Journal of Criminology*, 29, 317–335.

Tarling, R. (1993). *Analysing Offending: Data, Models and Interpretations*. London: HMSO.

Theobald, D. and Farrington, D.P. (2009). 'Effects of getting married on offending: Results from a prospective longitudinal survey of males'. *European Journal of Criminology*, 6, 496–516.

—— and —— (2011). 'Why do the crime-reducing effects of marriage vary with age?' *British Journal of Criminology*, 51, 136–158.

Tong, L.S.J. and Farrington, D.P. (2006). 'How effective is the Reasoning and Rehabilitation programme in reducing offending? A meta-analysis of evaluations in four countries'. *Psychology, Crime and Law*, 12, 3–24.

Tonry, M. and Farrington, D.P. (2005). 'Punishment and Crime Across Space and Time'. In M. Tonry and D.P. Farrington (eds), *Crime and Punishment in Western Countries, 1980–1999* (pp 1–39). Chicago: University of Chicago Press.

Walters, G.D. (2006). *Lifestyle Theory: Past, Present and Future*. New York: Nova Science Publishers.

Weisburd, D. and Waring, E. (2001). *White-collar Crime and Criminal Careers*. Cambridge: Cambridge University Press.

Van Mastrigt, S.B. and Farrington, D.P. (2009). 'Co-offending versus age, gender and crime type: Implications for criminal justice policy'. *British Journal of Criminology*, 49, 552–573.

—— and —— (2011). 'Prevalence and characteristics of co-offending recruiters'. *Justice Quarterly*, 28, 325–359.

Welsh, B.C. and Farrington, D.P. (2009). *Making Public Places Safer: Surveillance and Crime Prevention*. Oxford: Oxford University Press.

—— and —— (eds) (2012). *The Oxford Handbook of Crime Prevention*. Oxford: Oxford University Press.

Welsh, B.C., Loeber, R., Stevens, B.R., Stouthamer-Loeber, M., Cohen, M.A. and Farrington, D.P. (2008). 'Costs of juvenile crime in urban areas: A longitudinal perspective'. *Youth Violence and Juvenile Justice*, 6, 3–27.

West, D.J. and Farrington, D.P. (1977). *The Delinquent Way of Life*. London: Heinemann.

Wolfgang, M.E., Figlio, R.M. and Sellin, T. (1972). *Delinquency in a Birth Cohort*. Chicago: University of Chicago Press.

Zara, G. and Farrington, D.P. (2009). 'Childhood and adolescent predictors of late onset criminal careers'. *Journal of Youth and Adolescence*, 38, 287–300.

Zimring, F., Jennings, W.G., Piquero, A. and Hays, S. (2009). 'Investigating the continuity of sex offending: Evidence from the second Philadelphia birth cohort'. *Justice Quarterly*, 26, 58–76.

Index